The Normandy Camp

Bringing together essays on key aspects of the Normandy campaign from leading names in military history, this book re-examines the crucial issues and debates of the D-Day campaign.

Although it was the most important campaign fought by the Western Allies in World War II and was pivotal in determining the outcome of the war, there remains much to debate about D-Day and subsequent operations in Normandy. This volume tackles a range of core topics, placing them in their current historiographical context, to present new and sometimes revisionist interpretations of key issues. How effective was the deception plan used against the Germans? Can it be said that the German army was superior to the American, British and Canadian forces? Why did the Allied armies become bogged down for two months and to what extent, if at all, was the stalemate a product of poor Allied operational technique or German tactical flair? How have we come to see or interpret the Normandy campaign through the media of cinema and TV?

As World War II is increasingly becoming a field of revisionism, this book sits squarely within growing debates and brings current thinking from leading military and strategic historians to a wider audience.

This book will be of great interest to students of World War II, and of military and strategic studies in general.

John Buckley is Reader in Military History at the University of Wolverhampton, UK. He has written widely on various aspects of military studies, particularly World War II, the interwar era and air power. He has recently published *British Armour in the Normandy Campaign 1944* (2004).

ROUTLEDGE Series: Military history and policy
Series Editors: John Gooch and Brian Holden Reid

This series will publish studies on historical and contemporary aspects of land power, spanning the period from the eighteenth century to the present day, and will include national, international and comparative studies. From time to time, the series will publish edited collections of essays and 'classics'.

The Normandy Campaign 1944

Sixty Years On

Edited by John Buckley

Routledge
Taylor & Francis Group

LONDON AND NEW YORK

First published 2006
by Routledge
2 Park Square, Milton Park, Abingdon, Oxon, OX14 4RN

Simultaneously published in the USA and Canada
by Routledge
270 Madison Ave, New York NY 10016

*Routledge is an imprint of the Taylor & Francis Group, an informa
business*

Transferred to Digital Printing 2007

Typeset in 10/12pt Times NR by Graphicraft Limited, Hong Kong

British Library Cataloguing in Publication Data
A catalogue record for this book is available from the British Library

Library of Congress Cataloging in Publication Data
The Normandy campaign 1944 : sixty years on / edited by John
Buckley.
      p. cm. — (Military history and policy, ISSN 1465-8488)
   Includes index.
   ISBN 0–415–36931–2 (hardback)
   1. World War, 1939–1945—Campaigns—France—Normandy.
2. Allied Forces.   3. Germany—Armed Forces—History—
World War, 1939–1945.   4. Normandy (France)—History, Military.
I. Buckley, John (John D.)   II. Series.
D756.5.N6N695 2006
940.54′2142—dc22
                                                                2005033264

ISBN-10: 0–415–36931–2 (hbk)
ISBN-10: 0–415–44942–1 (pbk)
ISBN-10: 0–203–02888–0 (ebk)

ISBN-13: 978–0–415–36931–2 (hbk)
ISBN-13: 978–0–415–44942–7 (pbk)
ISBN-13: 978–0–203–02888–9 (ebk)

Contents

Contributors

Stephen Badsey is Senior Lecturer in the Department of War Studies at the Royal Military Academy Sandhurst, and a Senior Research Associate of the Centre for Defence Studies, Kings College, London. He is a specialist on military theory and on media presentations of warfare, and he has also made particular studies of airborne and amphibious operations. He has written or contributed to over 60 books and articles about warfare, including *Utah Beach, Omaha Beach, The Battle for Caen, Arnhem 1944*, and *Normandy 1944*. He appears frequently on television as a military and media historian.

Mary Kathryn Barbier is Assistant Professor of American Military History at Mississippi State University. She received her Ph.D. from the University of Southern Mississippi in December 1998 and subsequently won a two-year postdoctoral fellowship from International Security Studies at Yale University. She is the author of *Kursk: The Greatest Tank Battle Ever Fought, 1943* (2002, also published in German) and, with Andrew Wiest, *Strategy and Tactics: Infantry Warfare – The Theory and Practice of Infantry Combat in the 20th Century* (2002). She was recently invited to present a paper, 'When is the Use of Military Force Acceptable Internationally?' at the Couchiching Institute on Public Affairs public policy conference in Canada.

John Buckley is Reader in Military History at the University of Wolverhampton, UK, and has written widely on many aspects of military history. He is the author of *British Armour in the Normandy Campaign 1944* (2004) and in 2006 will publish *Normandy 1944* for Brassey's Campaigns in Focus series. He is currently working on the British tank industry in World War II and an analysis of the Second British Army in Northwest Europe 1944–5.

Terry Copp is Professor Emeritus and Director of the Laurier Centre for Military Strategic and Disarmament Studies, Wilfrid Laurier University, Waterloo, Ontario, Canada. He is the author of *Fields of Fire: The Canadians in Normandy* (2003) and the soon to be published sequel *Cinderella Army: The Canadians in Northwest Europe*.

James S. Corum is a professor at the US Army Command and General Staff College, Fort Leavenworth, Kansas. He previously studied at Brown,

Oxford and Queen's University Canada and was a visiting fellow of All Souls College, Oxford, from January to July 2005. Dr Corum is the author of four books on military and airpower history – *The Roots of Blitzkrieg* (1992), *The Luftwaffe: Creating the Operational Air War* (1997), *The Luftwaffe's Way of War* (1998) and *Airpower and Small Wars* (2003) – as well as dozens of journal articles and book chapters. His most recent book, *Quelling the Beast: A Counterinsurgency Strategy for America* will appear in 2006.

Ian Daglish read History at Trinity College, Cambridge, where his thesis was 'Napoleon Bonaparte and the Invasion of England'. After writing a number of articles about the Normandy campaign of 1944 and a short history of the American 82nd '*All American*' Airborne Division in Normandy, Ian has focused in recent years on the British sector of the Normandy campaign. For some years he has been a familiar sight in the Normandy battlefields, researching and leading groups of both serving and veteran soldiers. He is the author of *Operation BLUECOAT: The British Armoured Breakout* (2003), *Operation GOODWOOD: The Great Tank Charge* (2004) and *GOODWOOD: Over the Battlefield* (2005).

Nigel de Lee read History, War Studies and International Relations at Leeds, King's College, London, and Cambridge. He taught War Studies at Sandhurst for 30 years, and is now teaching War and Security Studies at the University of Hull. He has also taught at the US Naval Academy, Annapolis, and the Krigsskolen in Oslo, and since 1982 has carried out oral history interviews for the Imperial War Museum Sound Archive. He has conducted staff rides of Normandy and other theatres of war for the Army Staff College, RMA Sandhurst, US 29th Division and other clients, both military and academic.

John Ferris is Professor of History at the University of Calgary, and has published widely on military, diplomatic and intelligence history. Among his works are *The Evolution of British Strategic Policy, 1919–1926* (1989), *The British Army and Signals Intelligence During the First World War* (1992) and (with Christon Archer, Holger Herwig and Tim Travers), *A World History of Warfare* (2001). His most recent work is *Strategy and Intelligence: Selected Essays* (2005).

Peter Gray is a serving Royal Air Force officer with extensive operational and staff experience. He has worked in the Cabinet Office, in various MoD departments and spent three years as the Director of Defence Studies. He is currently the Director of the Defence Leadership and Management Centre. He has edited four books and published worldwide on air power topics.

Marc Hansen is a Research Associate and doctoral candidate at the Institut für Geschichte und ihre Didaktik, University of Flensburg, where he is also working as a teaching assistant in contemporary history. After completing his studies in Kiel and London he graduated in 2002 from the University of

Kiel with an MA and in his doctoral thesis, 'FeindBilder – Die Darstellung des deutschen Militärs in den zentralen Militärmuseen ausgewählter Siegermächte des Zweiten Weltkrieges', he provides a comparative analysis of how German armed forces are displayed in military museums of former enemy states.

Stephen A. Hart is Senior Lecturer in the Department of War Studies, The Royal Military Academy Sandhurst. Prior to this he lectured in the Department of European Studies at the University of Surrey and the Department of War Studies, King's College London. He is the author of *Montgomery and 'Colossal Cracks': The 21st Army Group in Northwest Europe 1944 45* (2000), *The Road to Falaise* (2004), and is co-author of several works on the German army in World War II.

Carsten Hennig (MA Media Studies) is preparing his dissertation on American war movies after 9/11 at the Institute for Media Research of the Academy of Visual Arts in Braunschweig, Germany. He works freelance as a consultant for systemic management, is an author on leadership, and a lecturer on war and the media. He lives with his family in Frankfurt am Main, Germany.

Mungo Melvin works in the Ministry of Defence as the Director of Operational Capability, responsible to ministers and the chiefs of staff for the collection and analysis of lessons from joint operations. He is a graduate of the German Armed Forces Staff College and is a former deputy director of the British Higher Command and Staff Course. His long-standing interest in military history, operational art and strategy has taken him to many battlefields across the world. He is currently writing a biography of Field Marshal Erich von Manstein.

Vincent Orange is Reader in History (retired), University of Canterbury, Christchurch, New Zealand. He is the author of seven biographies of airmen, notably Sir Keith Park, 'Mary' Coningham and Lord Tedder. His biography of Sir John Slessor is scheduled to appear in July 2006. As an Associate Editor for the *Oxford Dictionary of Biography* he contributed 19 articles and vetted 50 more.

Michael Paris is Professor of Modern History at the University of Central Lancashire, and a Fellow of the Royal Historical Society. His major research interest is war and popular culture in twentieth century. Recent publications include *Warrior Nation: Images of War in British Popular Culture* (2002), and *Over the Top! The Great War and Juvenile Literature in Britain* (2004).

Gary Sheffield is Professor of Modern History at King's College, London, based at the Joint Services Command and Staff College, Shrivenham. His most recent book is *Douglas Haig: War Diaries and Letters 1914–1918* (co-edited with John Bourne, 2005), and he is working on a study of the British soldier in World War II.

Acknowledgements

This volume is the product of two conferences held in 2004 to mark the sixtieth anniversary of the Normandy campaign: the first, 'Normandy 60 Years On: Lessons for Contemporary Doctrine', was a Ministry of Defence seminar organised by Colonel David Benest and held at Trenchard Lines, Upavon; the second, 'The Normandy Campaign 1944: 60 Years On', was held at the History and Governance Research Institute at the University of Wolverhampton, and was organised by myself. Both David and I found the experience rewarding and stimulating, and it was a great pleasure to be involved in bringing together so many leading scholars from all parts of the world. That such excellent papers were presented demonstrates that the Normandy campaign and the military history of World War II are now flourishing academic areas, ripe for further study and research. Hopefully, the two conferences have gone some way to highlighting some of the issues and topics for us to focus on in the following years. Indeed, many fascinating insights and points were raised in the final session at Wolverhampton – my particular thanks to Stephen Hart, Stephen Badsey and Mike Taylor for leading this discussion. As is often the case with conferences though, we posed as many if not more questions than we answered.

Grateful thanks are due to my colleagues here at the University of Wolverhampton who made the potentially hazardous and stressful task of organising an international conference that much easier. I am particularly indebted to Professor Mark Phythian, Professor Malcolm Wanklyn and Julie Hayward, and on a more personal note to Dr Julia Speht, who endured more 'war talk' than she probably deserved. In putting together this volume I was aided no end by David Benest, at a time when he was involved in other pressing matters. I would also like to thank Andrew Humphyrs and Marjorie Francois at Routledge/Taylor & Francis, who have shown admirable patience as I endeavoured to badger the finished versions of chapters out of certain individuals.

Finally, I would personally like to thank all those who attended the conferences be they leading academics, professionals, students, researchers, veterans or interested parties. Ultimately it is they who made this project worthwhile.

John Buckley,
History and Governance Research Institute, University of Wolverhampton

Introduction

John Buckley

It is now over 60 years since the Allies landed in Normandy in June 1944 and began the process of liberating Western Europe from the clutches of the Third Reich. It was a campaign that marked the beginning of the end of the Second World War and was the clearest indication yet that Hitler's regime was in the process of crumbling. Indeed, to many German soldiers and civilians, the greatest military achievement of the Nazi state had been to overwhelm France in the early summer of 1940, achieving in a few weeks that which had been denied to their predecessors in the Imperial German army for four years in the 1914–18 war. Yet, by the end of August 1944 all that had been undone and Allied forces had successfully liberated Normandy, recovered Paris and were pushing on into the Low Countries. The scale of the Allied victory was stunning. In the space of some 80 days they effectively destroyed two German armies to the extent that of seven armoured divisions only some 24 tanks and 1,300 troops escaped across the Seine to flee back to Germany.[1] Far more than any defeats on the Eastern Front, even Stalingrad, the loss of France in the summer of 1944 marked a huge and fatal psychological blow to Germany, one from which she would not recover. Defeating the Allied invasion that summer arguably had represented the Third Reich's last realistic hope of avoiding total defeat and though the struggle would continue into 1945, the crushing blow suffered in the Normandy campaign proved beyond serious doubt that the defeat of Nazi Germany had moved from a case of 'if' to 'when'.

Looking back after 60 years, on a number of levels the Normandy Campaign represents an excellent case study of how the war was won in the West and why the Germans were ultimately defeated. Indeed, the planning and preparation of the OVERLORD invasion, its prosecution, and the ensuing fighting, all demonstrated the considerable strengths and weaknesses of the respective belligerents, not only in the summer of 1944 but in the war more generally. The key factors behind the Allied victory in Normandy emphatically underscored the reasons why they had turned the tide of the war, and why the supposed attributes of the German war machine were no longer so relevant nor decisive. Moreover, the successful liberation of France proved that the Allies were dictating to the Germans the manner in which the war would now be fought, an approach which maximised Allied strengths and simultaneously minimised any areas of superiority the Germans were perceived still to retain. This in effect equated to emphasising the Allies' superiority in production, resources, planning, intelligence and air power, whilst limiting the impact of the Germans' greater operational experience and close-combat capabilities, particularly at the tactical level. Ultimately, the Normandy campaign starkly represented the total seizure of the strategic initiative by the Allies, which they retained until the war's end the following year.

Yet despite the scale of the Allied victory, the historical perception of the Normandy campaign is a battle yet to be resolved. Overwhelming though Allied success had been in the summer of 1944 it was still a qualified victory, one which raised many questions and provoked critical comment and debate in the ensuing years. Most obviously the Allied armies' apparently ponderous and clumsy efforts at dislodging the Germans from Normandy in the weeks following the initial landings, and their inability to close the neck of the Falaise Pocket as quickly as they might in August exposed them to criticism. For many historians and analysts the Allied armies had demonstrated a limited and unimaginative grasp of operational art, even in the later stages of the war, and had relied excessively on overwhelming strength in resources, artillery and air power to defeat the Germans; an army with more flair and skill would have seized battlefield opportunities with greater alacrity and scored a faster and more complete victory.[2]

Explanations for this soon began to emerge. Chester Wilmot and Basil Liddell Hart argued that Allied soldiers were uneasy engaging in heavy close combat and often sought refuge in cover until artillery and air-based fire support could be brought to bear to neutralise opposition. This reduced offensives to sluggish, wary affairs that lacked dynamism and drive. Liddell Hart even claimed that the 'lions led by donkeys' epithet of the 1914–18 conflict could be turned on its head in the Second World War, for it was now the soldiery, not the generals, who lacked vigour and determination. German accounts also seemed to support the view that the Allied armies did not demonstrate drive on the battlefield and that a few casualties would prompt a halt, allowing time for the Germans to improvise a further defensive position, causing yet more delay.[3]

A further interpretation highlighted the operational and tactical shortcomings of the Allied armies and leadership. Weaknesses in doctrine, particularly in the exploitation phase of a battle, repeatedly caused operations to bog down and grind to a halt. Structural flaws were in part to blame, but for many the key factor was primarily the approach of Montgomery and, to a lesser extent, Bradley: overly cautious, defensive and lacking in flair. Only George Patton showed the grip and vision necessary to match or outperform the Germans at their own game, it was claimed. Carlo D'Este developed this view in *Decision in Normandy* (1983), still probably the most widely read single volume on the Normandy campaign.[4] The lack of operational skill, partly supplemented by tactical shortcomings and inexperience, contributed to situations where Allied forces failed to seize opportunities on the battlefield, thus prolonging the agony and generating further casualties.

In contrast, it was argued that the German army had performed remarkably well in the circumstances. Despite being outgunned, outnumbered, denuded of air support and lacking strategic direction or support it had hung on grimly and obdurately, refusing to concede ground without exacting a heavy toll from the Allies. Eventual defeat had been brought about by the weight of resources being directed against the Germans, and it was this that had ultimately overwhelmed them. This was, and indeed still is, a view held by many. Max Hastings's *Overlord* (1984) certainly put forward the case that the Germans were, unit for unit, masters of the battlefield, while more recently Russell Hart effectively established a league table of fighting power in Normandy, with the Americans, British and Canadians trailing, in that order, behind the Germans. Robin Neillands, although pursuing a different agenda, also rated the Germans highest in operational and tactical terms in his popular 2002 history of the campaign.[5]

Many of the armed forces of the post-1945 Western world have also subscribed to the principles that supposedly underpinned the Germans' tactical and operational approach to fighting in the Second World War: command initiative, mission-based planning, devolved responsibility and manoeuvre rather than firepower-based techniques, for example. Much of this was based on necessity as NATO wrestled with the problems of confronting the numerically superior Warsaw Pact forces in the Cold War. For many, it appeared to be a similar problem to that confronting the German armed forces in the Second World War; how to avoid defeat against numerically larger opposing forces. Though the Germans had lost, it was contended that this had been a result of strategic mismanagement, and that the German army had retained its tactical and operational superiority until the final stages of the war. It had certainly shown the way in terms of manoeuvre-based warfare, a method which eschewed long, attritional fighting, something the Germans could not afford in the Second World War and which NATO likewise aimed to avoid in Central Europe. Thus, it was the German army's approach in the Second World War that elicited most interest in a professional and historical sense in the post-war world, and it was this fascination that helped to develop an orthodoxy that leant only grudging acknowledgement to the success of the Allied armies in Normandy.

However, a degree of revisionism has begun to emerge in recent years to challenge this relatively well-established view. David French's work, *Raising Churchill's Army* (2000), demonstrated that despite certain limitations, the British army recovered well and fought effectively in the second half of the Second World War. He argued that by Normandy the army had a generally clear view of what it was capable of and how to defeat the more experienced German forces it was facing. In 2002 Robin Neillands attempted to question the interpretation of many, in his view usually American, historians who claimed that the Allied armies' unsophisticated and clumsy showing in Normandy was in part due to the unwillingness of the British and Canadian armies to 'get stuck in' around Caen, principally because they were overly casualty-conscious. Moreover, Neillands repudiated the claim that Montgomery's excessive caution and lack of flair had contributed to the sluggishness of the front in Normandy for much of June and July in 1944, a view prevalent in the USA, particularly following the success of D'Este's book in 1983, and further popularised in the film *Saving Private Ryan*. Stephen Hart skilfully re-evaluated Montgomery's command methods in *Montgomery and Colossal Cracks: 21st Army Group in Northwest Europe 1944–5*, arguing that Monty's technique was largely appropriate to the strategic and operational environment as pertained in 1944–5, and that more importantly, although there were shortcomings to his approach, it was still the most effective method available, and was also a highly successful *modus operandi*. I have also attempted to salvage the reputation of British armoured forces in Normandy, arguing that they were a flexible fighting force that performed successfully during the campaign, and indeed adapted to the operating environment more effectively than their German counterparts. However, the most strident revisionist view was offered by Terry Copp in *Fields of Fire: The Canadians in Normandy* (2003). Here he argued that the Canadian army fought very effectively in Normandy and demonstrated tactical and operational flexibility and acumen, to a level previously unrecognised. Moreover, and perhaps most contentiously, he claimed that whilst the Germans demonstrated obduracy and grim determination, probably born of desperation and fear of retribution, they in fact displayed no great operational or tactical flair. He was particularly critical of the immediate counterattack, a doctrine repeatedly employed by the German army, even when it proved ruinously costly in the face of massive Allied firepower. Far from being the astute tacticians as widely popularised in Western military history since 1945, Copp argued that the Germans proved palpably unable to meet the challenge of the campaign in Normandy, principally because the Allies did not allow them to; and for this the Allies deserve considerable credit on strategic, operational and tactical levels.[6]

Contrasting views on this particular debate are represented in this volume. Mungo Melvin's chapter outlines the doctrinal factors behind the success of the German army at lower command level in the Normandy campaign and indeed the Second World War as a whole. Quite explicitly Brigadier Melvin seeks to explain '. . . why the Germans did so well in defence and the why the Allied forces made comparatively slow progress in attack' and concludes that superior doctrine and training were the key factors, linked with the skilful utilisation of helpful terrain and high morale. Terry Copp challenges this approach directly in his chapter on the performance of the Anglo-Canadian 21st Army Group in Normandy. Both Copp and Melvin agree that strategically the Allies proved superior in almost every respect, but they differ somewhat on the inability of the Germans to impose themselves on the campaign at the operational level. For this Melvin argues that Allied air power was decisive, but Copp rejects this and instead argues that it was the frontline fighting units – infantry and armour – that shouldered this responsibility. Copp even suggests that powerful and useful though Allied artillery proved, it was in no way so decisive as has been often believed. Moreover, he rejects the view that the Allied armies proved doctrinally deficient compared to the Germans; indeed he contends that the Allies had a clear idea of how to win and prosecuted their plans accordingly, demonstrating tactical flexibility along the way.

What has also been highlighted by the developing debate over the last few years is the scarcity of in-depth studies on many aspects of the campaign, most obviously from the ground-up as well as at higher command levels. Indeed, in order to assess the relative merits of the conflicting views of Melvin and Copp fully, a great deal of in-depth work is still required. For example, we still await analytical studies of Allied artillery and logistics in Normandy and incisive and rigorous investigations into the actual fighting strengths and abilities of German units in action, studies unfettered by preconceived notions of doctrinal superiority.

A number of key issues are addressed within this volume, however, demonstrating that this process in underway. Marc Hansen identifies many of the key failings in the German command structure: the compromised chain of command, the weak logistical support network and the Rommel/Geyr von Schweppenburg strategic controversy, yet argues that ultimately it was the failure of the German leaders, including those at the front, to respond immediately and decisively enough in the first hours of OVERLORD that decided the outcome of the campaign and indeed the nature of the war's conclusion. Hansen also underlines the view that German commanders were simply unwilling to come to terms with the real strategic and political plight of Germany by the midpoint of the war. In addition, he points out that many German commanders bemoaned the *kampfgruppe* system whereby troops were fed into the battle in an ad hoc fashion merely to maintain the front, as it ultimately surrendered operational initiative to the Allies. Paradoxically, this flexible system was and is much admired by Western armies, acclamation which rather obfuscates the point that it was a desperate response to Allied pressure and viewed as a very limited emergency compromise by the Germans.

The period immediately following the landings on 6 June, prior to the larger set-piece battles and operations, is a phase often passed over by historians, but Stephen Badsey challenges this oversight in his chapter. This was the crucial period in which the nature of the Normandy campaign was decided. Badsey, like Hansen, argues that German command failed on a number of counts, with different factions imposing their own ideas on how to react and defend against the invasion, down to tactical level. Moreover, Rommel himself and his staff failed to appreciate the importance of the Mulberry harbours and remained convinced that Cherbourg was the key to the whole campaign and that this was where the main German effort should focus. They were saved from this strategic blunder when Anglo-Canadian pressure and Hitler's orders forced them to commit their greater strength around Caen rather than in the more difficult terrain in the American sector.

However, the outcome of the battle for Normandy should not be predominantly viewed as a German failure; both Nigel de Lee and myself argue in our chapters that the Allies made considerable progress in adapting and developing their fighting techniques to the demands of the campaign. Contrary to some sources, de Lee demonstrates that the American frontline units devised, developed and adapted appropriate techniques for dealing with the demands of combat in the *bocage* (country characterised by small fields, high hedgerows and sunken lanes), to a degree hitherto little recognised. Moreover, he shows that this was a dynamic and fluid process, well suited to the military culture of the US army. It is interesting to note the nature of the tactical innovation and invention, which often emerged from the bottom (or hedgerow) up.

This was a pattern mirrored to a significant extent in British armoured units in Normandy. Since the end of the campaign, and perhaps more than any other arm, Anglo-Canadian mechanised divisions and brigades have endured a barrage of criticism. This has usually centred on inadequate equipment and inappropriate doctrine. In Chapter 6, I argue that this view is in need of revision, that in reality Anglo-Canadian armoured units played a crucial role in defeating the Germans in Normandy, one that fitted the operational and strategic approach of 21st Army Group. Furthermore, on a tactical level, British armoured units, like their American cousins, adapted their fighting techniques to the demands of Normandy, demonstrating considerable flexibility. In both cases, it should be noted that these armies were made up of largely inexperienced units and troops, and that consequently their doctrinal development is all the more impressive.

Allied efforts at developing and adapting their operational techniques during the Normandy campaign, whilst retaining the strategic initiative, are illustrated in two chapters. Ian Daglish analyses Operation BLUECOAT, a bitterly contested action fought in late July and early August. The intention was to pin German strength in the British sector and thus aid the burgeoning American breakout in the west. Daglish contends that BLUECOAT was a significant success, too often skimmed over by historians who prefer to focus on COBRA. Moreover, Daglish refutes Copp's claim that BLUECOAT represented arguably the greatest blunder of Montgomery's career. He argues that the British demonstrated the ability to respond quickly to a strategic need by setting up BLUECOAT at short notice; that Montgomery and Dempsey proved sufficiently flexible to shift the emphasis of their offensive in response to the flow of battle; and that ultimately the operation achieved most of its strategic objectives. Furthermore, BLUECOAT demonstrated that Allied tactical developments, notably in armour-infantry cooperation, were having a marked impact on the conduct of operations. Tactical refinements were also clearly apparent during Operation TOTALIZE, a dynamic and innovative plan principally devised by Guy Simonds, and the subject of Stephen Hart's chapter. He shows us that the Allied armies were capable of thinking through problems and devising solutions; yet, he also demonstrates that whilst many obstacles could be negotiated 'in theatre', there were limitations to what could be achieved. Indeed, the failure to exploit TOTALIZE's initial success, Hart argues, was partly attributable to Allied inexperience and fierce German resistance, but the operational techniques generated by the careful and cautious military culture of Anglo-Canadian armies also played a major role. When Simonds threw caution to the wind on the night of 8/9 August 1944, his forces were doctrinally and culturally ill-equipped to cope. Moreover, Hart explores the paradox that at times in the campaign, that at which the Allies excelled – planning, support and firepower – precipitated an approach and operational technique that actually imposed limitations on the ability of Allied forces to exploit the situations their strengths had created.

Whatever the operational and doctrinal debates and issues conducted at higher levels both then and since, for the soldiers at the front, mostly conscripts, the fighting in Normandy was a chastening experience. It is still not widely recognised that the British army endured a higher casualty rate in Normandy than it did at Passchendaele in 1917, nor that these casualties fell predominantly (in excess of 70 per cent) on the rifle companies alone. Gary Sheffield places the soldier's experience of war in the summer of 1944 into this context, demonstrating that despite the privations, the casualty rates and the increasing levels of battle exhaustion, the citizen soldiery of the British army reacted with stoicism to their time in Normandy. The widely held belief prevailed that the liberation of Europe was a job that simply had to be endured. Sheffield also amply demonstrates that junior leadership was fundamental to maintaining morale and battlefield effectiveness in Normandy, and that this job entailed a difficult balancing act of inspiration and bullying.

Although many historians have hitherto viewed the fighting on the ground in Normandy as an area in which the Germans had the edge, there has been less controversy over the superiority in other fields such as air power and intelligence. Yet a number of debates surrounding these two aspects of the campaign are raised in this volume which force us to question our assumptions on these issues. It is generally contended that German air power, all but snuffed out as an effective fighting force by the summer of 1944, had little chance of achieving anything meaningful in Normandy. Jim Corum partly refutes this claim, presenting the case that the Luftwaffe could have made a better fist of it than they did. He demonstrates that, as in so many other areas of their conduct of the war, the Germans focused too heavily upon special weapons and new technology, such as jets and guided bombs. Perhaps more importantly they also frittered away valuable resources on bombing England when such aircraft would have been far better employed deploying aerial mines against the Allied invasion forces. Corum also flags up an area of future research: the role and effectiveness of the flak forces in the Normandy campaign. Once again we have an area in which we may not know as much we think.

The role of Allied air power in determining the outcome of the Normandy campaign has been the centre of some debate in recent years. Although spectacular and immensely popular with ground forces the actual impact of tactical air power has been subjected to considerable scrutiny, as indeed has the part played by the strategic air forces.[7] Vincent Orange's study of Air Chief Marshal Arthur Tedder and the role he played in developing the transportation plan demonstrates, however, that this use of air power at least proved vital in bringing about the Allied victory in Normandy. Moreover, it is clear that Tedder was fundamental to its implementation and prosecution, and was later to be proved largely correct in his estimation that a concerted attack upon the German transportation network would yield rich rewards indeed in the months after Normandy.

However, air power did not always prove so beneficial or effective. Peter Gray's chapter on the bombing of Caen shows that a proposal can acquire an apparently irresistible and logical momentum, especially when propelled by events, personalities and strategic imperative. Yet, the plan or concept can fail because practical issues can remain unresolved; clearly the employment of strategic air forces to aid the capture of the pivotal city of Caen during Operation CHARNWOOD was a good idea *per se*, but translating the idea into a practical plan proved far more difficult than imagined, particularly with mounting political pressure demanding rapid results. It should be noted however, that the employment of strategic air forces improved considerably as the Northwest European campaign continued, and CHARN-WOOD was only the first step.

The intelligence war is a further aspect of the campaign in which the Allies proved successful, both in planning and prosecution. As ever, however, our orthodox view is in need of some redefinition, as explored in chapters by Kathryn Barbier and John Ferris. The broad aspects of the FORTI-TUDE deception are well known, from colourfully code-named double-agents such as 'Garbo' and 'Tricycle' to the establishment of the fictitious First US Army Group in Southeast England. However, as Kathryn Barbier argues in her chapter, too much attention has been focused on the mechanics of FORTITUDE, not its effects. In examining the impact of FORTI-TUDE Barbier shows us that although many facets of the Allied deception plan functioned properly, they did not necessarily drive the German high command's decision to maintain 15th Army in Pas de Calais area for some weeks after D-Day. Perhaps, therefore, we have been beguiled by FORTI-TUDE's complexities and 'cloak and dagger' activities into attributing to it greater importance than is merited.

John Ferris analyses the role played by intelligence in the planning and conduct of the invasion itself and shows us that although there was a good deal of information available, it was patchy in quality and then interpreted in contrasting manners by a host of different analysts, themselves shaped by national and cultural approaches. Therefore, the effectiveness of winning the intelligence war was itself uneven and did not translate easily into battle-field successes. Ferris contends, however, that the intelligence gathered was good enough, and that in any case even if it were better it would have made little difference; Operation CRUSADER in the western desert had already demonstrated that superb intelligence meant little if the armed forces them-selves could not conduct effective operations. In Normandy, the picture of the enemy may have been less comprehensive, but by 1944 the Allied armies had learnt how to fight the Germans and could deal with problems as they emerged on the battlefield.

Understanding the impact and feel of war – what it was like to be there – is all but inaccessible to the historian, especially with the passage of six decades, but sources are available to us to throw light upon the impact of D-Day and the Normandy campaign on the participants. Michael Paris argues that film can get us closer than any other source to certain aspects of the campaign in a way that even written testimony cannot. Nevertheless, the innate scepticism of the historian about the use of film as a valid source, coupled with the excesses of commercial film makers, have limited the util-isation of film in building our understanding of D-Day and Normandy. Paris focuses on the range of documentaries produced during the war and since and concludes that there is indeed much of value, despite the need to treat some productions with scepticism. It is also worth noting that as we are unlikely to see the likes of series such *The World at War* being made again for major network television, the increasingly popular docudrama may be the future for presenting and defining history to large audiences.

Undoubtedly the most important event in broadening interest in D-Day, the Normandy campaign and the Second World War more generally to the public, has been the relatively recent release of feature films such as *Saving Private Ryan* and television series such as *Band of Brothers.* However, the relationship between the makers of film drama and the historian is a difficult and at times fraught affair. Carsten Hennig's discussion of the influences shaping the progression of films portraying some aspects of the Normandy campaign nevertheless emphasises the point that drama is a potent tool for aiding our understanding of how we see the past. New forms of communica-tion media have often been the cause of much debate but ultimately, and indeed because of this, they constitute a valid source.

As we move into an era when veterans' associations begin to disband and the living link with the Second World War loosens ever more it is worth reflecting that popular and professional interest in D-Day and the Nor-mandy campaign is enjoying a renaissance. Moreover, perhaps unlike the fortieth anniversary, the sixtieth sees the subject in a state of thoughtful reassessment. The military conduct of the Second World War is unlikely ever to carry the same cultural and emotional baggage as the Great War, not in Britain at least, but it is clear that much work remains to be done.

There are still large gaps in our detailed knowledge of how the campaign was fought and this volume, and the conferences from which the chapters were drawn, have contributed in part to a process of re-evaluation. For future researchers the field is, nonetheless, very much open.

Notes

1 Martin Blumenson, 'General Bradley's Decision at Argentan (13 August 1944)', in *Command Decisions*, online edition, Center of Military History, Department of the Army, Washington, 2000 (originally published in 1959) www.army.mil/cmh-pg/books.
2 John Ellis' *Brute Force: Allied Strategy and Tactics in the Second World War* (London: Andre Deutsch, 1990), pp. 373–88 is an excellent example of this trend.
3 Chester Wilmot, *The Struggle for Europe* (London: Collins, 1952), pp. 130–1, 427–8 and 463–5; Basil Liddell Hart's comments can be found at the Liddell Hart Centre for Military Archives (LHMCA), Liddell Hart 11/1944/43–52, 'Lessons of Normandy' (1952); a much cited example of German views is Kurt Meyer, *Grenadiers* (Winnipeg, Manitoba: j. J. Federowicz, 1994), pp. 280–98.
4 Carlo D'Este, *Decision in Normandy* (London: HarperCollins, 1983), introduction and chapter entitled 'The Price of Caution'.
5 Max Hastings, *Overlord: D-Day and the Battle of Normandy* (London: Pan, 1984); Robin Neillands, *The Battle of Normandy 1944* (London: Cassell, 2002); and Russell Hart, *Clash of Arms: How the Allies Won in Normandy* (Boulder, CL: Lynne Rienner, 2001).
6 Revisionist style views: Stephen Hart, *Montgomery and Colossal Cracks: 21st Army Group in Northwest Europe 1944–5* (Westport, CT: Praeger, 2000); John Buckley, *British Armour in the Normandy Campaign 1944* (London: Frank Cass, 2004); Terry Copp, *Fields of Fire: The Canadians in Normandy* (University of Toronto Press, 2003).
7 See Ian Gooderson, *Air Power at the Battlefront: Allied Close Air Support in Europe 1943–45* (London: Frank Cass, 1998), the best single volume on this topic.

1 The 21st Army Group in Normandy

Towards a new balance sheet

Terry Copp

The purpose of this chapter is to offer further evidence in support of the view that the combat performance of the Anglo-Canadian armies in Normandy has been greatly underrated and the effectiveness of the German forces vastly overrated. This argument informs my study of the Canadians in Normandy, published under the title *Fields of Fire*,[1] but the intention here is to consider questions about combat between British and German units in Normandy.

My views on this subject were influenced by my long association with the late Robert Vogel and the work we shared in researching and writing a basic narrative of the campaign in Northwest Europe published in the 1980s. When we began our decade-long project, I had little knowledge of military history. Vogel, who was a military historian, introduced me to Clausewitz and other theoreticians but I soon decided that a social historian escaping a world dominated by Marxists was entitled to be suspicious of yet another nineteenth-century authority figure.

We agreed that history at the battalion, brigade and divisional level might best be understood by a careful reading of the primary sources and my first visits to Normandy convinced me that one of the most neglected sources was the actual ground, especially when supplemented by 1944 maps and air photos.[2] The study of the Normandy battlefields suggested to me that the basic question to answer was how the Allied soldiers overcame a powerful enemy, defending ground of its own choosing, in just 76 days. Other historians had answered the question by referring to the decisive role of air power and the application of brute force to the battlefield, but few of them seemed to know very much about what actually happened at the operational and tactical levels.

When our five-volume narrative was complete I began to work on three separate but related subjects: a study of a single infantry brigade; an inquiry into battle exhaustion; and an analysis of the role played by tactical air power in Normandy. The later project led to an interest in operational research in both the air force and army and I was able to interview a number of the most important operational research specialists.[3]

By the mid-1990s, I was convinced that the Allied campaign in Normandy required re-examination. It was evident that air power, strategic or tactical, had not been the decisive factor in Normandy or elsewhere. Evidence from operational research had also demonstrated that the anecdotal evidence on the vulnerability of Allied armour and the limited effectiveness of Allied tank gunnery was all too true. It was equally apparent that the principal Allied weapon systems, field and medium artillery, were rarely able to inflict damage on prepared enemy positions and were not always able to achieve temporary neutralisation.[4]

These severe limitations in Allied weapons technology helped to explain why the Battle of Normandy produced so many physical and mental casualties but brought us no closer to understanding why the enemy was so quickly defeated. The OVERLORD planners prepared for a campaign that would proceed in a series of managed phases. After the invading troops were ashore they were to establish and defend a bridgehead, defeating the German counter-attacks with naval, air, and artillery fire. The bridgehead was, if possible, to include the city of Caen, the centre of the road and rail network in Normandy. If Caen could not be captured before German reinforcements arrived, the city was to be masked until the build-up of Allied forces was sufficient for a set-piece attack.

South of Caen, the country was open, with good roads leading to the Seine and Paris. The planners assumed that the enemy would defend this area in strength, as a breakthrough here would cut off German forces in the west and bring a quick conclusion to the Battle of Normandy. If the enemy behaved rationally, there would be a fighting withdrawal to a new defensive line at the Seine, with the ground south of the Caen sector held as a pivot.

The OVERLORD plan called for the American army to capture Cherbourg and then fight its way south, turning west into Brittany to capture Brest and create a new port at Quiberon Bay. With the Brittany ports and Cherbourg available, the Allied forces would complete the build-up necessary to liberate France by the autumn of 1944. All of this was the basis of Montgomery's 'master plan', a broad concept that proved to have little operational significance except that it focused attention on Brittany.[5]

If 21 Army Group could be maintained at full strength, there would be ten infantry and five armoured divisions available to wage war against the German forces on the eastern flank. Even with five additional armoured brigades available to support the infantry divisions, the prospects of achieving the force ratios necessary to overcome the enemy in this vital sector were bleak. The presence of three or four German armoured divisions and a like number of infantry divisions would make it impossible to achieve the 3:1 ratio thought to be necessary for successful attacks on well-defended positions. The planners hoped to compensate for this weakness by fighting on Allied, not German, terms. This meant employing the largest possible amount of artillery in the bridgehead. Each corps was to be supported by an Army Group Royal Artillery (AGRA) with 4.5- or 5.5-inch medium guns. Air observation pilots flying light aircraft were to direct this fire, and there were to be abundant allotments of ammunition for both the medium and field artillery. Fully 18 per cent of the men in 21 Army Group were gunners; just 15 per cent were to be wearing infantry flashes. If the allocation of ancillary services is taken into account, fully a third of the army's manpower was committed to the artillery.[6]

This approach to war required commanders to emphasise logistics, elaborate fire plans, and centralised command and control. If shells were to be substituted for men's lives, they had to be delivered to the right places at the right times. Little attention has been paid to the pre-Normandy investment in survey regiments, air photo interpretation, meteorological reports, sound ranging, flash spotting and other elements of the gunner's war, but these efforts were an essential part of the preparations for victory at a blood price the Allies could afford. The gunner's war deserves much more attention than it has received.[7]

While the assault divisions prepared for an attack on the beaches of the Calvados coast, the divisions committed to the follow-up role prepared to 'attack, wear down and destroy German troops who would fight a series of defensive battles on ground of their own choosing'.[8] There was broad agreement on how this was to be accomplished and when Lieutenant-General Guy Simonds decided to issue a directive on operational policy to his inexperienced Canadian divisions, he sent copies to Dempsey, the Second British Army Commander and to Montgomery, both of whom read it with 'complete agreement'.[9] British senior officers were a bit puzzled by the Canadian tendency to prepare written papers outlining the obvious but the Canadians with their earnest staff officers and abundant supply of typewriters, clerk typists and duplicating machines produced a written record of considerable value to soldiers and historians.

Simonds's statement of Allied operational doctrine called for centralised control of virtually every aspect of the battle. The enemy was to be overcome by attacks that were 'carefully organised and strongly supported by all available artillery'. The Germans forward defences 'are not thickly held in terms of men, but are strong in automatic weapons and well supported by mortars sited up to three or four thousand yards' behind forward lines. The essence of the German system of defence was the counter-attack, and 'as long as fresh reserves are available the Germans will counterattack continuously, supported by self-propelled guns brought up to close-range. The success of the offensive battle hinged on the defeat of the German counter-attacks', and everyone was trained to deal with this reality. The preferred solution was to stage divisional attacks 'on a single thrust line, disposed in depth on a one-brigade front'. Brigades would be passed through one another to maintain momentum, with the frontage of the attack 'limited to that on which really heavy support can be given'. When the enemy concentrated its strength across the thrust line, a reserve brigade could be 'thrown wide of the leading brigade' to dissipate the enemy's strength. The weight of artillery support would then be shifted to the reserve brigade.

The infantry division, always and only when supported by the artillery, was the 'sledgehammer' in the Allied arsenal. The armoured division was 'a weapon of opportunity', capable of dealing with enemy rearguard positions and developing a breakout, but it was too weak in infantry to carry out an attack in depth. Everything experienced in Italy suggested that Allied armour could not be used to lead attacks against prepared German positions given the effective range of their tank and anti-tank guns.

There was no similar doctrine on the tactics to be employed in carrying out Simonds's 'operational policy', partly because such training was carried out in divisional battle schools and partly because the operational doctrine left little room for traditional platoon or section tactics. By 1944, experienced Allied commanders knew that the one certain way of defeating the Germans was to find, fix and then neutralise the enemy with overwhelming firepower. This would allow the infantry to assault and occupy vital ground, which the enemy would then counter-attack. This 'bite and hold' doctrine depended on the development of centrally controlled, indirect artillery fire capable of concentrating the guns of a regiment, division or corps on a specific area. This technique provided the best possible answer to the enemy's doctrinal commitment to immediate and continuous counter-attacks and to German technical superiority in infantry weapons and armoured vehicles.

An artillery-based battle doctrine required the infantry to move forward at a steady pace, leaning into the barrage, so as to be on the objective before the enemy could engage the attackers. Rifle companies, supported by tanks, would clear and consolidate, bring the anti-tank guns forward, and dig in to meet counter-attacks from enemy infantry, who would be advancing behind tanks or self-propelled assault guns. Success depended largely on the ability of forward observation officers to direct the fire of the field and medium regiments at observed targets. This procedure, rehearsed in countless exercises, did not require the infantry to practise the fire-and-movement skills learned in battle schools. It did, however, raise questions about other aspects of infantry training. These issues were widely debated within the army, and on 20 April 1944 a four-day conference was held at the School of Infantry to exchange ideas and information.[10]

One of the most contentious questions was raised by a staff officer from 2nd British Army, who noted that present teaching placed too much emphasis on the use of infantry weapons in the attack, especially the Bren. Experience had shown that the ammunition problem was acute in the counter-attack phase. Ammunition fired in the attack was seldom aimed and was therefore wasted. The same officer insisted that though the rifleman used his weapon in defending a position, in the attack he was 'mostly employed as an ammunition carrier for the Bren'.

This realistic view of the impact of operational doctrine on tactics directly challenged the traditional emphasis on teaching the infantry to fight their way forward, with their own weapons, by fire and movement. This approach was evident in a discussion of the implications of the decision that all troops should carry a shovel and a pick into battle. Obviously, the additional weight would limit the ability of the soldier to fight his way forward; yet without entrenching tools, no position could be held against enemy counter-attacks and mortar fire.

The critics of 21 Army Group's pre-invasion training are quite right when they argue that the army's leadership 'failed to enforce a coherent and effective tactical doctrine'.[11] But was this a weakness or a strength? There was agreement on operational doctrine, and a flexible approach to tactical problems encouraged officers to seek solutions based on specific battlefield conditions, especially analysis of the terrain using air photographs. A problem-solving approach to combat has little appeal to military theorists, but it proved to be an effective method of dealing with the enemy.

The discussions at the Infantry School barely touched on the role of the armoured regiments assigned to work with infantry battalions. This was the result of an earlier decision that the armoured commander, at the regimental, squadron or troop level, 'is the sole arbitrator of how he can best employ his resources'. This meant that the armoured commander decided where to employ his tanks in support of an infantry attack, which was itself largely determined by the artillery fire plan created at division and corps. Although 'the primary role' of tanks cooperating with infantry was 'to close with the enemy', armoured doctrine permitted indirect support 'on account of the unsuitability of the ground' or for other reasons. Armoured officers were also reminded that 'everyone, and particularly the infantry, should understand that the tank is designed with the primary object of destroying or neutralising enemy unarmoured troops'.[12]

Again, it is clear that those who criticise the Commonwealth forces for failing to develop the kind of integrated tank-infantry battlegroup doctrine practiced by the German army are correct. The British approach, as it was understood in May 1944, allowed everything and forbade nothing. It was up to individual commanders to develop methods of employing their tanks effectively, and as we shall see they did so.

The Anglo-Canadian army that fought the Battle of Normandy was well prepared for the kind of warfare they encountered. The only real surprise was the enemy's stubborn, almost mindless persistence in continuing to mount counter-attacks after it was evident that the Allies were well prepared to deal with them. Willing soldiers led by courageous leaders were repeatedly sacrificed in obedience to a doctrine that the German army ought to have abandoned. In Normandy it was the Allies not the Germans who worked out new ways of carrying out the intent of their orders.

This approach to the Normandy battle was developed during 20 years of research on the Canadian rather than British army, but the Canadians were a small part of a larger force so it was necessary to analyse specific British operations at corps, divisional and battalion level. Canadians have a special interest in the British divisions that served in First Canadian Army as well as 53 Welsh and 59 Staffordshire Divisions, formations that fought along-side the Canadians.

Let us begin with some comments on the performance of 51 Highland Division in Normandy. The Highland Division's record in North Africa and Sicily has won universal praise but there is near-universal agreement that it failed to function effectively in Normandy. I had the opportunity to present a contrary view in Edinburgh in 1996.[13] The audience included a number of veterans who had retired holding senior rank but who were platoon or company commanders in 1944. They were familiar with the negative view of the division recently highlighted by Carlo D'Este and Max Hastings and curious to know what a Canadian might have to say.

We reviewed the historiography and then focused on Montgomery's much-quoted letter to Alanbrooke dated 15 July 1944 in which an exasperated Monty wrote, 'Regret to report it is considered opinion of Crocker, Dempsey and myself that 51st Division is at present not battle worthy . . . and had failed in every operation it has been given to do'.[14] Montgomery's solution was to remove Major-General Bullen-Smith and replace him with a veteran jock, Tom Rennie. Few of the veterans present accepted the idea that Bullen-Smith had failed and that Rennie transformed the division, but there was agreement that getting away from Crocker's I British Corps and being given an operational-level task in TOTALIZE had a powerful effect on morale.

The orders given to the division in June and July required the defence of the vital Orne bridgehead coupled with limited battalion-level actions to secure additional ground. A difficult and costly business for anyone, Allied or enemy. Let us focus on two such actions: the battle for Ste. Honorine la Chardonnerette on 23 June and the attempt to secure Colombelles on 11 July.

The village of Ste. Honorine, or what was left of it, had been attacked, captured and lost during a bloody encounter in mid-June. 21 Panzer Division had counter-attacked with large forces and Bullen-Smith had wisely decided to withdraw and allow his artillery to deal with the enemy.[15] On 23 June, 152 Brigade (2nd and 5th Seaforths and 5th Camerons) organised a carefully-staged night attack which won them complete control of the village.[16] The inevitable counter-attacks began with first light – company-size battlegroups with tanks and self-propelled guns. This time the 13/18 Hussars provided a squadron of tanks, including Firefly 17-pounders, and the FOOs never lost contact with the field and medium artillery. The Cameron's *War Diary*[17] contains a detailed account of their part in this very successful action which devastated Panzer Group Luck, forcing Luck to 'rebuild the entire formation'.[18] This battle, marked by careful preparation, limited objectives, close infantry-tank cooperation and a fire plan designed to inflict maximum damage on an enemy whose patterned response was easy to prepare for, is one of scores of examples of successful brigade-level actions in Normandy that need to be studied.

A different fate awaited 153 Brigade (5th Battalion, The Black Watch; 1st and 5th/7th Battalion, The Gordon Highlanders) on the night of 10/11 July when Montgomery ordered Crocker to stage an attack on Colombelles, one of the industrial suburbs of Caen. The object of the action was to destroy the tall chimney stacks that provided the enemy with an unobstructed view of the Orne bridgehead. No detailed account of the battle is possible here but since this was the action that prompted Montgomery's letter to Alanbrooke, we need to at least note that both division and brigade, not to mention the 5th Battalion of The Black Watch, who were to carry out the first phase of the attack, knew that the Germans had reinforced their defences after Operation CHARNWOOD forced a withdrawal from Caen.[19]

The limited fire plan laid on by corps and patrol reports of dug-in tanks and anti-tank guns added to everyone's concern. Lieutenant-Colonel Thompson, The Black Watch commanding officer wrote an account of the battle which is appended to the *War Diary*. He described the efforts to dig-in on the first phase objectives under constant, accurate mortar and Nebelwerfer fire. The news that The 1st Gordons had been unable to reach all of their objectives explained the heavy fire coming from the battalion's right flank but brigade promised a new attack would begin at first light. Enemy infantry attacks were readily repulsed but German armour, including at least two Tigers, dealt a devastating blow to 148 Regiment RAC Shermans destroying 10 of their 11 tanks. The available 17-pounders had either been blinded by enemy defensive fire or destroyed and played no role in the battle. Thompson concludes:

> I spoke to the Brigadier and told him that to hold the positions of my leading companies would result in their destruction piecemeal as the anti-tank defence had collapsed and my own 6-pounders could not be brought to bear. He then ordered me at about 0800 hours to withdraw to St Honorine and this move was completed under continuous smoke by 0930 hours.[20]

Bullen-Smith supported this decision, infuriating Crocker and prompting Montgomery to claim that the division 'cannot fight the Germans successfully'. Montgomery was wrong. The Black Watch withdrawal from Colombelles was not a failure but a rational response to the realities of the battlefield.

Men in combat continually engage in cost-benefit analysis. Orders are ignored, amended or renegotiated as decision-makers engage in calculations of risk versus gain. This reality offends senior commanders whose plans are not carried out and military historians who seem to believe that actions that do not go as planned 'fail'. But the primary responsibility of the commander is to advance the goal of winning the war while the historian's job is to explain what happened not to issue pass/fail grades.

The experience of the 53 Welsh Division has attracted little attention and even less is known about Major-General R.K. Ross who commanded it throughout the war. My interest was sparked by the close cooperation between 2 Canadian and 53 Welsh during the advance to Falaise, but the divisional war diaries offer other insights into other operations in Normandy. The division took up positions west of the Orne in early July and one of its brigades fought under 15 Scottish during the battle for the Evrecy spur, but for the rest of the month the Welsh Division fought a series of battalion-level engagements with elements of 10SS Panzer Division and the 277 Infantry Division.

Ross quickly adapted to this limited role, ordering each battalion to thin out their forward positions and create large left out of battle (LOB) parties. Faced with heavy casualties from constant mortar fire, Ross reorganised his counter-mortar organisation and used his heavy mortar platoons to strike enemy locations. He also insisted on detailed preparation for company-level night raids designed to kill the enemy and prevent his own troops from becoming browned-off by having to sit in slit trenches, being mortared and shelled without retaliation. The raids appear to have accomplished their primary purpose and to have provoked the kind of enemy counter-attacks the divisional artillery and anti-tank regiments planned and prepared for. One such counter-attack on 22 July resulted in 10SS regaining control of the Bon Repas-Evrecy road, a clear victory in a win-lose narrative but a typical German defeat in any cost-benefit analysis. The Welsh division losses in July (over 250 killed and close to 2,500 wounded) speak of the character of the Normandy battle even when no major offensive operations were underway.[21]

Let us turn to the curious case of 49 (West Riding) Division. The 49th was part of First Canadian Army for most of the campaign and their commitment to the long left flank meant that the division experienced prolonged periods of limited action. Patrick Delaforce's recent history *The Polar Bears*[22] has helped to rescue the division from obscurity but many questions about its performance in combat remain. Brigadier Trevor Hart Dyke, the author of one of the very best memoirs of the campaign in Northwest Europe, *Normandy to Arnhem: A Story of the Infantry*,[23] provided some answers in a 1982 interview.

Brigadier Hart Dyke found the notion of German battlefield superiority curious. He had read Hastings and D'Este but was quite certain that the Hallams and their sister battalions in 146 Brigade had been consistently effective in combat against well-regarded German formations. He drew particular attention to the success of the Hallams and indeed the brigade at Fontenay-le-Pesnel and Tessel Woods. These actions, part of 49 Division's Operation MARTLET, an attack in support of EPSOM, created a three-kilometre deep penetration in the seam between 12SS and Panzer Lehr.[24]

MARTLET was designed to accomplish two purposes, distraction and attrition. The division carried it out with considerable skill. Those who insist that the British army never mastered the art of infantry-tank cooperation should examine the role of 24th Lancers (8 Armoured Brigade) at Tessel Wood. After assisting the assault battalions into Fontenay they reformed and worked closely with the 1/4 KOYLIs, employing all three squadrons in a close support role. With darkness falling, one squadron remained on the western edge of the woods to protect the right flank and later sent a troop to a threatened sector, forcing three Panthers to withdraw. The next morning the Lancers flushed snipers from the hedgerows, helping the infantry to consolidate.[25] The later phases of this battle, involving major German counter-attacks on 70 Brigade's positions at Rauray are described in detail in Kevin Baverstock's superb book *Breaking the Panzers*.[26] This account of the Tyneside Scottish in action offers a classic description of courage and skill in defeating powerful enemy counter-attacks. It should serve as a model for studies of other battles in Normandy and beyond.

Brigadier Hart Dyke's comments on battalion- and brigade-level operations prompted a discussion of the Hargest Report,[27] one of the key documents used by authors critical of the combat effectiveness of the British soldier. His first reaction was to note that Hargest's one reference to a 49th Division battalion, the Lincolns, was laudatory. He insisted that there were no problems of poor morale in his battalion or the brigade and was surprised by the bitter tone of Hargest's comments on the armoured regiments which he had thought superb.[28] Could 50 Division's experience have really been so different?

Hart Dyke was also puzzled by the New Zealander's stereotype of aggressive self-sufficient Dominion soldiers whom he claimed were very different from the 'hesitant Tommies'. Perhaps the report by Brigadier James Hargest, written by a brave soldier of the Great War, who had made a series of disastrous command decisions in Crete before his capture and imprisonment in Italy, was not an entirely dispassionate document. The Hargest Report along with the propaganda on the inferiority of Allied soldiers routinely produced by German staff officers needs to be examined critically as David French began to do in *Raising Churchill's Army*.[29]

If we are to revise the balance sheet on the performance of the British army in Normandy, a great deal of work needs to be done. When *Fields of Fire* appeared in 2003 an American colleague asked, 'When will you Canadians stop endlessly analysing your three division army. No one else,' he observed, 'knows the names and personalities of divisional, brigade and even battalion commanders. Why don't you look at the larger picture?'

The answer is that before we can really look at the larger picture in 21 Army Group, we need studies of the British army at corps, divisional and brigade level so that we have a firm basis for addressing questions about leadership, command, morale, combat motivation and combat effectiveness. Those who do study the campaign from the ground up will almost certainly come to the conclusion that the officers and men serving in 21 Army Group demonstrated a remarkable ability to apply their doctrine and training to the battlefield. They also demonstrated an ability to learn and innovate. The

British and Canadian response to casualties from mortar fire, 70 per cent of total losses, is a case in point. New measures were promptly introduced and a longer-term initiative to create counter-mortar radar batteries quickly approved.[30] The development and employment of the Kangaroo armoured personal carrier, the Wasp and Crocodile flame-throwers, the institution of CABRANK within the tactical air force, the evolution of Firefly tactics and the forward employment of self-propelled 17-pounder anti-tank guns all point to an army able to learn from experience. It is time for historians to follow their example.

Notes

1 Terry Copp, *Fields of Fire: The Canadians in Normandy* (Toronto: University of Toronto Press, 2003).
2 The Laurier Centre for Military Strategic and Disarmament Studies (LCMSDS), Wilfrid Laurier University, Waterloo, Ontario, Canada holds a large collection of wartime air photos and maps providing coverage of most of the areas of Northwest Europe in which the First Canadian Army operated. (www.canadianmilitaryhistory.com).
3 Terry Copp and Robert Vogel, *Maple Leaf Route*, 5 Volumes (Alma: Maple Leaf Route, 1983–8); Terry Copp, *The Brigade: the 5th Canadian Infantry Brigade* (Stoney Creek: Fortress Publications, 1992); Terry Copp and Bill McAndrew, *Battle Exhaustion: Soldiers and Psychiatrists in the Canadian Army 1939–1945* (Montreal: McGill University Press, 1990); Terry Copp (ed.) *Montgomery's Scientists: Operational Research in 21 Army Group* (Waterloo: LCMSDS, 2000).
4 'Accuracy of Predicted Fire', in Copp (ed.) *Montgomery's Scientists*, pp. 293–330.
5 The OVERLORD plan is outlined in L.F. Ellis, *Victory in the West*, Volume 1 (London: HMSO, 1962).
6 Ibid, p. 536.
7 Shelford Bidwell, *Gunners at War* (London: Arms & Armour Press, 1970) is a valuable introduction but a comprehensive study of the development of Anglo-Canadian artillery is yet to be written. The reports of the Army Operational Research Group (AORG) PRO WO291 are an indispensable source for such a project.
8 The full text of Simonds's Directive on operational policy is reprinted as an appendix in Copp, *Fields of Fire*.
9 The letters from Montgomery and Dempsey are in the National Archives of Canada (NAC), Record Group (RG) 24, Volume 10797.
10 'Infantry Training Conference: Record of Discussion', 15 May 1944, NAC RG 24, Volume 13241, Ottawa; PRO WO 204/1895.
11 Timothy Harrison Place, *Military Training in the British Army, 1940–1944* (London: Frank Cass, 2000), p. 169.
12 Great Britain, War Office, *The Tactical Handling of Armoured Divisions* (London: HMSO, 1943).
13 I wish to thank Colonel Diana Henderson, Ph.D. for inviting me to Edinburgh on this occasion.
14 Montgomery Papers, Imperial War Museum.
15 War Diary, 51 Highland Division, 16 June 1944, PRO WO 171/527.
16 See report on operations, 23/24 June in 51 Highland Division Intelligence Summery, 24 June 1944, PRO WO 171/527.

17 *War Diary, 5th Battalion the Queen's Own Cameron Highlanders*, Appendices 'A' and 'B', PRO WO 171/1270.
18 The quote is from H. von Luck, *Panzer Commander: the Memories of Colonel Hans von Luck* (New York: Praeger, 1989).
19 51 Highland Division Intelligence Summaries, 30 June 1944, 10 July 1944, PRO WO 171/527.
20 War Diary, 5th Black Watch, July 1944 PRO WO 171/1266.
21 War Diary, July 1944, 53rd (Welsh) Division, PRO WO 171/553.
22 Patrick Delaforce, *The Polar Bears* (Stroud: Alan Sutton, 1995).
23 Trevor Hart Dyke, *Normandy to Arnhem: A Story of the Infantry* (Sheffield: Privately Published, 1966).
24 Delaforce, op. cit. pp. 58–102.
25 *War Diary*, June 1944, 1/4 King's Own Yorkshire Light Infantry, PRO 171/223; see also Leonard Willis, *None Had Lances: The Story of the 24th Lancers* (Old Coulsdon: 24th Lancers Old Comrades Association, 1985).
26 Kevin Baverstock, *Breaking the Panzers* (Stroud: Sutton Publishing, 2002).
27 Brigadier James Hargest, 'Notes' PRO CAB 106/1060.
28 Letter Brigadier Trevor Hart Dyke to Terry Copp, 1987, author's archives.
29 David French, *Raising Churchill's Army* (Oxford: Oxford University Press, 2000).
30 Terry Copp, 'Counter-mortar operational research in 21 Army Group,' *Canadian Military History*, 3(2), (1994), pp. 6–21.

2   The German perspective

Mungo Melvin

Introduction

In the many studies of the Normandy campaign of 1944 there have been numerous attempts to explain why the Germans did so well in defence and why the Allied forces made comparatively slow progress in attack. None of this critique should mask the undeniable fact, however, that the campaign was won by the Allies and that the bulk of the German army in the West was defeated in the process. The best strategic cards, and most of the operational ones, were held and played by the Allies throughout three bitter months of fighting. Allied air supremacy, in particular, severely restricted German operational manoeuvre throughout the campaign. Furthermore, the Allies enjoyed relative logistic 'plenty' in comparison with widespread German deprivation. However, in the realm of combined arms tactics, and of fighting power at formation level, the Germans often showed themselves as superior opponents on the battlefield. This chapter aims to indicate how superior doctrine and training, if linked to appropriate equipment and organisation, can have a profound effect on the outcome of engagements, battles and major operations, if not campaigns. If the beneficial effects of defensive terrain and high morale (fighting spirit) are added, then the German defeat in Normandy was by no means certain. As the Allied planners of Normandy had rightly predicted, the campaign was to turn out (in modern phraseology) 'no cakewalk'. The British, with perhaps the honourable exception of Montgomery, had their own doubts as to the success of the enterprise.

Doctrine

German Army Regulation 300, *Truppenführung*, the first part of which was published in 1933, is arguably one of the most significant pieces of doctrinal writing in military history.[1] It set the intellectual framework and provided the detailed guidance for the manner in which the German army planned and conducted war at the tactical level. But it would be inaccurate to describe the document in simple terms as 'Field Service Regulations' or

'Formation Tactics'. It was a more forward-looking document. The introduction, for example, stands today as enduring testimony to the far-sightedness of its authors, its sentiments as relevant to 2006 as to 1933:

> 1   War is an art, a free and creative activity founded on scientific principles. It makes the very highest demands on the human personality.
> 2   The conduct of war is subject to continual development. New weapons dictate ever-changing forms. Their appearance must be anticipated and their influence evaluated. Then they must be placed into service quickly.
> 3   Combat situations are of unlimited variety. They change frequently and suddenly and can seldom be assessed in advance. Incalculable elements often have a decisive influence. One's own will is pitted against the independent will of the enemy. Friction and errors are daily occurrences.[2]

Most significantly, the concluding sentence of *Truppenführung*'s short introduction contains an important clue as to the remarkable powers of the German Army to regain the initiative:

> 15   . . . *The first criterion in war remains decisive action. Everyone, from the highest commander down to the youngest soldier, must constantly be aware that inaction and neglect incriminate him more severely than any error in the choice of means.*[3]

Of course doctrine alone does not provide fighting power in battle. To the conceptual component must be added the moral component of leadership and morale, and not least the physical means to conduct the fighting – combat power. Further, doctrine has to be learnt and practised through training. As we shall see, inconsistencies in doctrine and training within the British army reduced its fighting power in Normandy and hence its operational effectiveness. However, the fact remains that whatever the differences of training standards among German units – and there was a very wide range within the German army by June 1944 – the doctrine was at least uniform and applied fairly uniformly.

Doctrine under test

In Normandy, the German army was placed on the defensive, strategically, operationally, and for the most part, tactically. German defensive tactics had been developed from practical experience of the First World War, particularly in facing British and French offensives on the Western Front. By 1944, moreover, the German doctrine of 1933 had been supplemented by much further practical experience, and particularly that hard-won over three years on the Eastern Front against the Soviet army. So in the face of Allied air power, naval fire support and field artillery, how did the Germans resist for three months? Again, a few short extracts from *Truppenführung* indicate the German approach:

> 427   The defensive [*Abwehr*] is based primarily on firepower. The defender, therefore, must try to produce the maximum fire effect. Accomplishing this requires a detailed knowledge of the battle area, which in turn facilitates the use of terrain by means of field fortifications. Such positions provide better cover and make possible superiority of fire against the moving attackers.

Apart from obvious significance of firepower and fire effect, the use of terrain to best advantage is given particular emphasis:

> 429   The defensive terrain itself dictates the position of the forward elements. Good observation for the artillery and the infantry heavy weapons is usually the most important consideration for effective fires. Terrain that provides concealment for the infantry from enemy observation may be an overriding requirement.[4]

More interestingly, the enemy's perspective is also considered, noting that 'when the situation permits', terrain should be reconnoitred from the enemy's point of view. Specifically:

> 430   When the natural strength of the ground is used skilfully and the positions are well camouflaged, the natural terrain picture can be preserved. This in turn will hinder the enemy's reconnaissance efforts. In certain situations, less favourable terrain can be more advantageous than stronger terrain from which the enemy can easily determine the organization and intent of the defender.[5]

So when one wonders how the Germans managed to block VIII (Br) Corps' armoured phalanx attack during Operation GOODWOOD (18–20 July 1944), part of the reason surely rests in the skilled application of a well-considered defensive tactical doctrine to a piece of well-selected terrain. A bitter foretaste of German defensive prowess had already been given during Operation EPSOM (25 June–1 July 1944) in which 15th Scottish Division had received a bloody nose at the skilled hands of 12th SS Panzer Division.

German planning for the expected British break-out in the Caen sector had anticipated a tank-heavy assault and had designed a deeply echeloned defence accordingly. With a depth of over 15km, this was twice the figure that British intelligence had estimated before the battle. Even Major General Feuchtinger, the commander of 21st Panzer Division who was better known in the German army for his loyal organisation of Hitler's prewar rallies (*Parteitage*) than for his tactical abilities, had recognised the defensive potential of the area and, prompted by Rommel, had developed it into a very carefully prepared 'tank-killing zone'.

Truppenführung Part I (1933) devoted no less than 17 pages of detail in its Chapter VIII on the planning and conduct of the defence. The preparation of a 'main battle area' was based on the careful identification and setting out of a 'main line of resistance' (*Hauptkampflinie* (*HKL*)), which was protected by the 'main outpost line'. In turn, this line (a set of interlocked positions) was protected by a series of 'advanced positions' that denied the enemy close reconnaissance of the main defence. Additional lines to the rear of the *HKL* could provide further depth to the defence. Additional detail on defence against enemy armoured vehicles was added in the first chapter of *Truppenführung* Part II (1934). While tactical situations such as those prevailing in Operation GOODWOOD ten years later could not have been fully predicted, the doctrinal guidance of *Truppenführung* held good, stressing the integrated roles of artillery and anti-tank guns in particular:

756   In combat the enemy normally will deploy his armoured vehicles in great numbers and with the advantage of surprise. Defences, therefore, must be prepared as strongly as possible at all points where enemy attack is probable.

757   Artillery must engage enemy armoured vehicles when they are preparing for attack, approaching, or in the process of attacking. The fire of multiple batteries should be massed whenever possible. Artillery fire should be registered-in to cover the zones where enemy armoured attack is most likely . . . When infantry antitank guns are committed, their function is to destroy enemy armoured vehicles before they succeed in breaking through to the main infantry positions. Anti-tank guns should be deployed in concealed firing positions that provide mutual supporting fire.

758   Enemy tanks that break through are engaged by anti-tank guns deployed in depth and by the reserve. The preparation of a defence against such an attack is the responsibility of the divisional anti-tank battalion commander, based on the guidance of the division commander.[6]

In 1933/4 this doctrine was written largely from the perspective of an infantry division conducting defence. Regimental anti-tank companies protected their respective regiments, while the divisional commander retained control of the anti-tank battalion as a mobile reserve. When greater numbers of tanks and self-propelled guns became available during the course of the Second World War, defensive tactics were modified accordingly to exploit their hitting power, protection and mobility.

German equipment was also well suited to the defensive battle, which was designed around 'support weapons'. From the infamous 8.8cm dual purpose anti-aircraft and anti-tank gun to the heavy Tiger tanks; to the ubiquitous *Schuh* and *Teller* mines; to the numerous 50mm and 81mm mortars; to the *Nebelwerfer* multi-barrelled rocket launchers; and not least to the superb MG42 general purpose machine-guns (with over twice the firepower of the British Bren light machine-gun, and issued at twice the scale), the German army was well equipped if not well manned. In terms of unit firepower, a German infantry battalion had heavier weapons than its British or American counterparts.

In German doctrine, particular emphasis was given to the counter-attack in the conduct of the defensive battle. The relevant paragraphs from *Truppenführung* are well worth quoting in full:

> 463   Should a portion of the main battle area be penetrated and taken by the enemy, all efforts should first be made to eliminate them with fires. Friendly infantry elements and supporting weapons in the immediate area of the penetration [should] attempt to eject the enemy through hasty counter attacks before he can establish himself. These elements can be supported effectively by artillery fire laid in the rear of the enemy. These elements, however, should not be dependent upon artillery support.
>
> Should these measures fail, or should the enemy make a major penetration, the senior commander decides whether a deliberate counter attack will be made to restore the position or whether the main battle area is to be reestablished farther to the rear. Whenever possible, the counter attack is launched against an enemy flank. The counter attack requires thorough preparation, especially when launched by strong forces. A single commander must control the assembly areas, timing, objectives, boundaries, artillery support, and the commitment of armoured vehicles and air units. Too much haste leads to failure.
>
> Reserves intended for the counter attack must be so assembled, or during the course of the attack so shifted, that they are readily available.[7]

Of special significance was the German distinction between an immediate or *hasty* counter-stroke (*Gegenstoss*) and a planned or *deliberate* counter-attack (*Gegenangriff*). Broadly speaking, the former was a sub-unit or unit responsibility, whereas the latter was a formation one.[8] As an example of German command responsibilities, Major Hans von Luck – on the main effort of 21st Panzer Division's defence during Operation GOODWOOD – was able to direct his defensive battle, including calling on all available divisional and corps reserves, without having to refer to his divisional commander for advice or authority.

German doctrine was very clear about the committal of reserves in both offensive and defensive operations:

> 47   During the course of a battle the commander influences the action most directly by the increase and concentration of fire and the commit-

ment of his reserve . . . Assessing the strength of the reserve, constituting the reserve, and committing the reserve requires careful consideration. Mobility increases the opportunities for its commitment . . . By committing his reserve, the commander plays his last card regarding the shock elements at his disposal. He must not be led into doing this too early. On the other hand, he must not hesitate if committing the reserve means achieving a decision or if the battlefield situation requires it. Once the reserve is committed, the rapid formation of a new reserve is critically important.[9]

So in viewing the German army's performance in defence during the Normandy campaign, a number of factors stand out from a consideration of its doctrine:

- the careful selection and adaption of terrain to best advantage;
- through active security measures (screening) and passive ones (such as camouflage), to deny (and if necessary destroy) enemy reconnaissance efforts;
- an emphasis on delivering effective fire throughout the depth of the defensive battle zone, to break up the momentum of the enemy's assault;
- a clear responsibility to counter-attack, either on a hasty or deliberate basis;
- despite the skilled use of terrain, a *focus on the enemy throughout* and his defeat;
- flexible *tactical* command and combined arms cooperation throughout – despite significant operational- and strategic-level shortcomings;
- pragmatic *decision in battle* – based on thorough application of doctrine, good leadership, training and grip.

For all its many shortcomings, not least in its very generous treatment of Montgomery and British tactics, the British official history gave due (if not grudging) praise to the German defence:

Apart from the fatal defects in their command, German operations were fought under the insuperable handicap of the Allies' mastery in the air. No single factor did so much to assist the Allied armies' victory as the sustained air attack which seldom ceased and which rose at times to almost unbearable intensity. In this branch of warfare the German air force could neither hit back with comparable blows nor defend itself effectively. Yet in spite of this appalling handicap and others that have been recognized, the German armies in Normandy deserve credit for the tenacity and discipline with which they fought and the manner in which they held up the Allies' progress. That their fight ended in defeat was partly due to factors which soldiers in the field could not control. It is true that a significant number surrendered or were taken prisoner but many fought their way back and were to fight another day. The battle of Normandy was not only lost by the German Army's heavy defeat in the field but by Hitler's way of fighting it.[10]

The German influence on British theory and practice

It remains one of the ironies of British tactical method since the Second World War that the flexibility inherent in German combined arms battle groups (*Kampfgruppen*) was institutionalised in a rather inflexible manner. Today we still think in terms of fixed battalion-sized groupings rather than the variable groupings and command level required for the mission at hand. Von Luck's 'battlegroup' of the 21st Panzer Division, for example, was a reinforced *Panzergrenadier* regiment which contained at least four infantry and armoured battalion equivalents, with additional artillery and armoured support. Whilst this was an example of predetermined task organisation, a German *Kampfgruppe* could also be thrown together in combat as a hasty ad hoc grouping in the face of the enemy's (Anglo-American or Soviet) numerical superiority, particularly in fluid situations. For the Germans to make a virtue out of tactical necessity is one thing; for the British to apply it rigidly thereafter as an organisational principle is quite another matter.

Yet inculcating a combined-arms mentality within a formation is not just a matter of providing the appropriate training and operational experience. If the basic doctrine is ill-founded in the first place, or misapplied in action against a determined enemy, then the results can be disastrous. The combat performance of the battle-hardened 7th Armoured Division, which had fought well in North Africa and Italy, was poor in Normandy. Its oft-quoted first offensive action in 1944 at Villers-Bocage warrants only brief re-examination. Suffice it to say, the 22nd Armoured Brigade's advance guard of the 4th County of London Yeomanry (Sharpshooters) was hit very hard on 13 June 1944 by Obersturmführer Michael Wittman, a company commander of 101st SS Heavy Tank Battalion. The infamous action took place in the vicinity of Point 213, a high point north-east of Villers-Bocage on the road to Caen. However, what is remarkable about this one-sided engagement in which one German Tiger tank commander managed to destroy a squadron's worth of British Cromwells bunched-up non-tactically, is the higher-level confusion surrounding the employment of 7th Armoured Division as a whole.

In fact, the 'Desert Rats' *had* adopted a flexible combined arms structure of tanks and infantry which the 11th and Guards Armoured Divisions were only to adopt after Operation GOODWOOD. The problem was greater: demonstrable indecision in command. After the initial rebuff, 22nd Armoured Brigade did manage to defeat the determined German counter-attacks from elements of the Panzer Lehr and 2nd Panzer Divisions, but neither the 131st Lorried Infantry Brigade nor the balanced divisional reserve (an armoured regiment and an infantry battalion) was effectively employed. Furthermore, the divisional commander, Erskine, withdrew 22nd Armoured Brigade prematurely, blaming the commander of XXX Corps, Bucknall, for failing to provide adequate reinforcements. And the army commander, Dempsey, hardly covered himself in glory at this critical early stage of the campaign. Coherent command was not in evidence, and the fine theory of *FSR III* (Field Service Regulations) was not applied in practice:

> In dealing with his subordinates, a commander will allot them definite tasks, clearly explaining his intentions, and will allow them liberty of action in arranging the methods by which they will carry out these tasks. Undue centralization and interference with subordinates is harmful, since they are apt either to chafe at excessive control or to become afraid of taking responsibility.[11]

Some weeks after the battle both Erskine and Bucknall were sacked by Montgomery (and rightly so in the opinion of many writers). The whole very confused affair at Villers-Bocage and its set of associated bitterly contested engagements is now treated by many historians as a damning indictment of British tactical incompetence – demonstrated by a particularly disappointing performance of a veteran division 'living on its reputation'. Further, the corps (XXX) and army (Second British) levels of command had displayed weaknesses in handling their subordinate formations that were to take many weeks of fighting and bitter experience to resolve. The principles of 'freedom of action', and 'unity of effort', understood today as fundamental to mission command, were not applied.

What is even more remarkable about the Normandy campaign from a British perspective is that Montgomery only issued *Some Notes on the Conduct of War and the Infantry Division in Battle* in November 1944.[12] This useful pamphlet, which drew heavily on the experiences of the Normandy campaign, together with its sequels *Some Notes on the Use of Air Power in Support of Land Operations and Direct Air Support* and *The Armoured Division in Battle*, would perhaps have saved many lives had 21st Army Group as a whole trained on something similar *before* the campaign.[13] However, at no time was sufficient doctrinal emphasis placed on the planning and conduct of corps-level and army operations at the interface of the tactical and operational levels of war. What was emphasised throughout was a focus on capturing ground, and not on defeating the enemy. Yet Montgomery's doctrine did rely on some German terms to make up for the paucity in British military thought. Montgomery was remarkably open-minded in this respect. *The Armoured Division in Battle*, for example, in describing 'basic points of any operation' directed: 'In all offensive operations endeavour to hit hard on a narrow front and keep on hitting, penetrate deeply, and then turn outwards, i.e. the *Schwerpunkt* and the *Aufrollen*. The momentum of the attack must be kept up at all costs'.[14] But if one thinks of all the fuss doctrine writers face today in introducing new terms for new concepts, one wonders whether we would get away with lifting expressions directly from other military languages!

Significantly, neither the British nor the Americans (unlike the Germans and Russians) recognised in 1944 the crucial role of operational art in linking and sequencing tactical actions to strategic objectives. The Anglo-American inability to plan and to execute encirclement operations was a significant failure of doctrine and practice, and the battle of the Falaise Pocket compares badly with equivalent Soviet operations. The German ability to extricate forces out of the Pocket reflected their experiences on the Eastern Front, both in victory and in defeat. German doctrine stressed the importance of envelopment, reflecting Moltke the Elder's dictum of envelop, encircle and destroy (*Umfassen, Einschliessen, Vernichten*).

FSR III, however, contains guidance on envelopment, penetration and pursuit in the context of the offensive battle but does not once mention encirclement. Rather, a typically 'phased' approach is emphasised, which despite the authors' warning note, became the hallmark of Montgomery's way of war:

> No fixed rules for battle can be laid down, but generally the offensive battle will have the following phases: the preparatory stage; the main attack on the enemy's position, carefully organized and prepared; the period of exploitation by the reserves after initial success or of reconstruction after failure; and pursuit, when the enemy is driven from the battlefield. Though these phases are treated separately in this manual in order to show the differences in methods that each demands, they will seldom be as clear-cut and distinct in actual practice, and will often tend to merge into each other, without any marked interval.[15]

In any broad analysis of British doctrine and tactical performance in Normandy, in comparison with the German, a number of common threads can be identified:

1   In the Second World War, British army doctrine and training methods were confused by a multiplicity of steadily-revised sources. Lessons were not systematically incorporated: they were *identified but certainly not learnt*!

2   Lacking a single, coherent and authoritative *taught* and *understood doctrine*, units and formations adopted different methods in battle. Drills for combined arms groupings at battlegroup level did not become standardised until the latter stages of the Normandy campaign.

3   In practice, *manoeuvre was often conducted on a piecemeal basis*: battalions were given brigade tasks, brigades given divisional tasks and so in – an enduring fault identified in North Africa, Sicily and mainland Italy.

4   *Local tactical successes were rarely exploited* with sufficient resolve and vigour. Undue brave risks were often taken at the lower tactical levels whereas divisional and corps operations were predominantly conducted in a risk-averse manner. Mission command was the exception, not the rule. Too little freedom of action was given at all levels of command.
5   That said, British 'bite and hold' tactics, combined with heavy and largely very effective air, naval and land-based artillery fire support did wear down and defeat the majority of German formations opposing 21st Army Group.

The German influence on American doctrine

The US army in Normandy started the campaign as a junior partner but by its end had become the senior one. Facing even worse terrain than the majority of British formations, the Americans adapted to the particular demands of close combat in the *bocage*. From the 'battle for the hedgerows', they then demonstrated a flair for deep armoured manoeuvre in breaking-out from the western flank (Operation COBRA) and exploiting deep into northern and eastern France. Critics of the American approach point to an over-dependence on firepower and logistics. This view was not shared by the German formations facing them, however! Yet the foundation for this flexibility in an army that had grown at a faster rate than the British was a combination of pragmatism, doctrine and training method. Although slow to adopt specialist armour in the preparation of the campaign (and this failure contributed to their heavy losses at Omaha Beach), the Americans were quick to incorporate hedge-busting rams to their tanks in the *bocage*.

Doctrinally, it is a gross but nonetheless fair interpretation to set the US army as somewhere between the German and British armies. This is hardly surprising as the *Field Manual 100-5 Operations* (*FM 100-5*) was largely based on the German *Truppenführung*. Furthermore, the US army had paid close attention to the reports sent by its students attending the German War College (*Kriegsakademie*) before the Second World War. As an aside, one of the American students, Albert C. Wedemeyer, wrote a very detailed analysis of German doctrine and training before the war and then went on to plan from his office in the Pentagon War Plans Division the massive expansion of the US army based on the imperative of raising a continental army to fight a decisive campaign in Europe against the German army.

According to the editors of the recently published English edition of *Truppenführung*, the German doctrine was translated into English by US Army Intelligence in the late 1930s, and 'greatly influenced the 1940 and 1944 editions of *FM 100-5*'. Indeed, the 1940 version of *FM 100-5* 'was organized in a very similar manner' and even more remarkably, 'its writers even lifted entire sentences from *Truppenführung*'.[16] The US army's links to German doctrinal thought were developed further after the Second World War. Captured German general staff officers under the leadership of

Generaloberst Halder reviewed the 1944 edition of *FM 100-5* and published a report on it in April 1953.

So rather than analysing extracts from *FM 100-5*, the German view on US army doctrine is perhaps more illuminating, as the following extract from Halder's report illustrates:

> Uniformity of doctrine is a prerequisite of independent action within the overall operational framework. If, however, doctrine is uniform and a subordinate commander has, accordingly, been given freedom to act in the spirit of his mission, then any additional instructions hamper his initiative. The manual [*FM 100-5*] frequently attempts to foresee or forestall possible developments in a combat situation by the use of an order and to arrange details in advance. This tendency cramps the initiative of a commander who, being on the spot, has a better chance of assessing the situation. Thus, it robs the troops of one of the major prerequisites of success. For instance, to make every single decision to withdraw from a sector of the front dependent on permission from the immediate superior is unjustifiable and conducive to irresolution . . . According to our [German] experience, the method of assigning broad missions is the best, provided a trained officer corps is available. According to this method, clear and unambiguous missions are assigned, but their execution is the responsibility of the subordinate commander. As a result it may be said that 'Orders should confine themselves to what is necessary to achieve their objective'.[17]

Surely this view holds true today – even in an increasingly digitized era. The Halder report also stressed the need for clarity in tactical expression. It is a fact that military English is not as rich as military German, and thus it is more difficult for the English speaker to be as precise and succinct in oral or written orders as his German counterpart. As we have seen, even Montgomery had to resort to German terms in the *Armoured Division in Battle*. Few Germans would need to debate *Schwerpunkt* in the way that 'main effort' is discussed in British military circles – and often in a confused manner whether at a staff college course or in a formation headquarters.

Conclusions

This chapter has not attempted to provide a comprehensive survey of German and Allied doctrine in 1944. Rather, it has suggested a number of dominating themes discerned from German and British theory and practice. Lack of space has precluded an equivalent or balanced perspective of US army doctrine, except to indicate its surprising German origins. However, there are several broad enduring issues that warrant more detailed reflection, discussion and debate. It is suggested that the following matters be discussed further:

- What is the purpose of doctrine – to educate or to train? At what level should it be pitched?
- How general should doctrine be – 'broad brush' or specific in terms of detailed tactics, techniques and procedures? What emphasis should be given to clarity of expression?
- When should one discard existing doctrine and issue new material? What are the risks involved in having too much or too 'fresh' doctrine, and of having too many bodies involved in its production and dissemination?
- How can a 'lessons identified' process best be linked to the production of doctrine?
- What have we to learn from the different approaches adopted by the German and Allied armies in the Second World War, particularly in terms of combined arms tactics and command styles?
- What can we learn from the need to *exploit*?

Finally

The final question is surely to consider the broader lessons of a study of the Normandy campaign to the development of contemporary joint and multinational doctrine. Whilst the Allies excelled at joint operations, in fire support and in logistics, the Germans often more than held their own at the tactical level. Part of the reason for this German asymmetric success surely rested on their sound combined arms doctrine, usually interpreted flexibly as the situation and terrain dictated. But no amount of tactical- (or even operational-) level virtuosity could make up for significant strategic deficiencies, not only in material and personnel resources, but also in terms of high command. It is against this background that the Normandy campaign of 1944 remains a rich treasure trove of relevant and stimulating issues for an examination of contemporary warfare and the study of high command. To dismiss it in the modern context of 'effects-based operations' and 'network-centric warfare' is to ignore the enduring aspects of war, including human factors, friction and chance. Any doctrine that denies these essential truths is surely flawed. Regardless of the scale of effort, enemy or terrain, military success depends on the appropriate blending of the conceptual, moral and physical components of fighting power. Over 60 years on, all this doctrinal bedrock surely endures!

Notes

1 *Truppenführung, Heeresdienstvorschrift* (*German Army Regulations*) 300 Part I (1933). Translations of both Part I and II (1934) are contained in Bruce Condell and David T. Zabecki (eds) *On the German Art of War: Truppenführung* (Boulder, CO: Lynne Rienner, 2001). All page references refer to the 2001 translation; all paragraph numbers refer to the German original editions. *Truppenführung* is best translated – if not somewhat clumsily – as 'Unit/Formation Command and Tactics'.

2 Ibid., p. 17.
3 Ibid., p. 19. Emphasis as in the original.
4 Ibid., p. 119.
5 Ibid., p. 120.
6 Ibid., p. 196.
7 Ibid., p. 128.
8 German, British and American terminologies differed in 1944 and continue to cause some confusion today. In military German, the unit (*Einheit*) refers to company equivalents. Formations (*Verbände*) included battalions and regiments; divisions and larger formations were termed *Grossverbände*. The Germans employed 'brigades' at the beginning and at the end of the Second World War, but fought as regiments and divisions for the most part. The British 'unit' is the battalion equivalent, the 'formation' is a brigade or larger organisation. Only the British army continues to interchange 'battalion' and 'regiment' depending on cap badge. The US army of 1944 did not have brigades: infantry divisions were composed of three regiments; armoured divisions normally fought as two mixed armour and infantry 'Combat Commands'. In current US army terminology, a 'unit' may be used to describe a battalion, brigade or division. The Second World War term Regimental Combat Team (RCT) survives today in the US Marine Corps usage.
9 *Truppenführung*, op. cit., p. 26.
10 L.F. Ellis, *Victory in the West – Volume I* (London: HMSO, 1962), p. 490.
11 *Field Service Regulations Vol. III. (FSR III) Operations – Higher Formations*, 1935 (London: HMSO, 1936), p. 9.
12 *Some Notes on the Conduct of War and the Infantry Division in Battle* (Bernard Montgomery, 1944).
13 *Some Notes on the Use of Air Power in Support of Land Operations and Direct Air Support* (Bernard Montgomery, 1944).
14 *The Armoured Division in Battle* (Holland: 21st Army Group, December 1944), p. 11, Sub-paragraph 22 (c). The original text was set in capital letters for emphasis.
15 *FSR III*, p. 37.
16 Bruce Condell and David T. Zabecki (eds) *On the German Art of War: Truppenführung* (Boulder, CO: Lynne Rienner, 2001), p. 10.
17 Ibid., p. 282. Annex E of the Condell and Zabecki edition contains the first three chapters of Halder's report, highlighting the key differences between German and American military thinking.

3   The German commanders on D-Day

Marc Hansen

Most D-Day 1944 publications intended for a wider general audience focus largely on the Allied Forces. But, since a historical event such as 'Normandy 1944' demands an analysis from a multinational perspective, it is rather important to take specific aspects of both sides into consideration or, to put it in the words of Field Marshal Sir Arthur Wellesley, 1st Duke of Wellington: 'to look at the other side of the hill'. In recent years there has been a vivid discussion within the community of German military historians as to whether the German public, the military and the political elite of the Third Reich saw the Allied landings and the Battle for Normandy as *the* decisive battle of the Second World War.[1] Of course, we historians know by now that the turning point in the European theatre came in 1941. The strategic concept of a global *blitzkrieg*[2] – that is, a series of successive tactical operational successes featuring rapid armoured formations – has to be seen as a failure by the end of 1941 at the latest, when the German Operation BARBAROSSA was brought to a standstill shortly before Moscow. This signified the loss of the Third Reich's only chance to decide the war in its favour, though of course it must be kept in mind that such conclusions always represent a retrospective analysis. Nevertheless, the prevailing opinion now held by the majority of today's military historians in Germany is that the turn of the war was indeed in 1941. But in 1944, this perception did not loom large in the experiences of the majority of Germans, or of many representatives of the military and political elite. We have to consider the possibility, indeed probability, that they simply did not believe that the outcome of the war was decided by June 1944.[3]

Continuing this train of thought, a key question arises regarding the Allied landings in Normandy in June 1944. If, for the majority of the leading elite, the war was not decided at the time of D-Day, then one should consider if the invasion was viewed as the decisive battle in a Clausewitzian sense.[4] Specifically, this thesis asks us to consider whether senior military leaders privy to the true war situation viewed the invasion as the decisive battle of the war because of true inner conviction or for other reasons. Maybe they did it as '*l'art pour l'art*', maybe to prevent a recurrence of a 'November 1918', or maybe they found themselves hopelessly obliged to the oath of allegiance they swore to their Führer. In order to assess this thesis it is therefore crucial to examine the specific opinions and views of these German general officers, most obviously those who deployed in France on the most likely invasion front. Therefore it is the aim of this chapter to present a critical discussion of the differing personal attitudes of German commanding officers to the Allied invasion who were deployed in France in June 1944.

Due to space constraints, it is not possible to deal with all German commanding officers in Western Europe. This analysis will therefore concentrate on the main decision-makers in *Oberbefehlshaber* West (OB West), Army Group B, Seventh Army headquarters and the divisional commanders of the infantry and tank divisions stationed directly on the invasion front. The most important sources are the unpublished files from the Bundesarchiv/ Militärarchiv at Freiburg, Germany. In addition, the compilation *Foreign Military Studies*, kept in the BA/MA has been accessed, with due regard to its possibly questionable historical authenticity.[5]

As early as November 1940, the OB West[6] Generalfeldmarschall Gerd von Rundstedt determined that any defence against enemy attempts at landing on the Western European coast had become considerably more difficult due to lack of organisation among the senior and lower ranking leadership *in situ*. Commands given from the *Oberkommando der Wehrmacht* (OKW),[7] especially the Führer's orders No. 40 and No. 51,[8] were intended to facilitate a unified execution of command in the West; indeed, they were to regulate the orientation of all armed force activities for defence against an Allied landing attempt. But for reasons inherent within the inadequate internal leadership structure of the German armed forces, they never worked properly regarding the preparation to repulse an Allied invasion of Western Europe.

The OB West was responsible for preparing and implementing the defence of the coast of the occupied western region, but to this end only army troops were under its direct control, which proved a clear disadvantage for preparation of defence. All air force and navy units deployed in France were under OB West control only as far as they were intended for operative war activities, otherwise they were exclusively subject to the orders of the SS Führungshauptamt *Oberkommando der Luftwaffe*[9] or the *Oberkommando der Marine*.[10] Indeed, those navy and air force units stationed at the Atlantic and channel coast sectors of France (*Luftflotte 3* and *Marinegruppenkommando* West) did everything to retain an independent status.

Within this organisational chaos – described in the literature as *Befehlschaos* (confusion of command) – von Rundstedt and his chief of staff, General der Infanterie Günther Blumentritt, recognised the impossibility of mounting a successful defence against any landing attempt by Allied forces. That this landing attempt would take place and that it would be 'successful on every front',[11] as Blumentritt remarked, was never substantially doubted at any time by either of these commanders. However, they were also both clearly convinced that defeating this invasion would be the deciding point of the war. The OB West and Blumentritt's chief of staff held this view of an Allied landing based on two reasons, one political and one strategic. A failure to open a second European front would represent a massive loss in credibility for the Western Allies *vis-a-vis* the Soviet Union, who already had a very fragile and complicated relationship with each other. The possibility of a separate peace with the Western powers – albeit perhaps disadvantageous for the Third Reich – was a distinct possibility if a second front failed. On a strategic level, the entire staff at OB West saw an opportunity for the Allies by way of landing in Northern France – as long as the landing occurred at the Pas de Calais – to open the route to the Rhine and Ruhr areas essential to Germany's war economy. According to Blumentritt, the entire hinterland behind the lines of the 15th Army to the Rhine was 'practically free from troops capable of fighting'.[12] In the view of OB West, a landing at the Pas de Calais – which according to Blumentritt would be successful particularly due to Allied air superiority even against the relatively strong 15th Army – was potentially *the* decisive strategic option for the Allied forces. The erroneous belief that the Allies would not actually make use of this 'golden opportunity' was the main reason for the OB West's decision to retain 15th Army forces at the Pas de Calais for defence against the anticipated main strike. Naturally, with the benefit of hindsight, it is easy to criticise von Rundstedt and Blumentritt for adhering to that decision for too long a time.

However, the deciding error of the staff at OB West was the complete misidentification of the size of Allied force concentrations in and around the beaches on D-Day itself. The lack of information relayed from the landing area prevented most higher commanders from identifying where enemy concentrations were located and whether the action was a major landing or a diversionary manoeuvre. The window of opportunity for a successful defence against the invasion – at least as it still appeared in theory – closed on the evening of D + 3 at the latest. From this date onwards, the plans of OB West and all other German commanders in the West did not correspond with the reality of the situation. Their plans and their actions once more confirmed Napoleon's hypothesis that land could always be regained, but never time.

Regarding the famous *Panzerkontroverse* (tank controversy),[13] which carried on long after the war had ended, both von Rundstedt and Blumentritt in principle considered Geyr von Schweppenburg's view as the correct defence strategy. The issue was whether defending against the invasion could have been better achieved had all tank reserves been stationed directly in potentially endangered landing sections – a proponent of this position being Generalfeldmarschall Erwin Rommel, Commander-in-Chief of the *Heeresgruppe* B (HG B) – or whether it would have been more effective to position tanks centrally at a distance from the coastal regions and then apply them in a concentrated manner once enemy intentions were identified. The main proponent of this position was the commander in chief of the *Panzergruppe* West (PzGr West), General der Panzertruppen Leo Reichsfreiherr Geyr von Schweppenburg.

Correctly, they all considered the so-called Atlantic Wall to be a comforting Potemkin village put forth as part of the lies of propaganda for both the German population and ordinary soldiers. In particular, they also considered Frederick the Great's central military theorem highly important: 'He who defends everything, defends nothing'. In all these points, the views of these commanders were diametrically opposed to those of the supreme commander in chief of the Wehrmacht, Adolf Hitler, and the OKW.[14] An analysis of the conception and implementation of the defence against an Allied invasion in the OB West region demonstrates that both the principles of the strategy and the direction of its tactical implementation was influenced far more by outside factors, i.e. a direct influence of the ongoing battle by Hitler himself or by Generalfeldmarschall Keitel and Generaloberst Jodl at the OKW. This interference hampered any free operational-tactical decision-making by the military leaders in charge of command in the western areas considerably. Von Rundstedt and his staff certainly did not receive the necessary authority for taking appropriate action in defending France against a concentrated, air supported landing by enemy amphibious craft and paratroopers. In addition, the OB West was faced with the pressing considerable problem of Allied troops moving quickly inland protected by a screen of artillery provided by the invasion fleet, which would require immediate response and action on the part of the defending Germans. Following the successful landing, the OB West would be forced to move from a mixed static-mobile forward defence on the coast to conducting a moving battle from deep inland. However, this elastic defence, which would require the operative use of tank reserves, was likely to be made untenable by the undisputed Allied air superiority. Nevertheless, von Rundstedt is open to criticism for not extending the scope of authority of his command more substantially.

At first glance, the overall concept of Generalfeldmarschall Rommel appears to have been the only possible defence strategy to combat the overwhelming superiority held by the Allies.[15] In his April 1944 dictum to his adjutant, Hauptmann Hellmuth Lang, Rommel stated: '*Wir haben nur eine Möglichkeit, den Gegner zum Stehen zu bringen: wir müssen ihn fassen, solange er noch im Wasser ist und sich an Land vorkämpft. Ersatz wird sich niemals bis an die Kampflinie herankommen; es ist Unsinn überhaupt damit zu rechnen*' ('The war will be won or lost here on the beach. We have only one possibility, to bring the enemy to a stop: we must get him as long as he is in the water and is fighting to get to land. Reinforcement troops will never be able to get to the battle line; it is foolish to even count on this').[16] This reveals two things. Rommel correctly recognised that the initial 24 hours – the famous 'longest day' – was the window of opportunity during which the Allied landing troops were most vulnerable. If it were at all possible to defeat the invasion, it could only be achieved before they could establish an operating base in the invasion area that they could hold and defend. However, this concept of a fixed forward defence required setting up insurmountable barriers for the enemy, comprising of pre-beach obstacles, bunkers and so forth, which must be attacked frontally without sufficient cover. One could say that Rommel – who is meanwhile internationally presented as an admirable proponent of modern military strategy, featuring tactical operational use of rapid tank groups – here fell back on strategic concepts from 1915–17. It is clear that for Rommel, the Allied landing was essentially a decision *par excellence*. Winfried Mönch expressed Rommel's thoughts:

> *An einem Tag, an einem bestimmten Ort, zu einer bestimmten Stunde, fällt die militärische Entscheidung, ohne daß irgend welche abstrakten Potentiale zu dieser Zeit an diesem konkreten Ort zum Tragen kommen können. Dazu kommt noch eine dezisionistische Unerbittlichkeit . . . wenn es nicht gelänge, den gelandetet Feind innerhalb einer kurzen Frist wieder ins Meer zu werfen, ist nicht allein ein Gefecht, eine Schlacht, ein Feldzug, sondern der ganze Krieg verloren.* (On one day, at one specific location, at one specific hour, a military decision is made without any abstract potential coming into play at this time at this particular place. An inevitable outcome is also added to this . . . if the landed enemy fails to be thrown back into the sea within a short period, not only is a skirmish, a battle, a campaign lost, but an entire war.)[17]

There has been much speculation about Rommel's absence on the day of the invasion.[18] In theory, it should have played no significant role, since all alarm and mission plans conceived by Rommel were already in place at headquarters of HG B. In reality, however, with the absence of Rommel, the active command was temporarily transferred to the chief of staff of HG B Generalleutnant Dr Hans Speidel. The basic tone of his reaction to the landing operation once underway is summarised effectively by the *Kriegstagebuch* (war diary) of the HG B: '*Chef des Stabes Heeresgruppe B der Ansicht, daß von größerem Unternehmen vorerst keine Rede sein kann*' (Chief of Staff Army Group B is of the opinion that for the time being no larger undertakings will take place).[19] Speidel's actions on D-Day were largely characterised by orders to wait, clarify and analyse. In the initial hours of Operation OVERLORD, the HG B headquarters could have used a real troop commander instead of a general staff officer.

Geyr von Schweppenburg disagreed with Rommel's opinion as to the best strategy to defend against invasion; most obviously he was also diametrically opposed to Rommel on the issue of moving tank reserves.[20] However, he did agree about the decisive character of invasion defence with respect to how the war would end. Von Schweppenburg stated: 'The invasion must result in a decision', thus implying that he believed it possible to have a successful battle serving the ability of the German Reich to further engage in war.[21] He was strongly convinced that the battle could be won – if he were given free hand and could concentrate his forces in ready-to-use assembly areas, but not on the coast itself, and could use these tanks as part of an elastic-style combat. Among all German generals, von Schweppenburg felt most strongly that he was restricted operationally by Hitler's strategy of 'holding out at any cost and to fight until the last bullet'. He stated that Hitler, as a World War I lance corporal and now a supreme army commander, was characterised by an 'obsession with a closed front'.[22] When von Schweppenburg was asked after the war what effects and consequences this conflict of opinions had, he merely answered by quoting Horace: '*Quidquid delirant reges, plectuntur Achivi*' (Whatever madness their kings commit, the Greeks take the beating).

After analysing the unfolding of the Allied attack on D-Day, Geyr was convinced that the reserves on hand would be able to lead an operational level counter-attack. He therefore planned to launch a full-scale counter-attack that would drive the British and Canadians back into the sea, but on 10 June (the original intended date of the offensive), Geyr's headquarters were attacked and destroyed by Allied fighter-bombers. Geyr himself was wounded and many of his staff officers were killed, forcing the cancellation of the attack. It remains a question of counterfactual history whether an offensive by *Panzergruppe* West would have been successful. Given the Allies' overwhelming aerial superiority, it is highly doubtful that such powerful German forces could have been assembled for the proposed offensive.

'*Es unteriegt keinem Zweifel, daß die anglo-amerikanische Invasion des europäischen Festlandes die militärische und politische Entscheidung im Zweiten Weltkrieg gebracht hat*' (There is no doubt that the Anglo-American invasion of the European mainland was militarily and politically decisive in the Second World War), said Generalmajor Rudolf Freiherr von Gersdorff, the successor of Generalmajor Pemsel as the chief of staff of Seventh Army.[23] Gersdorff's statement is a prime example of the general view of the *Armeeoberkommando* 7[24] (AOK 7) that the invasion, should it take place mainly against Seventh Army, would unavoidably lead to the defeat of the Wehrmacht in the West. With the forces made available to him, the commander of Seventh Army, Generaloberst Friedrich Dollmann, believed it impossible to stop an invasion. Seventh Army was significantly reinforced in the spring of 1944 but consisted on D-Day mainly of units of poor to indifferent quality. Its preparations against the airborne landings were ineffective, its state of training was poor, and its overall reaction to the invasion was sluggish. In addition, Dollmann believed, as Rommel did, that reserves could not be brought up to the main line of resistance during the initial critical battle phases.

In any case, one can accuse the AOK 7 of holding on to the notion for too long that an invasion at the Pas de Calais could still be launched, despite receiving strong indications that the major landings had indeed already occurred. In the case of AOK 7, the cause of this misinterpretation was an analysis by the *Marinegruppenkommando* West, who claimed that a landing in the Seine Bay area appeared 'as good as ruled out' due to coastal conditions. In addition, there appeared to be no operational deep-water harbour for shipping and heavy equipment. These factors demonstrate that the Allied Mulberry harbour concept was a great success and surprised the operations and planning staff of AOK 7 completely.[25]

In contrast to memoir literature and earlier historical depictions Erich Marcks, the commanding general of Seventh Army's LXXXIV Corps, *General der Artilleri*, based in St. Lô, was the only commander to recognise the full implications of the incoming messages regarding the air and sea landings on 6 June. Marcks's prophetic foresight subsequently gained him some fame in the international literature of OVERLORD. In February, he had conducted war games with the AOK 7, and in the role of the attacker, had played through scenarios of large-scale landing operations on the Normandy and Calvados coasts. A result of these fictitious operations was the annihilation of Seventh Army. There is no doubt that General Marcks had exceptional strategic and tactical operational abilities, and only his past as one of the most prominent and committed political and military figures of the Weimar Republic prevented him from attaining a higher position within Hitler's army.[26] Marcks also regarded the invasion as a decisive battle of the war and he was also convinced that the armed forces would only have a real chance of defeating a landing attempt in north-west France if the political leaders were prepared to give up southern France and clear it of German troops. In addition, Marcks – entirely in line with Rommel – revealed himself to be a keen supporter of the forward defensive system.

On D-Day itself, LXXXIV Corps was the highest German command structure directly affected by the actions on and around the beaches. Following the Allied landing, it was quickly apparent that the coastal troops could not fend off the invasion for very long: the landing of enemy troops was not being continuously hindered by German sea and air forces, and the pre-beach barriers and shore-based resistance nests did not create the insurmountable barrier as conceived by Rommel in his defence plans. Nevertheless, Marcks demonstrated that he was the most active and capable commander in the entire invasion area, and as the initiator and organiser of 21 Panzer Division's counter-attack north of Caen, he came extremely close to establishing a stable right defensive wing on D-Day. Since General Marcks fell in battle on 12 June in an Allied fighter attack on his vehicle column, one can only surmise that he would have had a significant influence on the subsequent battle for Normandy.

When we analyse the mindset of the German divisional commanders directly at the invasion front, we gain the impression that we are dealing with professional soldiers who dedicated themselves to a task where difficulty and complexity were acknowledged, but not further reflected upon. In contrast to the views of almost all other German commanders in the West, *Generalleutnant* Josef Reichert, commander of 711 Infantry Division (attached to Fifteenth Army) was '. . . *persönlich durchaus nicht überzeugt, daß überhaupt eine Invasion über den Kanal erfolgen würde*' (. . . personally not convinced that an invasion via the Channel would occur at all).[27] Reichert even believed that: '*Bis etwa Mai lag der Küstenabschnitt in voreiligem Frieden. Aber die Invasionspsychose – ich hielt sie damals dafür – hielt an . . . Ich war persönlich mehr geneigt, alles für einen Riesenbluff zu halten . . . mit dem Zweck, dem russischen Verbündeten durch die Fesselung starker deutscher Kräfte zu helfen*' (until around May the coastal sections were in a state of expectancy. But the invasion psychosis – which I thought it was at the time – continued . . . I was personally more inclined to consider everything a huge bluff . . . with the aim of helping Russian forces by containing stronger German forces).[28]

However, on the morning of 6 June he was forced to revise his opinion based on what he witnessed: British paratroopers landed only a few metres from his own headquarters. Like Marcks in particular, Reichert saw that the only possibility to influence and then defeat the invasion would be to lead a rapid, concentrated armoured counter-attack on both sides of the Orne on the day of the landing. At the same time, Reichert was enough of a realist to recognise that '*der der Küstenverteidigung gestellte Auftrag, eine feindliche Anlandung zu verhinden hieß: . . . das unmögliche Verlangen um Mögliches zu erreichen*' (the order to coastal defence forces to prevent an enemy landing meant: . . . the impossible desire to achieve the possible).[29] Reichert considered himself as abandoned in terms of his defence efforts, after his division was forced to give up troops and material successively to ad hoc formed battle groups on D-Day and over the weeks that followed. Reichert laid the primary blame with the navy and the Luftwaffe since these partial forces did not succeed in interfering with the invasion fleet in a lasting manner.

On D-Day, 709 Infantry Division under the command of Generalleutnant Karl-Wilhelm von Schlieben formed the left-most wing on the German invasion front. The task of this division was to secure the right half of the Cotentin peninsula with the major harbour of Cherbourg. Von Schlieben, formerly commander of 18 Panzer Division on the Eastern Front, was extremely unhappy with his new command duties. He regarded the transfer from a strong fighting tank division to an aged, static infantry division only used for coastal protection as a demotion in his military career. In addition, von Schlieben found it very hard to accept that due to a lack of high quality reserve units, OB West was forced to reinforce 709 Infantry Division in large part through elements of the 'Ost Battalions'. Von Schlieben's well known comment, 'we are asking rather a lot if we expect Russians to fight in

France for Germany against Americans', reveals his inner conflict.[30] There is no doubt that von Schlieben's strength lay at the operational-tactical level of war and although he did not command tanks in the battle for Normandy, his personal leadership in the counterstrike on St-Mère-Église reveals exceptional bravery and courage under fire in addition to his ability to lead infantry formations into battle. However, of crucial importance in determining the poor performance of 709 Infantry Division on D-Day itself was von Schlieben's absence in Rennes on the night of the Allied landing. The lack of determined leadership in the first, crucial hours of the invasion contributed greatly to the outstanding success of 1 US Infantry Division landing at Utah Beach.

709 Infantry Division also failed to prevent the fall of Cherbourg.[31] The organisation of the defence of the Cherbourg citadel – a command given to von Schlieben directly by Hitler on June 17 – was condemned to failure right from the start; indeed, lacking sufficient logistical support the losses suffered by *Kampfgruppe* 'von Schlieben' could not be immediately replaced, thus jeopardising the defence. The well-known controversy on the retreat to the actual Cherbourg fortification area 'in one move' (v. Schlieben/OB West) or 'through slow surrender of wide ranging closed all-around defence' (Hitler/OKW) played only a secondary role in the failure. The role of von Schlieben in defending Cherbourg has, however, remained in dispute; since the war, he has been accused of not fighting for the city with complete determination. However, along with Dieter Ose, it can asked whether: '*der General aber, ohne Aussicht auf Verstärkung und mit dem noch zur Verfügung stehendem Personal anders hätte handeln können . . . immerhin war ja der Hafen, der Hauptzweck der Festung, nachhaltig zerstört worden*' (the General could have acted differently, without hope of reinforcements and with the personnel he had available . . . after all the harbour, the main target of the citadel, was completely destroyed'.[32]

716 Infantry Division was practically destroyed on D-Day, and there was virtually nothing Generalleutnant Wilhelm Richter, the commander of the division, could have done to prevent this fate. The division was struck by the full weight of the attack of British Second Army. As it was, on 6 June elements of 716 Division were involved in the fighting on Omaha, Gold, Juno and Sword Beaches. On the latter three, 716 Division alone provided the sole defence until units from 21 Panzer Division entered combat later that day. Richter's division, made up of replacement units, was designated a static division whose primary purpose was to build and occupy fixed defensive positions in its assigned sector. Its fighting value has to be estimated as very low.

In March 1944, Richter completed a risk analysis for 716 Infantry Division, in which he highlighted a series of concerns: the overstretched area it had to cover (the 34km long coastal sector north of Caen), especially the insufficient depth of defence positions in coastal areas; the lack of any aerial reconnaissance; the lack of air support; and an insufficient or incorrectly applied artillery plan. Richter especially referred to the increasing conflict between the *Seekriegsleitung* and the army commanders in arranging the fireplans for the many German coastal batteries which were under the command of the navy. The navy preferred an alignment only against sea targets whereas the army wanted to use the heavy guns also against targets inland. Despite the fact that Richter's leadership was very important in delaying the British advance on Caen in the first hours and days of OVERLORD, his performance as a divisional commander had obviously been judged as inadequate and he was relieved of his command in September.[33]

Organisationally, 352 Infantry Division was better off than most German divisions in 1944. At that time, as a result of severe personnel losses, German infantry divisions were generally reduced by one infantry battalion per regiment, yet 352 Division retained its full complement of nine battalions. However, just two days after the invasion, Generalleutnant Dietrich Kraiss, the Commander of 352 Division, must have recognised the futility of his efforts. Almost half of 352 Division was fighting whilst heavily outnumbered against the British at Bayeux; several other sections of the division were involved in heavy skirmishes with American paratroopers near the Vire and with Rangers at Pointe du Hoc. The remainder of the 352 was practically annihilated at Omaha Beach. Kraiss acknowledged that his situation was becoming worse by the hour. Enemy reinforcements of troops and *materiel* were delivered to the invasion coast *en masse*, while few German reinforcements arrived and then only intermittently. In addition, reinforcements were immediately used in mixed battle groups in an ad hoc manner. In Kraiss's opinion, this approach would lead to a real weakening of the effectiveness of all fighting groups as a whole. Like Marcks, Kraiss, who had served as a company commander during World War I and led 169 Infantry Division during the June 1941 invasion of the Soviet Union, was also one of the typical 'fighting generals'. Like others he believed D-Day to be the decisive battle of World War II and put his life on the line for it. He displayed both personal bravery and a clear sense of what the situation required.[34] Kraiss was mortally wounded on 2 August at his command post near St Lô and this represented a major loss of military experience and leadership ability for further German armed forces operations in the West.

Neither Kraiss nor Generalleutnant Wilhelm Falley, the commanding officer of 91 Airlanding Division, survived the initial stages of the Battle of Normandy. Falley had been killed by paratroopers of US 82 Airborne on his return from the planned wargame at Rennes. There has been much speculation about the performance of the 91 Airlanding Division which was specially trained to intervene against enemy airborne troops. One could argue that if Falley, who was described as an excellent tactical commander, had been present until D+3 the 91 Airlanding Division might have taken more energetic action against the American airborne troops and therefore might have hampered the landings on Utah more effectively.

After being destroyed in North Africa, 21 Panzer Division was reformed in June of 1943 at Rennes and remained stationed in France for the next year, being deemed unfit for service on the Eastern Front. On 6 June 1944, it was the only German armoured division in the immediate vicinity of the Allied landing beaches in Normandy. Confusion reigned as Generalleutnant Edgar Feuchtinger, the commander of the 21 Panzer Division, was not at divisional headquarters, but in Paris. The lack of firm leadership, along with total Allied air and sea superiority, all contributed to the 21 Panzer Division making a sluggish and ultimately unsuccessful counter-attack against the Anglo-Canadian beachheads on D-Day. Samuel W. Mitcham provides an excellent characterisation of Feuchtinger: 'There is nothing in Feuchtinger's record to suggest that he was remotely qualified to command a Panzer division, he owed his promotion solely to political considerations . . . By any measure, he had been one of the least qualified and least successful of the German tank commanders'.[35] Oberst Hans von Luck described his superior officer in his memoirs: 'General Edgar Feuchtinger, an artilleryman, had no combat experience [in World War II], and none at all of Panzer units. He had become known in Germany as the organiser of the military part of the so-called *Reichsparteitage*, the national party rallies, and through that was very familiar with Hitler and the party apparatus'.[36]

Assuming the theory is correct that the only chance to beat the Allies was in the first 72 hours after the initial landings, it becomes clear that 21 Panzer Division – the only reserve capable of fighting back on D-Day – was led by the most unsuitable man for this task. Feuchtinger 'lost the day for the Germans' and was quickly made responsible for the disaster. One can argue this especially since the counter-thrust of 21 Panzer Division requested in confusion by Generalleutnant Richter (716 Infantry Division) on D-Day was not arranged through the initiative of its commanding officer Feuchtinger, but on the orders of General Marcks. Feuchtinger was a live and let live person. He was fond of all the good things of life, for which Paris was a natural attraction. Knowing that he had no combat experience or knowledge of tank warfare, Feuchtinger had to delegate most things; that is, leave the execution of orders to his experienced commanders. The question whether Feuchtinger saw the invasion as the decisive battle of the war is purely hypothetical, for he simply did not seem to care. His primary motivation as a commander of a fighting unit was to survive the war in a prestigious and comparatively secure position.

Conclusion

After overrunning the German beach defences, the Allies rapidly expanded the individual beachheads, and were able to reinforce the lodgement with extra troops, ammunition and supplies. The window of opportunity to defeat the invasion definitively closed on D+3 and most of the commanders, all of them professional soldiers for many years, were well aware of this situation. Many of those D-Day commanders believed that the war was still not lost in June 1944, though they accepted that it would not end in complete victory. They hoped more for a political division within the anti-Hitler coalition, a possibility as long as they were able to keep the Western Allies contained within their lodgement for long enough and with heavy enough losses. It should be borne in mind that democracies even in wartime have a very limited willingness to sustain heavy casualty rates over a long period of time. Nevertheless, the idea of negotiating a separate peace with the Western powers, in whatever shape or form, clearly reveals that the German commanders in the West were professional soldiers but not trained in foreign affairs. Hitler – always more politician than military commander – assessed the situation much more realistically when he stated, '*Mit mir macht niemand Frieden*' (No one makes peace with me).

The chaos of command – that is, the sometimes confused and conflicting command structures in the OB West section, the supply problems, the often destructive intervention of the OKW in OB West areas of expertise and the tank controversy between Rommel and von Schweppenburg prior to the start of the invasion – did not really come to bear during the Battle of Normandy. Prior to 6 June 1944, all German commanders were of the opinion that defeating the invasion was to be the decisive battle of World War II, yet on the day of the invasion, none – maybe with the exception of Marcks – reacted decisively enough to match the dangers they perceived to exist. In addition, the fixed thinking of German generals, who only focused on operations, led to an oversight of many factors which normally determine the long-range course of a highly technical, modern war. The military elite developed very little sense of politics and economic and logistical relationships, though their operational and tactical leadership qualities were no doubt excellent. However, this often did not count for much on the Western European stage. Other factors which the Allies paid so much attention to – such as air superiority, access to information, deception plans and integrated command structures across navy, army and the air force – more than balanced the advantages of excellent German leadership. Ultimately, the events of June 1944 had only one consequence for the German public and most German military commanders in the West, an acceptance of impending defeat, and this emerged once the euphoric hope of a German victory in the face of an Allied landing gave way to deep feelings of despair when it became clear that the Allies had been able to establish a secure bridgehead in Fortress Europe.

Notes

1 See Michael Salewski, 'Die Abwehr der Invasion als Schlüssel zum Endsieg?' in Rolf-Dieter Müller and Hans-Erich Volkmann, *Die Wehrmacht – Mythos und Realität* (München: Oldenbourg, 1999), pp. 210–24.

2 For an introduction to the concept of *Blitzkrieg* see Charles Messenger, *The Art of Blitzkrieg* (Shepperton: Allan, 1976).

3 See Norbert Frei, 'Der totale Krieg und die deutsche Heimatfront', in Günter Bischof and Wolfgang Kreiger (eds) *Die Invasion in der Normandie 1944: Internationale Perspektiven* (Innsbruck: Studien Verlag, 2001), pp. 17–32.

4 For a definition of the term *Entscheidungsschlacht* see Carl von Clausewitz, *Vom Kriege* (München: Studien Verlag, 2003), pp. 238–55.

5 Historical Division Headquarters, United States Army, Europe: 'Foreign Military Studies'. Begun in Europe while the authors were Allied prisoners of war, the Foreign Military Studies were completed in the 1950s under the auspices of what is now the US army's Office of the Chief of Military History.

6 *Oberbefehlshaber* West – commander in chief West.

7 *Oberkommando der Wehrmacht* – Armed Forces High Command.

8 Walther Hubatsch (ed.) *Hitler's Weisungen für die Kriegsführung 1939–1945* (Bonn: Nebel Verlag, 2000), pp. 176–83, 233–41.

9 *Oberkommando der Luftwaffe* – Air Force High Command.

10 *Oberkommando der Marine* – Naval High Command.

11 Foreign Military Studies: MS, B-284, Normandie '6 Juni – 24 Juli 1944' Gen. d. Inf. Günther Blumentritt (Chef des Stabes OB West).

12 Ibid.

13 Dieter Ose, Die Panzerkontroverse in *Wehrwissenschaftliche Rundschau*, Bd. 31, No. 6, 1982, pp. 189–195.

14 *Oberkommando der Wehrmacht* – Armed Forces High Command.

15 See Detlef Vogel, 'Deutsche und Alliierte Kriegführung im Westen', in Militär-geschchtliches Forschungsamt (ed.) *Das Deutsche Reich und der Zweite Weltkrieg Band 7, Das Deutsche Reich in der Defensive* (Stuttgart: Deutshe Verlags-Anstalt, 2001), p. 463.

16 Quoted in Dieter Ose, *Entscheidung im Westen 1944: Der Oberbefehlshaber West und die Abwehr der alliierten Invasion* (Stuttgart: Deutsche Verlags-Anstalt, 1982), p. 49.

17 Winfried Mönch, *Entscheidungsschlacht 'Invasion' 1944? Prognosen und Diagnosen* (Stuttgart: Steiner, 2001), p. 136.

18 See Vogel, p. 536.

19 KTB – Ia/Heeresgruppe B, 06.06–04.07. 1944, BA/MA: RH 19 IX/ 2 bis 3.

20 Hans Wegmüller, *Die Abwehr der Invasion: Die Konzeption des Oberbefehlshabers West 1940–1944* (Freiburg: Rombach Druck und Verlaghocus, 1986), pp. 142–58.

21 Foreign Military Studies: MS, B-258 Geschichte der Panzergruppe West Gen. d. Pz.Tr. Leo Freiherr Geyr v. Schweppenburg.

22 Ibid.

23 Foreign Military Studies: MS, B-122 Allgemeine Bemerkungen zur deutschen Invasionsabwehr Gen. Maj. Rudolf Freiherr von Gersdorff (AOK 7).

24 *Armeeoberkommando* – Army Command Staff.

25 Alfred B. Stanford, *Force Mulberry. The Planning and Installation of the Artificial Harbor Off U.S. Normandy Beaches in World War II* (New York: Morrow, 1951).

26 Reinhard Stumpf, 'Marcks, Erich' in David G. Chandler and James Lawton Collins Jnr (eds) *The D-Day Encyclopedia* (New York: Helicon, 1994), pp. 350–1.

27 Foreign Military Studies: MS, B-403 Der Einsatz der 711. Infanterie-Division.

28 Ibid.

29 Ibid.

30 Foreign Military Studies: MS, B-845 Die 709. Infanterie-Division.

31 For a German perspective of the fall of Cherbourg see Ose, *Entscheidung*, p. 140

32 Ibid.

33 Samuel W. Mictham Jr, 'Richter, Wilhelm', in Chandler, p. 458.

34 Günther Hiller, 'Kraiss, Dietrich', in Chandler, p. 334.

35 Samuel W. Mitcham Jnr, 'Feuchtinger, Edgar', in Chandler, p. 231.

36 Hans von Luck, *Panzer Commander* (Westport, CT: Praeger, 1989), p. 87.

4   Culture, controversy, Caen and Cherbourg

The first week of the battle

Stephen Badsey

'It had always been impossible' according to the historian of 3rd British Infantry Division, 'to imagine D plus 1'.[1] Compared with the drama of D-Day, the events of the subsequent week have received very little attention. The typical history of the Battle of Normandy starts with the debates over its planning on both sides of the English Channel, then the narrative swoops down onto the experiences of the soldiers on D-Day for a chapter or two, either to end on the beaches or to pull back up into the stratosphere of the debate on how the senior commanders conducted the remainder of the battle. While much has been made of Montgomery's insistence on being in overall command on D-Day, and of Rommel's absence from the battlefield (actually from his headquarters at la Roche-Guyon Château, over 150 miles from the beaches) before the late afternoon, the joining up of the Allied lodgements has been treated largely as a foregone conclusion, coupled perhaps with a mild scolding at their failure to achieve the inevitable more quickly, or to capture Caen at the first attempt. Narratives that continue past D-Day generally rush through this first week to pick up again at 13 June, with the remarkable but massively over-written action by Obersturmführer Michael Wittman at Villers-Bocage.

This is a view of the Battle of Normandy that even after 60 years still conforms very much to the agenda set by the senior officers on both sides, through their own memoirs and the writings of compliant aides and journalists during and immediately after the war. However, it is possible to break away from this, even if to do so inevitably leads to speculation and some presently unanswered questions. On 7 June Montgomery, Bradley (who engaged in a perilous boat journey in order to confer with his two corps commanders) and Eisenhower (who toured the beaches with Admiral Ramsey in the minesweeper HMS *Apollo*), all issued essentially the same orders: that the Allied priority had been changed from an advance directly inland to linking up the beachheads.[2] There were no other orders that they could possibly have given, and both their orders and even their presence were rendered largely irrelevant by circumstances for the next few days. On the German side, the few decisions that Rommel could make also made little difference to the battle's actual conduct. What happened between D-Day and the securing of an Allied continuous front on about 12 June depended almost entirely on the unspoken assumptions inherent in the planning of the battle, the structuring and training of the formations that fought it, and on military and broader national 'cultures', a term including but not limited to the military idea of doctrine as presently understood.

This is important to our understanding of the Battle of Normandy, because it was in its first week that the battle was won and lost. D-Day as it was fought could not have failed, in the sense that without some radical and large-scale change made months beforehand the best German performance imaginable could not have wiped out all the Allied lodgements.[3] By 14 June, after committing 12th SS Panzer Division and Panzer Lehr Division alongside 21st Panzer Division against the British and Canadians, and 17th SS Panzergrenadier Division against the Americans at Carentan, the Germans achieved a brief equality in numbers of divisions with the Allies and were able to contest any further advance inland. It was this which led Air Chief Marshal Tedder to advise his senior officers that day that the situation had the 'makings of a dangerous crisis'.[4] But the apparent stalemate was an illusion based on divisional numbers which masked the great Allied superiority across the front and at all levels. German commanders who expressed an opinion, including General Erich Marcks commanding LXXXIV Corps (killed on 12 June by an Allied air attack), agreed that 9 or 10 June was the critical last day on which the Allies could have conceivably been defeated.[5] On 10 June, the SHAEF planners advised that the best way to break any future stalemate was to use air power in support of an attack out of the beachhead: and this was the method used in Operation CHARNWOOD on 8 July, Operation GOODWOOD on 18 July and Operation COBRA on 25 July to achieve a successful breakout for the Allies.[6] On 14 June, while Tedder was expressing his concerns, US VII Corps launched its major attack out of the Utah beachhead, not as the Germans expected directly north from the Montauban-Quinéville ridge towards Cherbourg, but west to cut the Cotentin peninsula. Thereafter the succession of Allied attacks was delayed or weakened only by the weather: either Montgomery's set-piece attacks of corps size or more at approximately weekly intervals from late June onwards, or the more continuous actions on a wider front preferred by First US Army prior to Operation COBRA.[7]

The verdict that Normandy was already a lost battle was confirmed at the German higher commanders' conference on 17 June at Margival near Soissons, the closest that Hitler ever travelled to the Normandy battlefield, at which he rejected pleas by Rommel and von Rundstedt for a retirement, demanding that Cherbourg must be held at all costs. To attempt to retire behind the Seine in June might or might not have produced a better result for the Germans in the long term; but once these facts are grasped most historiographical controversies about the generalship of the battle either vanish into irrelevance or are reduced to their proper size. The exact reasons for Hitler's decision were not something for which his generals felt able to ask. They may have been based on a genuine assessment that without Cherbourg the Allies would run out of supplies and be forced to scale back their offensive, or on a wider political conviction that the Third Reich could not be seen to fail in battle. Regardless, Hitler's decision condemned the troops of Army Group B to a further two months of repeated defeat. After its first week, Normandy was a hard-fought battle, but it was never a close-run one. Unless the Allied commanders committed some unthinkable and colossal blunder, there was no chance of the Germans holding their line in the face of the relentless firepower to which they were subjected. Senior German commanders were fully aware of this, and continued to demonstrate their concerns, most spectacularly Colonel-General Friedrich Dollmann of Seventh Army in his despairing suicide on 28 June. True to their own military culture, they were puzzled only by what they saw as the Allied reluctance to take greater risks, not realising that their indifference both to the destruction of French life and property and to the loss of their own soldiers could not be shared by their Allied opponents.

All accounts of the Battle of Normandy also include a brief and sometimes florid passage acknowledging the importance of the Normandy terrain and of the weather, particularly on D-Day itself, to the conduct of the battle; although having mentioned these, most proceed to neglect them in favour of deciding which senior Allied officer deserves bouquets or brickbats. Uniquely, only Field Marshal Sir Alan Brooke among the senior Allied commanders had first-hand knowledge of both the beaches and the *bocage*, from visits before the war.[8] It is one of the many paradoxes of our present historiography that Eisenhower is praised for what Montgomery's official biographer calls his 'greatness'[9] in taking the courageous decision to launch the invasion on 6 June in only marginal weather, but that Montgomery is then roundly condemned for failing to achieve all the Allied D-Day objectives, as if the bad weather and its impact on the battlefield were not a factor. In fact the marginal state of the weather on D-Day meant that all the Allied airborne landings suffered from some scattering, and all the beach landings suffered from eastward drift due to wind and current, although these conditions affected the western landings of First US Army more than those of Second (British) Army. The problem was least evident at Sword Beach, where the prominent landmark of the Canal de Caen-River Orne estuary and the mudflats to its far side largely prevented eastward drift, although the narrow beach required 3rd British Infantry Division to land the equivalent of five brigades sequentially on a one-brigade front, instead of the two-brigade fronts at Juno, Gold and Omaha. But the presence of a prominent landmark, although it gave the assault craft a target for which to aim, did not always work to the Allied advantage. Steering towards the church steeple at Vierville-sur-Mer on the western edge of Omaha Beach, the strongest part of the Omaha defences, led to the slaughter of many of the first-wave troops who landed there. At Utah Beach on the Cotentin the initial landing was also made on a one-brigade front, although there were no obstacles to prevent a landing by two or even three brigades abreast. Although histories and sources are strangely silent on the reason for this, the most probable explanation for the single-brigade front at Utah is a shortage of assault landing ships and landing craft. In fact, at Utah the impact of the bad weather on the offshore tides and currents, and the lack of prominent landmarks, meant that the first landings by US 4th Infantry Division took place about 2,000 yards south-east of the intended point, but the lie of the land prevented observers for the most powerful German batteries from seeing that subsequent waves of craft were turning southwards close inshore, and much of the German fire fell on the wrong beach. After the first landings, the rapidly incoming high tide, also due to the bad weather, reduced all the Normandy landing beaches to narrow strips of sand (or in the case of Omaha, obliterated the beach altogether), precluding the swift movement of armoured firepower inland, and delayed further landing of troops and supplies for several days. By far the greatest problem after D-Day for US V Corps moving off Omaha was the limitation imposed on movement by the slow landing of follow-up formations and supplies. But even on the comparatively successful Juno Beach the follow-up British formation on D-Day, 51st (Highland) Division, did not complete landing until D plus 7.[10] This is a large part of any explanation for the nature of the Allied advance inland both on D-Day and for days afterwards.

If it was hard at the time to envisage D plus 1, then from the perspective of 60 years on it is equally hard to appreciate the Battle of Normandy from the perspective of D minus 1. With the knowledge of hindsight, the record of senior Allied figures, most notably Eisenhower and Brooke, bracing themselves for heavy casualties or a disaster, makes them appear pessimistic in the extreme.[11] The story of the Allied deception plan, Operation FORTITUDE, has been told so often and so well that its success has come to be regarded as inevitable. The impression persists that surprise on the morning of D-Day was absolute, and – if only from television re-runs of the fictionalised feature-film version of *The Longest Day* (1962) – that the first the Germans knew of the Allied invasion fleet was when Major Werner Pluskat of Artillery Regiment 352 looked out from resistance nest WN-62 on Omaha Beach at dawn at 5.56 a.m. to see the whole of Task Force O coming straight for him. In fact, from OB West downwards the German defenders of Normandy in Seventh Army, and Fifteenth Army further north, moved to various stages of alert in the course of the night of 5 June and the following morning. The Allied success in achieving surprise required a total, triple, failure of the Luftwaffe reconnaissance effort, the patrol craft of the Kriegsmarine from Le Havre and Cherbourg (a failure to which the high seas in the bad weather contributed), and also of *Abwehr* military intelligence. Given that one German success could have provided the information that the Allied invasion fleet was in mid-Channel, this was unlikely, especially in the light of the E-Boat incursion into Operation TIGER off Slapton Sands on the night of 28 April.[12] Although senior commanders put on a brave face for the troops, before D-Day a realistic Allied assessment was that the Germans would have anything from 12 to 24 hours prior warning of the seaborne invasion. This was long enough to move at least some elements of 12th SS Panzer Division and Panzer Lehr Division from reserve to join 21st Panzer Division in counter-attack positions south of the Caen-Cherbourg road. It would also probably have meant heavy casualties from Luftwaffe nightfighters for the transport aircraft carrying the Allied airborne divisions. That the actual result on 6 June was almost freakishly favourable for the Allies puts both the controversy over the disposition and command of the German reserve Panzer divisions, and the complaints about Allied failures, in their proper perspective.

All accounts of Normandy also acknowledge the early capture of Cherbourg as a supply base as the fundamental first objective for the Allies. Once Normandy was agreed for the landing area, Operations NEPTUNE and OVERLORD were a compromise between this and the decision to land on the Calvados coast rather than chiefly in the Cotentin peninsula. This decision was partly based on operational military considerations: the distance across the peninsula from Lessay in the west to Carentan in the east is only 17 miles, and the Germans could too easily seal up the area. Partly it was a function of the Cotentin terrain, chiefly its unsuitability for airfields.[13] The Cotentin was also unsuitable for large armoured formations, and First US Army's plans did not include landing any armoured divisions at Utah during this first week. The German defensive scheme was also based on protecting the ports of the Channel coast, and what became the Normandy beach defences were actually the southern defences of Le Havre in Fifteenth Army area and of Cherbourg in Seventh Army area respectively. On 6 June three of LXXXIV Corps' six divisions (plus one paratrooper brigade and two weak armoured battalions) and the bulk of its heavy artillery were positioned to defend both sides of the Cotentin. Also, the Kriegsmarine had advised LXXXIV Corps that landing across the offshore shoals of the Calvados coast was impractical. German military doctrinal orthodoxy was that a major port was needed to sustain an Allied invasion. This belief that Cherbourg was the Allied *Schwerpunckt* (point of main effort, a fundamental concept in German military culture) did not change even when, from late on D-Day onwards, they could see from land and air the Gooseberry blockships being sunk and Mulberry harbours being built. On 7 June Third Air Fleet was ordered that 'no possibility is to be left untried' in attacking Allied ships off the beaches,[14] although there was little that the Luftwaffe could do in the face of Allied air superiority except drop a few bombs and sea-mines. But beyond that, the German response to the Normandy landings for the first few days, including Hitler's position at Margival on 17 June, was predicated on the idea that the Allies were vulnerable until they had secured Cherbourg. Nowhere in Seventh Army and Army Group B records is there any indication that Rommel or any other senior German officer grasped the operational, rather than logistic, significance of Mulberry:

that it had freed the Allies from the *early* capture of Cherbourg. This was a major blind spot in the German response to the Normandy landings.

The need for a large port remained of course a high priority in the Allied plans: their famously controversial phase lines called for Cherbourg's capture by D plus 16 and unloading to start on D plus 19; Cherbourg was in fact captured on D plus 21 (27 June) although only 31,000 tons were discharged in July and about ten times as much – half what had been expected – for each month thereafter. Also, and with perfect hindsight, Mulberry itself was less important for Allied supply purposes than the direct landing of supplies across the beaches, particularly after the abandonment of 'Mulberry A' off Saint Laurent after the 'great storm' of 19–21 June, leaving only 'Mulberry B' (Port Winston) working off Arromanches. But the German lack of response to the significance of Mulberry in terms of the battle is only explicable in the context of their military doctrine and culture of the time, which stressed tactical and operational prowess while neglecting and undervaluing logistics,[15] and a military orthodoxy that simply fixated on the nearest major port to the Allied landings.

Protracted arguments about the German defensive scheme for the Battle of Normandy have focused almost entirely on Rommel's plans for defence on the beaches, and so on the compromise over the deployment and command of the reserve Panzer divisions inland. As already pointed out, this argument would have been much less significant without the unexpected total surprise achieved by the Allies. But the emphasis placed on the Panzer divisions, together with the repeated use of the German propaganda term 'Atlantic Wall' to describe Rommel's beach defence concept, has also obscured the fact that both were only part of a much more sophisticated doctrinal debate among the German commanders. The Eastern Front veterans (*Ostkampfer*) whose influence transformed LXXXIV Corps after November 1943 believed in a defensive doctrine which had originated on the Western Front in the First World War and had been further developed fighting against the Red Army, based on a thinly-held infantry front line, a series of infantry and anti-tank artillery battle positions a few thousand yards further back, and armoured counter-attacking forces in reserve.[16] Rommel and other veterans of battle against the western Allies in North Africa and Italy argued that vulnerability to Allied firepower, including airpower, made this kind of elastic defence impossible, and static forward defence the only option. The result was an unhappy doctrinal compromise typical of Hitler's Third Reich, in which neither scheme was adopted wholeheartedly. Although the construction of the beach defences absorbed most of the steel, concrete and labour resources available, they were never as strong as Rommel wanted: Sword Beach was defended by two infantry companies (each of about 100–150 men), Juno Beach and Gold Beach by three companies each, Omaha Beach by four, and the landing area at Utah Beach by only one. Given that Task Force O (for Omaha) alone included 386 seagoing ships and craft plus a further 33 minesweepers and 585 support vessels, the grim German joke on D-Day that the Allies had more ships than they had men may have been, at the water's edge, literally true. But the real strength of the German defences lay not only in these resistance nests but in a second line of defences set on a dominating ridge about 90–150 feet high (actually the prehistoric sea-cliff from the time of the last ice age), varying from 2,500 to 4,000 yards inland. On this ridge the Germans deployed the reserve companies of their front-line infantry battalions, and also most of their artillery. The defensive scheme at Utah was slightly different from that along the Calvados coast, with the counter-attacking reserve coming from the two-company 795th Georgian Battalion (an *Ost* battalion that fought very well on D-Day), and a second line of battalions deployed to defend the Cherbourg road chiefly north of Montebourg. On the morning of D-Day, all these reserve companies launched counter-attacks against the Allied landing troops as they moved inland, although mostly they were so savaged by Allied firepower that the attacks went almost unnoticed, with one exception. This was a company-sized attack with some armour towards Ste-Mère-Eglise from the south, identified by 82nd Airborne Division as the most serious threat to its positions that day.[17]

The German artillery defending the beaches were chiefly field guns protected by earth and wood, but also included a few concrete casemated batteries, of which the most important were at Merville inland to the south-east of Sword and both Crisbecq and Azeville to the north-west of Utah, all of which continued to function as miniature fortresses for the Germans after D-Day. These artillery positions were mostly sited along the inland ridgeline, with only a few batteries along the cliffs that separated Omaha from Gold to the east and from the mudflats of the River Vire estuary to the west, such as the battery at Longues-sur-Mer in the Gold Beach sector, and at the Pointe du Hoc. What was conspicuously missing from this defensive scheme was a third line of mobile counter-attacking armoured battalions or brigades held near the main Caen-Cherbourg road (the 'lateral road' in Allied planning), except for the brigade groups of 21st Panzer Division south of Caen. This was largely a result of Rommel's forward defence doctrine. His order to 352nd Infantry Division to move forward from Saint Lô in March 1944 to take over what became the Gold Beach and Omaha Beach sectors more than halved the coastline frontage defended by 716th Infantry Division, at the cost of removing any substantial counter-attacking reserve in the sector between Bayeux and the Vire estuary.

A combination of German military culture, which stressed independent thinking on the part of lower-ranking commanders, and a certain contempt for Rommel himself and his humble social origins, led to Eastern Front veterans openly condemning Rommel's tactical scheme; Major General Karl-Wilhelm von Schlieben, commanding 709th Infantry Division, claimed after his capture to have done so in front of Rommel himself and his staff.[18] They criticised the lack of concrete defences and strongpoints further inland and at roadblocks, and the way in which working on the beach defences exhausted their troops and left inadequate time for training. In partial defiance of Rommel, both 709th Infantry Division and 352nd Infantry Division contrived to create small mobile reserves, in the latter case an engineer battalion and some assault guns held near Cerisy forest. This division also provided LXXXIV Corps' mobile reserve of three battalions (two on bicycles and one in French civilian transport) as Battle Group Meyer, held south and east of Bayeux. In 709th Infantry Division sector the local reserve was Infantry Regiment 1057 (belonging to 91st *Luftlande* Division) deployed west of the River Merderet together with a few tanks, mainly obsolete French models, and *Fallschirmjäger* Regiment 6 at the base of the Cotentin.

As with any conventional set-piece land battle of the First and Second World Wars, the Allied success on the morning of D-Day depended on the extent to which they could suppress not only the immediate German beach defences but also the supporting artillery pieces and reserves, by using firepower coupled with a rapid advance to occupy the German battle positions. What made the first few days of Normandy an unusual battle was that the Allies had to start this process from the sea, and that a large part of their supporting gunfire came from ships offshore. The Allied reliance on the shock of firepower was deeply rooted in their own doctrines and military cultures. For the United States this went back to their Civil War; while a British version had developed on the Western Front in the First World War, and had been adopted by Montgomery as the so-called 'Colossal Cracks' approach, and also accepted by Simonds for the Canadians.[19] Although British amphibious doctrine preferred night landings with surprise away from the main enemy defences,[20] the British planners were perfectly aware that the terrain of the landing beaches and Rommel's beach defences made this option impractical. The Anglo-Canadian forces landing on Gold, Juno and Sword were faced with a problem unique in military history: fighting house-to-house from the water's edge through the seaside villages, for which heavy firepower and armour was essential. On D-Day, Allied airpower and the heavy guns of the larger warships were directed chiefly at the German second line of defences on the inshore ridge, leaving 'beach drenching' from destroyers and landing craft together with specialist armour including the 'DD' (for Duplex Drive) amphibious Shermans to overcome the immediate beach defences. The lightest Allied casualties came at Utah Beach, where beach drenching almost destroyed the defending heavy weapons of resistance nest WN-5, and the reserve gun line was destroyed or suppressed by a combination of paratroopers, airpower and naval gunnery. The heaviest Allied casualties came at Omaha, where the amphibious tanks of one of the two leading battalions largely foundered offshore, the initial beach drenching failed, but even more importantly the previously undetected gun line of Artillery Regiment 352 behind the beaches was not suppressed until about midday, and not completely eliminated until D plus 1, along with the last of the beach defenders. There is even a suggestion that some German guns simply ran out of ammunition.

The Allied success on D-Day on each of the landing beaches depended heavily on the support given by specialist troops and equipment to each of the assaulting divisions. All five beach landings were supported by the amphibious Shermans, with varying successes largely depending on the effect of the weather and sea currents. The problem created for Second Army by the defended chalets and houses on its three beaches was solved largely by the addition of specialist armoured vehicles, chiefly from 79th Armoured Division ('Hobart's Funnies'). In addition, the importance of airborne forces in identifying and engaging the German guns and reserve companies along the ridgeline was shown not only by their successes, notably those of 101st Airborne Division inland from Utah, but also by their absences, particularly the problems caused to 3rd British Infantry Division from Sword Beach by the inland Hillman and Morris positions, which played an important part in preventing the division from reaching Caen on D-Day. The two beaches where the Allies suffered their heaviest casualties, Omaha and Gold, were also the furthest away from the disruptive effects on the Germans of the airborne drop. As an extreme case, the bunker complex including the Luftwaffe radar station at Douvres-la-Deliverande just three miles inland from Juno Beach was not finally captured by British troops until 17 June. This raises the question as to why no thought was given to splitting the Allied airborne divisions to put airborne brigades down between Caen and Bayeux and directly south of Omaha, operations that would have carried no greater risk than those actually attempted. The answer is rooted in both British and American institutional military culture. The best and most flexible structure for the Allied airborne troops would have been independent mixed brigades of paratroopers and gliders, on the same model as the commandos or rangers (paratroopers by themselves were vulnerable to enemy armour, and needed the anti-tank weapons and ammunition carried by the gliders), rather than divisions, which were too unwieldy for their intended purpose. However, the institutional difficulties and complexities of establishing new forces in the Second World War were so great that without the creation of airborne divisions as a power base the British and American airborne forces might not have existed at all.[21]

The focus in the historiography of Normandy on the individual Allied beaches on D-Day has led to a neglect of some important aspects of their wider plan and its implications, especially for the days that followed. The original COSSAC plan for the battle was first presented in July 1943, and changes were made by SHAEF and 21st Army Group from mid-January 1944 onwards. There was a strong sense among Allied higher commanders in early 1944 of critical decisions being made under great time pressure, and of the need to maintain a consensus among themselves. The initial 21st Army Group plan for Operation OVERLORD was issued on 1 February 1944, confirmed two weeks later, and after that most of the effort went into revising details. The corps' plans were finalised by 27 March with a few late adjustments, of which the most significant was the change to the American airborne plan on 27 May in the light of new information on German dispositions in the Cotentin. A point often missed is that the two beaches added by SHAEF in February to the COSSAC plan were Sword Beach with its narrower frontage, as well as Utah Beach on the Cotentin.[22] But if Sword gave the British a problem, the addition of Utah completely changed the objectives for Omaha: as well as an advance south-eastward towards Bayeux to link up with Gold, a distance of about ten miles, the forces at Omaha were now also required to make a further simultaneous and even greater advance towards Isigny-sur-Mer and beyond to link up with forces from Utah. This problem was ingeniously solved by US V Corps at Omaha by landing two half-divisions side by side for its first waves, with the intention of 1st Infantry Division peeling off towards Bayeux and 29th Infantry Division towards Isigny-sur-Mer. But one effect of this command arrangement was to increase the confusion on Omaha when things went wrong on D-Day. Further, Omaha was not only the most critical beach in terms of the Allied plan and the most challenging in terms of German defences and natural terrain features, it was also the only beach where the landing troops received (other than the amphibious Shermans) no additional help at all in the form of either specialist armour or vehicles, or airborne troops.

What is even harder to explain is that, although the German military doctrine and culture almost instinctively identified Cherbourg as the Allied *Schwerpunckt* and therefore the link-up between US V Corps and VII Corps as critical, there was no such emphasis in First US Army's plan. Second Army landed two commando brigades with the specific mission of linking up their beachheads: 1st Special Service Brigade on Sword Beach on D-Day to reinforce 6th Airborne Division in the River Orne bridgehead, and 4th Special Service Brigade on Juno and Gold on D-Day and D plus 1 to tie in these beaches together with Omaha. But the First US Army plan called only for 116th Infantry Regiment to lead the push inland in the general direction of Isigny-sur-Mer, even though this was also one of the two leading assault regiments to hit the beaches. First US Army's plan actually weakened the COSSAC version, which had a British commando battalion landing to the east of Omaha and American paratroopers landing to the west. In addition, the VII Corps plan called for 4th Infantry Division from Utah to swing north and north-west towards Cherbourg on D-Day and D plus 1, leaving Carentan to be captured by 101st Airborne Division, assumed to be able to fight as a formed division on D plus 1 or soon after, despite the division's paratrooper regiments being dropped in darkness on D-Day, and contrary to all previous experience of the nature of airborne assaults. Unlike the British and Germans, US military culture of this period made little room for the possibility of unforeseen failures. The difference in military cultures between the two Allies was further highlighted by the British decision to suppress the Longues-sur-Mer cliff-top battery by airpower and naval gunfire alone, leading to its capture from the landward side on D plus 1, in contrast to the US decision to use its two elite ranger battalions and their associated landing craft to capture the Pointe-du-Hoc on D-Day by scaling the cliffs. This raises the issue of whether the ranger battalions, which were assigned their role at the Point du Hoc in the original COSSAC plan, would have been better employed, once that plan was changed by SHAEF, landing as a second brigade with the first wave at Utah, with a mission to push towards Carentan on D-Day.

By the fortunes of battle, the only Allied division to achieve all its major objectives on D-Day was British 6th Airborne Division, although it continued to have problems for some days afterwards. The story of the airborne landings is usually told in terms of objectives achieved on D-Day and the problems caused particularly for the two American divisions from the scattered night landing (for which the airborne forces and some historians have most unjustly blamed the pilots of their aircraft). But when seen from the German perspective this scattering of paratroopers across the Cotentin in the early hours of D-Day worked considerably to the Allied advantage. The threat to Cherbourg continued to impress Seventh Army, which recorded in its summary of events on 6 June that, 'It is the opinion of the chief of staff' Lieutenant General Max Pemsel, 'that the enemy intends to cut off the peninsula COTENTIN at its narrowest point',[23] a formal statement identifying the enemy *Schwerpunckt*. This impression was reinforced by American paratroopers landing in the Vire estuary and south of Carentan, and then by the Utah Beach landing. The defenders of the bunker complex at Grandcamp and Maisy, which was heavily shelled on D-Day, also seemed convinced that they had beaten off a significant Allied seaborne landing attempt, and until 8 June Army Group B continued to believe that a deliberate airborne landing had also taken place on the *western* side of the Cotentin. Before dawn on D-Day, even while Battle Group Luck, the leading formation of 21st Panzer, was having its first encounters with 6th Airborne Division east of Caen, LXXXIV Corps ordered attacks towards Sainte Mère Eglise, by two battalions of Infantry Regiment 1058 from Montebourg in the north, Infantry Regiment 1057 from the west, and *Fallschirmjäger* Regiment 6 from the south, in the classic German battle of encirclement. The corps also ordered its reserve, Battle Group Meyer, to move from south-east of Bayeux westward to the Carentan area. Shortly after dawn, as it became apparent that the immediate threat to Carentan had been exaggerated, Battle Group Meyer was turned around, and committed during the afternoon of D-Day north of Bayeux against the flank of 50th (Northumbrian) Division advancing from Gold, peeling off a battalion northward towards Omaha as it did so on the assumption that this was sufficient to eliminate a failed Allied landing there. If the attack by Battle Group Meyer had succeeded together with the attacks by 21st Panzer Division, these together with the arrival of 12th SS Panzer Division west of Caen on D plus 1 would have formed the basis for an encirclement of the whole of Second Army. This episode gives the almost certain answer to the often-raised question as to what would have happened at Omaha if a brigade of 12th

SS Panzer Division had been present to the south: it would have been sent elsewhere, either towards Sainte Mère Eglise or Bayeux.

For D plus 1 and the following days, attention has mostly been paid to 12th SS Panzer Division's prevention of 3rd Canadian Infantry Division reaching Caen from the west, while 21st Panzer Division blocked the British advance from the east. But across the Allied landing area the Germans, almost without formal orders being issued above divisional level, continued to launch the pincer-like double envelopments that were their classic (even stereotyped) manoeuvre. All these double envelopments failed to reach the beaches in the face of Allied firepower. Although airpower and artillery played their part, the most important Allied weapon was naval gunnery, which the Germans acknowledged as decisive in destroying or blocking any attempt on their part to manoeuvre north of the Caen-Cherbourg road, very much as Rommel had predicted.[24] Although the German armoured battle groups at least remained intact, by the end of D plus 1 *Fallschirmjäger* Regiment 6's counter-attack against Utah from the Carentan area had failed with heavy casualties, as had Battle Group Meyer's counter-attack against Gold. But the strong German doctrinal instinct for such counter-attacks led to attempts on D plus 1 to repeat Battle Group Meyer's attack with the last remaining available LXXXIV Corps reserve, Mobile Brigade 30 (mobile on bicycles), which was likewise effectively destroyed north of Bayeux. Counting this last attack, three battle groups of 352nd Infantry Division had been smashed by the British from Gold, and a further two by the Americans from Omaha, producing the brief gaping hole in the German centre on 8 June that became known as the Caumont Gap.

The Allied landing divisions also, after the shock of D-Day, behaved almost as if they were on autopilot to complete their objectives rather than responding to events around them. 1st Infantry Division pushed forward eastward from Omaha on D plus 1 quite unaware that in combination with 50th (Northumbrian) Division from Gold it was driving the remnants of the two failed German counter-attacks by Battle Group Meyer and Mobile Brigade 30 into a pocket north of Bayeux, from which the survivors broke out in the darkness of the early hours of 9 June, the junction between Omaha and Gold coming next day. Short of transport and even ammunition, the otherwise redoubtable 1st Infantry Division was so conscious of its own vulnerability to a large German attack from the south that before dawn on 8 June it reported one happening, and went briefly onto the defensive. It was not until 9 June that V Corps realised that 352nd Infantry Division had disintegrated in front of it, by which time the first units of II Parachute Corps were arriving to steady the German line. As 1st Infantry Division drove to the east, 29th Infantry Division pushed to the west along the coast and the northern side of the Lower Aure valley, driving the remains of 352nd Infantry Division back towards Carentan. This was a very hard advance: veterans of Omaha Beach considered that capturing the German bunker positions at Grandcamp on 8 June was the harder fight. But

V Corps orders still required 29th Infantry Division only to secure Isigny-sur-Mer. Early on 9 June its reserve formation, 175th Infantry Regiment, reached the town, sending patrols across the Vire estuary the next day.

Allied plans expected a full-scale German counter-offensive to start at any date from D plus 3 to D plus 7, with reinforcing divisions arriving in the interval. Rommel now found himself torn between his preferred object-ive and his biggest problem. While the immediate Allied threat was from the British and Canadians in front of Caen, Army Group B and Seventh Army were convinced that the Utah beachhead (or as the Germans inevit-ably thought of it, the Sainte Mère Eglise pocket) remained the Allied *Schwerpunckt* and also their chief vulnerability. This conviction was rein-forced by the German capture on 7 June near Omaha Beach of the order of battle and scheme of manoeuvre for V Corps, including information about the 'Mulberry A' harbour at St-Laurent, and on the morning of 8 June, from a landing craft beached in the Grandcamp area, of a comparable set of documents for VII Corps, including Carentan as a main objective. So, by the evening of 8 June, Army Group B had the complete plans for First US Army for the entire first week of the battle. These plans confirmed Rommel's views about the weakness of First US Army's position at Carentan, but he continued to ignore the evidence regarding Mulberry.[25] On the after-noon of 9 June he ordered all his forces facing the Calvados coast from the Orne to the Vire briefly onto the defensive, in favour of his belief that 'everything must be used to defend Cherbourg'.[26] Orders were also issued to the arriving Panzer Lehr Division to hold (in fact to retake, as it has already fallen) Isigny-sur-Mer at all costs.[27] The success of 50th (Northumbrian) Division from Gold led to Panzer Lehr Division being instead diverted to the Bayeux sector, preventing a very dangerous situation indeed developing for the Allies.

Meanwhile, and regardless of Bradley's new orders, in the Cotentin VII Corps' plan unfolded very much as it had been drawn up, with the main effort being made northwards led by 4th Infantry Division, leaving a weakened but very determined 101st Airborne Division (including its glider brigade, which had arrived by sea) to seize Carentan. Starting early on 9 June, the airborne troops attacked over some of the most exposed and difficult terrain on the Normandy battlefield against an even more weak-ened *Fallschirmjäger* Regiment 6. During the afternoon of 10 June the lead company of 327th Glider Infantry Regiment made the first fragile contact just west of the River Vire with 29th Reconnaissance Troop and 175th Infantry Regiment. According to one account, many of the American soldiers from both sides of the junction had adopted German transport methods and were riding horses.[28] 101st Airborne Division secured Carentan on the morning of 12 June after an epic fight supported by airpower, artil-lery and naval gunnery, after the town's abandonment by *Fallschirmjäger* Regiment 6 (according to its commander chiefly because his men were out of ammunition), and barely hours before the arrival of the leading elements of 17th SS Panzergrenadier Division as reinforcements. It was only circumstances and some extraordinary bravery that prevented an American failure to take Carentan rather than a British failure to take Caen being the great controversy of the Battle of Normandy.

Despite the jokes that it caused among Bradley's officers, Montgomery's message to him on 25 June that 'Caen is the key to Cherbourg' contained much truth.[29] On 11 June Army Group B planned 'to replace the Panzer units [opposite the British and Canadians] with infantry divisions and transfer its *Schwerpunkt* to the Carentan-Montebourg area in order to avert the danger to Cherbourg'.[30] Rommel was unable to do this because of the continued Anglo-Canadian threat to break out past Caen, and because of Hitler's opposition. On 12 June, in response to the fall of Carentan, Hitler ordered both absolutely no retreat, and for the Allied beaches to be rolled-up sequentially from the east starting with the Orne bridgehead. Despite repeated complaints by German senior officers about Hitler's interference in battlefield decisions, this order almost certainly saved Rommel's military reputation. Given the strength of the Anglo-Canadian threat in front of Caen, the unsuitability of the Cotentin for armour, and the difficulties involved in moving and supplying the Panzer divisions for such a redeployment, Rommel's plan would surely have led to a defeat even more rapid and complete than that which was eventually achieved. Even so, Hitler's orders on 12 June set the attritional agenda for the rest of a Battle of Normandy that he had already lost.

Acknowledgements

This chapter arose largely out of research for three volumes in the 'Battle Zone Normandy' series of combined history/battlefield guidebooks published by Sutton Publishing of Thrupp in 2004: *Utah Beach*, *Omaha Beach* and *The Battle for Caen*. I would like to acknowledge the work of my co-authors on two of these volumes, Tim Bean and particularly Dr Simon Trew. The chapter's conclusions are based chiefly on war diaries and other original documents in the National Archives of the United Kingdom (Public Record Office), the National Archives of Canada, and the National Archives and Research Administration (NARA) of the USA, including translations of German documents and the results of debriefings of German prisoners of war. The following official accounts of Normandy have been also been used: Ellis, L.F. *et al.*, *Victory in the West Volume I: The Battle of Normandy* (London: HMSO, 1962); Harrison, G.A., *Cross-Channel Attack* (Washington, DC: War Department, 1950); Stacey, C.P., *The Victory Campaign* (Ottawa: the Queen's Printer, 1960); *Omaha Beachhead 6 June–13 June 1944* (Washington, DC: War Department, 1945); *Utah Beach to Cherbourg 6 June–27 June 1944* (Washington, DC: War Department, 1947); together with the following recent editions of accounts by senior German officers as prisoners of war: Isby, D.C. (ed.) *Fighting the Invasion: The German Army at D-Day* (London: Greenhill, 2000); and Isby, D.C. (ed.) *Fighting in Normandy: The German Army from D-Day to Villers-Bocage* (London: Greenhill, 2001). For German dispositions on D-Day see the facsimile maps in Mehner K. (ed.) *Die geheimen Tagesberichte der Deutschen Wehmachtführung im zweiten Weltkrieg 1939–1945* (Osnabrück: Biblio Verlag, 1984–95), Volume 10; and also Chazette, A., *Le Mur de l'Atlantique en Normandie* (Bayeux: Heimdal, 2000).

Notes

1 N. Scarf, *Assault Division* (London: Collins, 1947), p. 93.
2 W.B. Brauer, *Hitler's Fortress Cherbourg: The Conquest of a Bastion* (New York: Stein and Day, 1984), pp. 98–9; D.D. Eisenhower, *Crusade in Europe* (Baltimore, MD: Johns Hopkins University Press, 1997), pp. 253–4; N. Hamilton, *Monty: Master of the Battlefield 1942–1944* (London: Sceptre, 1983), pp. 612–15.
3 Paradoxically, this view has been strengthened by experiments in counterfactual history attempting to produce a total Allied defeat on 6 June: it cannot be done. See P. Tsouras, *Disaster at D-Day* (Machanicsburg, PA: Stackpole, 1994); T.N. Dupuy, *Options of Command* (New York: Hippocrene, 1984), and S.E. Ambrose, 'D-Day Fails' in R. Cowley (ed.) *What Ifs?* (London: Macmillan, 1999), pp. 341–51.
4 Ellis, *Victory in the West Volume I*, p. 265; R.J. Kershaw, *D-Day: Piercing the Atlantic Wall* (London: Ian Allen, 1993), p. 237.
5 Isby, *Fighting in Normandy*, pp. 76–80.
6 Planning document PS SHAEF (44) 21 (Final) 10 June, cited in M. Blumenson, *Breakout and Pursuit* (Washington, DC: Department of the Army, 1961), p. 187.
7 See S.A. Hart, *Montgomery and 'Colossal Cracks': The 21st Army Group in Northwest Europe 1944–45* (London: Praeger, 2000); T. Copp, *Fields of Fire* (Toronto: University of Toronto Press, 2003); R.A. Hart, *Clash of Arms* (Boulder CO: Lynne Reinner, 2001).
8 F. Morgan, *Overture to Overlord* (London: Hodder & Stoughton, 1950), p. 163.
9 N. Hamilton, *Monty: Master of the Battlefield 1942–1944*, p. 593.
10 *Omaha Beachhead*, p. 116; J.B. Salmond, *The History of the 51st Highland Division* (Edinburgh: Pentland, 1953), pp. 139–41.
11 C. Ryan, *The Longest Day* (London: Victor Golancz, 1982), p. 207; A. Danchev and D. Todman (eds) *Field Marshal Lord Alanbrooke: War Diaries 1939–1945* (London: Weidenfeld & Nicholson, 2001), p. 554.
12 For Slapton Sands see R.J. Kershaw, *D-Day: Piercing the Atlantic Wall*, pp. 9–15; see also J.C. Masterman, *The Double-Cross System* (London: Pimloco, 1995); R. Hesketh, *Fortitude: The D-Day Deception Campaign* (London: St Ermin's, 1999), F.H. Hinsley *et al.*, *British Intelligence in the Second World War Volume 4* (London: HMSO, 1990).
13 E.P.F. Rose and C. Pareyn, 'British Applications of Military Geology for "Operation Overlord" and the Battle in Normandy, France, 1944', in J.R. Underwood Jr and P.L. Guth (eds) *Military Geology in War and Peace* (Boulder, CO: Geological Society of America, 1998), pp. 55–65. For a full description of the reasoning see 'Operation Overlord – Report and Appreciation July 1943' in CAB 106/969 'History of COSSAC' National Archives of the United Kingdom Public Record Office (PRO).
14 R. Bennett, *Ultra in the West* (London: Hutchinson, 1979), p. 73.
15 See M. van Creveld, *Fighting Power* (London: Arms and Armour, 1983) and T.N. Dupuy, *A Genius for War* (London: Macdonald & Janes, 1977). As may be guessed from their titles, both authors enthusiastically support this German doctrinal approach.
16 T. Copp, *Fields of Fire*, pp. 26–8; P. Griffith, *Forward into Battle: Fighting Tactics from Waterloo to Vietnam* (Chichester: Anthony Bird, 1981), pp. 78–82; D.M. Glantz and J. House, *When Titans Clashed* (Lawrence KS: University of Kansas Press, 1995).
17 *Utah Beach to Cherbourg* (Washington, DC: War Department, 1947), p. 34.
18 CSDIC (UK) 'Report on information obtained from Senior Officer PW on 13–14 Aug 44 – C/22 Generalleutnant von Schlieben – conversation between Schlieben and Broich'. I am grateful to Mitchell Yockelson of NARA for this reference. See also Isby, *Fighting the Invasion*, pp. 102–4.

19 S. Badsey, 'The American Experience of Armour 1919–1953', in J.P. Harris and F.H. Toase, *Armoured Warfare* (London: Batsford, 1990), pp. 124–44; Hart, *Montgomery and 'Colossal Cracks'*, Copp, *Fields of Fire*.

20 See A.R. Lewis, *Omaha Beach: A Flawed Victory* (Chapel Hill, NC: University of North Carolina Press, 2001), pp. 34–49.

21 N. Crookenden, *Dropzone Normandy* (Abingdon: Purnell, 1976), pp. 12–61; T.B.H. Ottway, *Airborne Forces* (London: Imperial War Museum, reprinted 1990); J.A. Hudson, *Out of the Blue* (West Lafayette, IN: Purdue University, 1972).

22 'Operation Overlord – Report and Appreciation July 1943', CAB 106/969 PRO; Hamilton, *Monty: Master of the Battlefield*, pp. 482–3; Morgan, *Overture to Overlord*, pp. 152–3.

23 German Seventh Army War Diary, entry for 6 June 1944, RG 407 – Box 24154 – ML488 NARA.

24 Ellis, *Victory in the West Volume I*, p. 239.

25 D. Kahn, *Hitler's Spies: The Extraordinary Story of German Military Intelligence* (London: Arrow, 1980), pp. 387–99; G.L. Harrison, *Cross Channel Attack*, (Washington, DC: Government Printing, 1951), p. 350.

26 Isby, *Fighting in Normandy*, p. 80.

27 Bennett, *Ultra in the West*, p. 77.

28 R.F. Weighley, *Eisenhower's Lieutenants: The Campaigns of France and Germany 1944–1945* (London: Sidgwick & Jackson, 1981), p. 98.

29 Quoted in D. Irving, *The War Between the Generals* (London: Penguin, 1981), p. 177.

30 Seventh Army War Diary, entries for 11 and 12 June 1944 RG 407 – Box 24154 – ML488 NARA.

5 American tactical innovation in Normandy, 1944

Nigel de Lee

Opinions of the tactical performance of the American army in Normandy differ widely. Apologists for the German army are inclined to be highly critical, ascribing the victory of the Allied armies to superiority of numbers and quantity of material resources alone. They imply that in a more equal contest the Germans would have won, as if any armed struggle had ever been equal. But some authorities from the Allied side are in agreement with this view. Albert Norman, the historian attached to the HQ of the US First Army wrote: '. . . the principle of mass was applied throughout the OVER-LORD campaign. At every chosen point of attack overwhelming manpower and material force was pitted against numerically weaker forces. That is how . . . the breakthrough at St Lo was achieved'.[1]

Major-General Richard Schimpff, commander of the 3rd *Fallschirmjaeger* Division claimed that in his sector, 'The purely numerical proportion of power was therefore estimated to be 1:4 to 1:5'.[2] Colonel Zerbel of the 352nd Infantry Division remarked that in mid-June, '. . . the enemy was only inclined to attack when he felt completely superior in material'.[3] The German field commanders were also very critical of the American tactics, although their comments in regard to this subject are inconsistent. Colonel Ziegelmann of the 352nd Division remarked on a general lack of audacity and enterprise on the part of the American troops. With regard to the fighting between 11 and 14 June he commented: 'Soon it became noticeable that the enthusiasm, which previously had prevailed during attacks was lessening . . . it became a practice with the enemy to spray each hedge with his MPs for longer and longer periods of time . . .'. In describing the fighting on 16 of June he noted: 'the tendency not to take advantage of success . . . stubbornly adhering to his plan . . . The caution and lack of daring prevailing in the American infantry was characterised by their stopping in small sub-sectors whenever they met with stubborn resistance, rather than by-passing it'.

But Ziegelmann also mentioned that on 16 June, 'the situation north of St Lo actually became rather serious . . . the intermingled and exhausted German units were threatened with a complete tearing-up of the weakened front . . .'. The HQ of the 352 Division at Le Mesnil Rouxelin was brought under direct fire by leading elements of the US 29th Division. According to

Ziegelmann the American infiltration of the German positions '. . . increased the beginning feeling of panic'.[4] He also remarked that the Americans used few tanks after having lost some to *panzerfausts* while stuck in the hedge-rows. He was critical of the failure of the 29th Division to use tanks to follow up the success of infantry supported by artillery and tactical aircraft on 16 June,[5] but in a comment on the fighting in July he acknowledged the fundamental reason for the American limited employment of armour, and the radical effectiveness of one of the technical measures taken to meet the difficulty:

> The fact that the enemy did not make use of . . . tanks, was due to the terrain. Their commitment was restricted to employment in numbers, and the use of a new kind of shoveling apparatus attached to their fronts which dug breaks into the rows of hedges, and furthermore made the hedgerows useless as protection for the infantry men.[6]

Schimpf agreed with most of the critical comments made by Ziegelmann. He stated of 10 June, 'If the Americans . . . had launched an energetic attack from the Forest of Cerisy, St. Lô would have fallen'. He also made a more general remark that the Americans 'only decided on extremely limited objectives and failed to exploit achieved successes by continuing their thrusts in depth . . .'. He found them generally predictable in tactical behaviour, saying, 'American tactics . . . were much more schematic and inflexible than the German, which fact often gave the defensive troops the opportunity to take appropriate counter measures'.

But, although struck by a tendency not to use covered approaches, stealth and surprise, he did admit that American raids of company strength could get to within 70 metres of his division's main line of resistance undetected, evading outposts by such techniques. He also admitted the advantage which the Norman terrain gave the defence: 'The terrain hindered the attacking enemy from fully developing his air and tank superiority . . .'.[7]

Some American scholars agree that the tactics were deficient, particularly in the early stages of the campaign. Doubler remarked that 'companies and battalions learned that spirited but ill-prepared attacks produced heavy casualties' – that mass and confidence combined were not enough to bring success.[8] Carafano stated that, with their insistence on 'winning the firefight', before attempting any decisive movement, 'U.S. Army tactics were ill-suited for hedgerow fighting . . .'.[9] More specifically he found that 'The US Army had not foreseen the requirement for close infantry-armor co-ordination, and did not have radios that allowed small infantry units and individual tanks to communicate'.[10] In his discussion of COBRA he was very critical of US artillery tactics: 'Artillery barrages, both before and during the opera-tion, were often ineffective. Artillery was only used to good effect when the U.S. infantry and armor could advance and see the enemy and then direct cannon fire directly onto the German positions . . .'.[11]

Doubler remarks that senior officers were unwilling to admit that the tactics were in need of change or improvement and quotes Bradley as claiming, 'Our tactics as taught at home are as sound as a dollar'.[12]

This curious but common military affectation, of claiming infallibility in a field in which practical flexibility has always been a supreme virtue, was followed by other official commentators such as the G-3 Division of SHAEF which stated in December 1944, 'basic pre-invasion infantry-tank doctrines still remain sound. They had to be applied with a bit of ingenuity and a tremendous amount of energy, but they did produce results even in the hedgerow country'.[13] The same line was taken by the commander of the 29th Division, Major-General Charles Gerhardt in his comments on the fighting in June 1944: 'Certain minor variations must be made to fit peculiar terrain requirements. However, this should not be allowed to influence tactics or organization once the need has passed'.[14]

Both Doubler and Carafano concede that despite the inherent conservatism of the higher commanders the US Army did adapt to the tactical requirements of Normandy. Carafano says, 'the US Army . . . adjusted to the requirements of Normandy fighting reasonably well . . . two months of hard fighting had provided stiff lessons . . .'.[15]

This judgement is too harsh. As Doubler argued, the American troops in action in Normandy began to adapt their tactics to concrete realities and the needs of survival and success much earlier. There is plenty of evidence that the necessary changes in practice began at low level, 'hedgerow level', and were gradually recognised and adopted by units and formations as they proved their value. The best-known are those which were approved by the higher levels and then discussed and disseminated in orders and journals, means which have left their traces in written form. Others have been recorded in regimental literature, memoirs and orally. Because this process was spontaneous and not officially inspired or controlled it was sporadic and patchy, often driven by particular local conditions and events. As standard tactical modes failed, troops who survived and had imagination devised new improvised forms of organisation and methods. This inherent adaptability had already impressed their great enemy Field Marshal Rommel who remarked: 'What was astonishing was the speed with which the Americans adapted themselves to modern warfare. In this they were assisted by their extraordinary sense for the practical and material and by their complete lack of regard for tradition and worthless theories . . . great imagination and foresight . . .'.[16]

Balkoski, the historian of the 29th Division observed, '. . . it took a few weeks for the squad leaders to grasp the significant differences between real war and "war by the book", and by then many of them were dead . . . men discovered that the infantry tactics they had been taught were in urgent need of modification'.[17]

According to the histories of the 115th Infantry Regiment and the 110th Field Artillery Battalion, which formed a Regimental Combat Team in the

29th Division the troops grasped the need for change on first contact with the enemy and the terrain in Normandy. The regiment had been in training for 18 months in England and, 'All of this training . . . was designed to teach them what to do without stopping to think. It was hoped that the men would become so familiar with the solutions to the problems that they would have to face that these solutions would be automatically carried out'.[18]

This is not what happened in Normandy. On 6 June, according to one sergeant, 'we moved forward along the hedgerows. We moved cautiously and hesitantly partly because of fear and partly because of the strangeness of the situation . . . it was not rare for a single well-hidden sniper to hold up an entire battalion'.[19] The artillery also found the country strange, as recorded in the Battalion history, 'the 110th advance parties found that the actual country differed vastly from their mental pictures . . .'.[20] They also rapidly had to improvise a new temporary order of battle, taking over control of four SP guns on 6 June and then a stray armoured car and six guns from an infantry cannon company the following day.[21] Later that month they acted as a fire control unit for other battalions combined with their own, incorporated a battery of light anti-aircraft artillery and developed experimental tactics to put fire onto hedgerows and also behind them in support of the infantry.[22] Artillery forward parties were used to lead infantry advances and safety margins were cut to stop enemy infiltration.[23] Intimate close support for the infantry proved invaluable on 12 June when most of the 3/115 had shown a little too much audacity by going through the enemy lines south of the Elle and were about to be cut off in the *bocage*, much reduced and having used all their ammunition. A timely and accurate barrage two hedges away allowed at least some to get back to their own lines.[24] The infantry learned a bitter lesson in an early attempt at close cooperation with armour. 'K' Company of the 3/115 advanced into St Laurent with tank support but had to retreat when German anti-tank fire drove back their armoured support. The company planned a new attack, with two tanks in support at night, but 'the tankers refused to bring their heavy vehicles back into St Laurent, fearing the enemy's high-velocity gun . . .'.[25]

By 20 June the 29th Division had devised a new scheme for the combination of tanks and infantry with engineer support in the attack. The new system was tried out by the 3/115 and 747 Tank Battalion in an attack on Sequeville, north of Villiers Fossard, but proved the need for more thought and training. According to the plan:

> The infantry was to clear a field, engineers . . . would then rush in and blow a gap in the hedge. Then a tank would move in, stick its cannon and machine-guns through the gap and blast the corner of the next field. Under cover of this fire the, the doughboys would advance up the lateral hedges, clear the remaining resistance, and then the tanks would move up and the entire process would be repeated . . . It sounded like a good plan but on this particular day it didn't work out too well.

The infantry and engineers managed to clear the first field and gap the hedge, but the tanks were impeded by mud while moving up and hit by 88mm anti-tank guns. They attempted to manoeuvre out of the line of fire but were hit again, when 'The tankers at this point became reluctant to proceed and despite the efforts of the CO of the 747th . . . the attack bogged-down and the troops became disorganised'. The infantry pushed on but were soon held up by machine-guns and mortars, and were recalled.[26] It was obvious that as yet the infantry and tanks lacked the mutual confidence necessary for effective cooperation. There were similar failures at other times and places in other formations. On 7 July the 83rd Division advanced on the area of Saintenay but, 'When tanks paced our infantry attack they were permitted to pass and the troops following them were fired upon, allowing the next enemy line of defence to engage the tanks'.[27]

On 11 and 12 July the 35th Division assaulted a most elaborate defensive position at Le Carillon. The 2/137 found the armoured support provided entirely ineffective. The tank destroyers were wrecked by mines and mortars, and of four tanks sent in, one was blown up on a mine and two became bogged in the mud.[28] These misadventures reflect the German policy of always separating enemy armour from infantry where they could do so. The 2/137 was more successful in changing tactical organisation and procedures for the infantry and their own and attached fire support weapons. Colonel O'Connell decentralised his forces, attaching a platoon of heavy machine-guns and a section of 81mm mortars to each company. The rifle companies were ordered to abandon conventional formation and create attack groups of four or five men. O'Connell remarked, 'The best tactic was to first place very heavy concentrations of mortar fire on all suspected enemy lines and then to follow this up with a liberal use of grenade launchers and hand grenades'.[29]

Of course, decentralisation made control much more difficult. The HQ VII Corps noted, 'The hedgerow country of small plots or fields made any large scale co-ordinated attack impossible'.[30] But some degree of control was necessary as remarked by the staff of SHAEF: 'Decentralization is necessary because limited visibility tends to isolate the fight in each field. Control is necessary to insure against exposure of a unit to flanking fire by a too rapid advance'.[31]

By July the 29th Division had worked out an effective way to combine infantry, tanks and engineers to clear *bocage*. The basic tactical team consisted of an infantry squad, a tank and four sappers. The 60mm mortar bombarded the field beyond the one under attack, the infantry tossed grenades over the hedge, the tank moved up to the hedge, fired its 75mm gun into the corners of the field and sprayed the hedgerow ahead with machine-gun fire. The infantry squad then advanced across the middle of the field to gain the next hedge. Once they had done so, the tank pulled back to allow the sappers to blow a gap in the hedge. The tank then advanced, escorted by the sappers, on watch to deal with mines and *panzerfaust* teams.[32] The division usually employed two such teams in echelon to sustain the effort, as reported in the 'Battle Notes' for July:

> The Divisional plan for Infantry-Armor tactics . . . one infantry squad, one tank and one field, proved itself a very practical solution . . . It was found that a pair of tanks in column, separated by at least one field, gave elasticity in the attack in that when a tank ran out of ammunition or gasoline or the demolition squad needed explosives, a new tank was leap-frogged through . . .[33]

On 11 July the 116th Infantry attacked via St Andre de L'Epine and up the Martinville Ridge, gaining some 3,000 metres in the face of the German 3rd *Fallschirmjaeger* Division, using these tactics.[34] A few days later, having made a number of unsuccessful formal attacks with massive support, both the 115th and 116th Regiments made infiltration attacks in darkness or mist to penetrate and compromise the German defensive positions on the western end of the Ridge. In the advance of the 3/116, silence was required: 'only two men in each platoon were permitted to fire, and then only in the event of an emergency. The others were to rely on their bayonets and hand grenades'.[35] When 'A' Company of 1/116 followed on, 'The Company advanced past Martinville in two columns, working along axial hedgerows one field apart and maintaining visual contact. Only occasional sniper fire was met. Each column left small combat groups of two men in every field passed through to hold the corridor open'.[36]

Finally, on 18 July the 29th Division improvised a mixed task force at three hours notice to dash into St Lô and disperse to seize key points in the town by a *coup de main* which relied on 'speed, boldness and surprise' to succeed. The motorised part of the force picked up 1/115 *en route* on the outskirts of the town which was secured before the enemy artillery could react in full strength.[37]

Other formations devised proposals and solutions of their own. The 3rd Armoured Division believed that the 29th Division system could be defeated by mines, *panzerfausts* and dug-in infantry. Brigadier-General Bohn proposed an alternative. In his scheme the attackers should advance on a road in column. The leading tank should be followed at a distance of 100 yards by the tank of the platoon leader, and the tank of the company commander should be 100 yards behind that of the platoon leader. Immediately behind the company commander should be a tank-dozer and then the rest of the tanks in close column with the infantry riding on them. If enemy anti-tank weapons opened fire on the lead tank the platoon leader would alert the company commander, who would order the dozer to open a gap in the hedge along the road. Next the tanks would go through the gap, and move up parallel to the road some 300 yards to the side, led by the dozer to make the necessary gaps on the way. Once this lateral column was within one field of the enemy anti-tank position, the infantry would dismount and infiltrate forward to attack it. The HQ staff of 3rd Armoured Division felt that Bohn's tactics themselves could not work against a strong enemy. The tactics they preferred involved advancing on a broader front, using one platoon of tanks, a squad of engineers and at least two tank destroyers in each assaulting unit. The tanks were to move through the fields, with infantry on the flanks and rear of each one, keeping at least 20 yards away from all hedges until that in front had been cleared by the infantry and gapped by the sappers. Artillery should be in support to suppress enemy mortars and heavy weapons.[38]

This system was described in more detail by the G-3 staff of SHAEF. They remarked that the artillery should fire a general preparation before the advance while the mortars hit suspected enemy anti-tank positions. On the advance, 'The tanks moved forward slowly on both sides of hedges paralleling the direction of advance, avoiding roads . . . they sprayed the hedges with machine-gun fire. Tanks, mortars and artillery shelled crossroads and suspected A/T gun locations. Artillery forward observers accompanied the leading wave of tanks'. This style of attack made the infantry auxiliary to the tanks. The infantry were to protect the tanks, mop up enemy remnants, put prophylactic fire into cover and destroy enemy anti-tank weapons by outflanking attacks or using mortars and machine-guns. A second echelon with the same organisation was to follow to give support against any counterattacks.[39]

The 2nd Division was active in developing new tactical procedures which were used most strikingly in the highly elaborate set-piece attack on Hill 192 on 11 July. The tactical innovations employed applied to the uses of artillery, tanks, engineers and infantry and were the product of reflection on the causes of failure of previous attacks on the hill. The divisional staff remarked in retrospect, 'The lesson learned from the initial operation on Hill 192 was the necessity for careful and meticulous planning if the enemy was to be dislodged . . .'.[40] The analysis of the attack on 16 June remarked,

> certain rough spots had shown up . . . The most serious of these was the failure of the tank-infantry team to function smoothly. In storming the hedgerows there had been occasions when the tanks and infantry had become too widely separated: the tankers wanted to pick their own terrain, which often did not agree with the doughboys' estimate of the situation. Often the tank would boldly advance where infantry feared to tread. When the two groups became separated and the tankers started firing at the enemy, there were several cases when friendly infantry got caught between. Such situations bred mutual distrust.

The cure applied was to design new tactics and train intensively in their application. From the end of June onwards the battalions chosen to attack the hill trained with the tanks and sappers who were to accompany them in the operation under the supervision of their executive officers. They used a cycle of explanation, demonstration, discussion and critique, and each went through the process three times over. As a result of the training, 'The smaller units could get used to operating closely together. The same tanks and their commanders operated with the same infantry squads . . . a mutual appreciation and trust was thus built up, which was reinforced as soon as the shooting actually started'.

The tactical procedure taught was as follows:

> Each hedgerow represented a new line of departure. With the tank firing its machine-gun at the next hedgerow, the infantry scouts went out along the sides of the hedge-bound field, also covered by the BAR team. Two of the four demolitions men followed behind, and the engineers and infantry squad leader would agree on the best place for the tank to go through. Having selected a suitable place . . . one of the demolitions men would signal back with a handkerchief. This message would be transmitted to the buttoned-up tank by one of the engineers who had remained with the tank. Special EE-8 phones were installed on the rear of the tanks and connected with the tanks' interphone system[s] . . . The two engineers remaining with the tank would protect it during its advance, scanning and firing at the side hedges to keep down bazookamen.[41]

During the fighting on 11 July the new tactics were used with great success by most of the companies in the attacking battalions. But even as they went forward they were making their own local variations as suited their particular tasks and circumstances, such as adjusting the use made of the light and heavy machine-guns in support of the assault squads.[42] The artillery fire plan for the attack on the hill was exceptionally massive but also highly flexible and allowed the assaulting infantry to hold, retard, advance or halt the rolling barrage. Control was facilitated by giving each battery a colour code, each phase line a letter, and every one of the plotted fields on the hill a number. The communications system allowed observers with the forward companies to signal direct to the batteries in support of them as well as to the central Fire Direction Centre. During the attack the guns fired 25,000 rounds which kept the enemy's heads down and destroyed at least some defensive positions. The Divisional Artillery Staff described the fire plan as, 'A World War rolling barrage with modern instincts'.[43] Later in July the Divisional Artillery used airburst over closed tanks to assist them in overrunning enemy dug-in positions around St Jean des Baisants.[44]

The relatively few examples cited above indicate that there was a great deal of tactical innovation in the US First Army in Normandy. Once under the stress of combat tactics are bound to evolve as an army, being human, is an organic entity, predisposed to change in order to maximise its chances of survival: this process is described in regard to the British infantry on the Somme during the First World War by John Lee.[45] Doctrine, that formal discipline of the mind, has its uses. It gives a sense of solidarity to believers and brings confidence and consistency to training and planning. It bears some relation to the actual conduct of operations, in the same way as drill did to minor tactics. But when soldiers are exposed to the realities of fighting, lethal disappointment inspires invention, and doctrine has to adapt to the new realities of battle behaviour or become completely irrelevant.

Notes

1 A. Norman, *Operation Overlord* (Harrisburg: Military Service Publishing Co., 1952), p. 209.
2 R. Schimpff, *Operations of 3rd Parachute Division*, precis of MS#B-541, US National Archives.
3 A. Zerbel in Ziegelmann, *The Fighting North of St Lô*, MS#B-241, US National Archives.
4 Ziegelmann, *The Fighting North of St Lô*, MS#B437, US National Archives.
5 Ibid.
6 Ibid.
7 Schimpf, *op. cit.*
8 M.D. Doubler, *Closing with the Enemy: How GIs fought the war in Europe* (Lawrence, KS: University of Kansas, 1994), p. 24.
9 J. Carafano, *After D-Day, Op COBRA and the Normandy Breakout* (Boulder, CO: Lynne Rienner, 2000), pp. 27–8.
10 Ibid., p. 48.
11 Ibid., p. 260.
12 Doubler, op. cit., p. 28.
13 G-3 Division SHAEF, 'Employment of Tanks and Infantry in Normandy', in *Military Review*, December 1944, p. 13.
14 H.Q. 29th Infantry Division, After Action Report, 6–30th June, 329-0-3, US National Archives.
15 Carafano, op. cit., p. 63.
16 B.H. Liddell-Hart (ed.) *The Rommel Papers* (London: Collins, 1953), pp. 521–2.
17 J. Balkoski, *Beyond the Beachhead: The 29th Division in Normandy* (Harrisburg, PA: Stackpole Books, 1989), p. 87.
18 J. Binkoski and A. Plaut, *The 115th Infantry Regiment in World War II* (Nashville, TN: Battery Press, 1988), pp. 4–5.
19 Ibid., p. 17.
20 J.P. Cooper, *History of the 110th Field Artillery* (Baltimore, MD: Maryland Historical Association, 1953), p. 93.
21 Ibid., pp. 94–5.
22 Ibid., pp. 111, 116.
23 Ibid., pp. 117, 119–20.
24 Binkoski and Plaut, op. cit., pp. 44–5.
25 Ibid., p. 24.
26 Ibid., pp. 61–2.
27 HQ VII Corps, History of VII Corps for the period of 1–31 July, 1944, RG407 VII Corps Records, Box 3827 207-0.3, US National Archives.
28 Lt. Col. G.T. O'Connell, O.C. 2/137, in G-3 Report to Adjutant-General, 4 August 1944, 35th Division, RG 407 Box 24042, Folder 106, US National Archives.
29 Ibid.
30 HQ VII Corps, op. cit.
31 G-3 Division SHAEF, op. cit., p. 15.

32 Balkoski, op. cit., p. 231.
33 HQ 29th Division, After Action Report for July 1944, 329-0-3, 113, US National Archives.
34 Colonel Dwyer, C.O., 116 Regiment, interview of 21st July, in 29th Division, Battle for St Lo, GL 405, 2, US National Archives.
35 Ibid, interviews with Colonel Dwyer and Captain Puntennay C.O. of 3/116, and Colonel G. Ordway C.O. of 115 Regiment.
36 Ibid., interview with Captain Rabbitt.
37 Task Force 'C' in Battle for St Lô, GL 405, 3, US National Archives.
38 XIX Corps, Reduction of the Villiers Fossard salient, operation of TF 'Y', 3rd Armored Division, RG 407 Box 24088 Folder, US National Archives.
39 G-3 Division SHAEF, op. cit., p. 16.
40 2nd Division Combat Interviews, RG 407-427-box 24014-Folder 12, US National Archives.
41 Colonel J.H. Stokes, Chief of Staff, 2nd Division, Interview of 1st December 1944, in Combat Interviews, RG 407-427 Box 24014, Folder 12,6, US National Archives.
42 Narrative of Attack, 1st Battalion, 23rd Infantry Regiment; Narrative of Attack, 1st Battalion, 38th Infantry Regiment; Narrative of Attack, 2nd Battalion, 38th Infantry Regiment; 2nd Division Combat Interviews, RG 407-427 Box 24014 Folder 12; 8,9,10, US National Archives.
43 2nd Division Artillery Staff, GL-405 in 2nd Division Combat Interviews; D.C. Little, 'Artillery Support in the Capture of Hill 192', in *Military Review*, March 1948 pp. 35–6; *Combat History of the 2nd Infantry Division* (Nashville, TN: Battery Press, 1979), pp. 32–3.
44 *Combat History of the 2nd Infantry Division*, p. 36.
45 J. Lee, 'Some Lessons of the Somme: The British Infantry in 1917', in Brian Bond *et al., Look to Your Front: Studies in the First World War – British Commission for Military History* (Staplehurst: Spellmount, 2000), pp. 79–87.

6   British armoured operations in Normandy, June–August 1944

John Buckley

As British armoured formations drove hard across Northern France and on into the Low Countries in August and September of 1944, exceeding the rate of advance achieved by the Germany army in May 1940, many tankcrew and commanders believed they had completed a good job in the most difficult and trying of conditions, winning out against a resourceful and recalcitrant foe. It had been a spectacular success, achieved in less than 90 days with tolerable casualties, and which had finally put paid to the ghosts of 1940. For the British tankcrews, following the disasters and frustrations of the first few years of the war, their contribution in Normandy represented a considerable achievement; or so it appeared to them. Yet, many historians and analysts studying the campaign in subsequent years did not regard it in the same way. Indeed, it has become something of an orthodoxy to view the performance of British armour in 1944 as disappointing, inadequate or even peripheral to Allied victory.

Basil Liddell Hart naturally had a judgement to pass, claiming that British units had demonstrated a poor grasp of armoured doctrine in Normandy, a view supported by commanders from opposite sides of the hill, such as Michael Carver and Kurt Meyer.[1] Later historians have also subscribed to this analysis: John Ellis in *Brute Force* (1990) was roundly critical of the armoured divisions, while in 1991 Jack English described the armoured arm as the 'weakest link in the Anglo-Canadian order of battle'. More recently still in 2001 Russell Hart claimed that 'British armour made little contribution to Allied victory in Normandy', and in the same year Roman Jarymowycz unfavourably compared Allied operational techniques, in particular their employment of armour, with Soviet late-war and German methods.[2] The consensus appeared to be that Allied armour had played a limited role in Normandy, and that this fitted with an overall picture of the Allied armies winning out against the Germans thanks to their overwhelming superiority in resources, artillery and air power, and not because of tactical or operational ability. Moreover, this view fortified the already apparently impregnable belief that the German army's tactical and operational flair and flexibility allowed it to hold back much larger and better-supported opposing armies for long periods from 1943 onwards, until they were overwhelmed by sheer weight of numbers and crumbling infrastructural support.[3]

Indeed, it is contended that when key operations of the Normandy campaign are examined, there is clear justification for such views. At Villers Bocage on 13 June the highly respected British 7th Armoured Division (the Desert Rats) was severely mauled by a much smaller German force (though not just one Tiger tank as still suggested in many sources), while during the first set-piece engagement, Operation EPSOM (26 June to 1 July), British armour signally failed to break out into the Orne Valley to the south of Caen. Subsequent battles around that pivotal city also underlined weaknesses in armour-infantry cooperation technique. Most famously of all, however, during Operation GOODWOOD on 18 July, following a huge supporting aerial and artillery bombardment, three British armoured divisions assaulted but failed to penetrate German positions to the east of Caen. Some progress was made but at a heavy cost; in excess of 400 tanks were knocked out and no breakthrough beyond the Bourguébus Ridge was achieved. During Operation BLUECOAT in late July and early August, slow and painful progress was made, but once again the armoured arm did not entirely cover itself in glory to the extent that 7th Armoured Division's GOC, Major General Bobby Erskine, and many of his senior staff were sacked in order to 'pep up' the unit. Canadian-directed operations in August – TOTALISE and TRACTABLE – showed some degree of innovation in operational technique and the employment of armour but, it is claimed, opportunities for bold and aggressive exploitation were yet again frittered away.

There are, however, many flaws and weaknesses in this prevailing view that British armour and operational methods were found wanting in Normandy throughout the summer of 1944. The contemporary sources raise a number of important issues of reliability, for example Liddell Hart's analysis is based upon his desire to highlight the positive pre-1939 influence he had on the German army's development of superior operational methods, as employed in the Second World War. His view, already considerably laced with egotism, was further underpinned by the opinions of German generals in post-war interviews. Such men were willing to tell Liddell Hart what they believed he wanted to hear in order to ingratiate themselves, and more importantly were determined to blame their defeat in the field on others; usually the Luftwaffe, frequently Hitler, but most often the Allies' huge superiority in resources and *materiel*. Indeed, largely unrepentant and unsavoury characters, such as Kurt Meyer, much preferred to pinpoint weaknesses in the Allied armies and highlight the superiority of their own troops and units. This type of evidence must be treated at the very least with a high degree of caution.

Furthermore, any analysis of operations in Normandy must examine the employment of armour in the context of the 1944 campaign as it existed, not how many subsequent writers would have preferred it. Indeed, much of the criticism levelled at British armoured formations in 1944 is based upon the erroneous notion that the Allies were attempting to fight a campaign quite different to the one that they did; or, even if they were not so doing, it is argued that they should have been. Too often the starting point of analyses has been that because Anglo-Canadian armoured and operational techniques did not mirror those of their much lauded German opponents, they were inappropriate and flawed.

Yet it is clear that 21st Army Group, under Montgomery's direction, did not endeavour to conduct armoured operations in a manner similar to their enemy. The Anglo-Canadian armies in Normandy strove to prosecute the campaign in a style which suited their strengths, whilst minimising the impact of their weaknesses: not for Monty and his generals were the type of bold yet risky ventures conducted by the Germans earlier in the war.

Operational methods in 21st Army Group were founded upon a number of assumptions made by Montgomery and his staff. Firstly, heavy combat casualties could not be sustained in Northwest Europe as the pool of personnel replacements would begin to dwindle by the summer of 1944. Secondly, concern was growing over the ability and willingness of Allied front-line soldiers to endure harsh and exacting close combat with their German counterparts and Montgomery was worried that a series of setbacks and costly defeats may rapidly undermine morale in his forces. Finally, the Allies held a considerable advantage in resources: artillery, tanks, fuel, ordnance, air support and transport to name but a few. In such circumstances it was entirely logical to conduct operations to maximise this superiority, and thus the Commonwealth and American armies attempted to attain victory over the Germans by employing high levels of equipment and firepower; 'let metal do it rather than flesh' as one put it.[4]

Consequently, 21st Army Group's doctrine reflected these three assumptions, employing particular operational methods in an attempt to force the Germans to fight as the Allies wanted, not as the Germans desired. The operational approach placed considerable emphasis on heavy concentrations of firepower focused across a narrow front to blast troops onto their objectives. Thorough planning was the key to the successful prosecution of such operations, along with commanders sticking to the plan and understanding clearly and unambiguously what was required of them. The second, and arguably most crucial aspect of operations would centre on defeating the almost certain German counter-attack; thus, getting troops, artillery and tanks into defensible positions once an objective had been seized was pivotal to making the doctrine effective. Moreover, it was in throwing back these counter-attacks, usually with heavy concentrations of defensive firepower, that the heaviest casualties were likely to be inflicted on the Germans. Thus, Anglo-Canadian operational planners aimed to seize the initiative; choose the most appropriate field of battle where possible; launch a well coordinated and firepower-supported set-piece attack; absorb and defeat the German counter-attack; and if possible exploit without taking too many risks.

It was an operational doctrine with shortcomings, but one that nevertheless played to the Allies' strengths and simultaneously exploited the weaknesses of the Germans.[5]

The extent to which armour conformed to and supported this operational technique, and indeed the degree to which this approach facilitated armoured warfare, is therefore crucial to any analysis of its overall effectiveness in the summer of 1944. Although there were clear and understandable reasons underpinning the operational methods in 21st Army Group, they did not always aid the employment of armoured forces. Montgomery and his staff planned to conduct tightly-controlled operations with heavy concentrations of firepower support, launched across a narrow front. Narrow front attacks allowed greater concentrations of suppressing firepower to be delivered upon the enemy and would allow follow-up forces to be deployed in depth to push forward once leading units had become worn down. Such attacks would also be tightly constrained and more easily controlled by senior commanders, particularly as officers would have been issued a set of clear and obvious objectives. There were obvious advantages to the approach, but for armoured forces, particularly the armoured divisions, there was a price to pay. Over-reliance on firepower became an issue as units increasingly ground to a halt and awaited artillery or air attack to deal with battlefield difficulties. Moreover, heavy concentrations of firepower often devastated ground and road networks, compromising the ability of mobile forces to manoeuvre and advance rapidly. In any case, commanders of armoured forces complained that they were often forced to deploy over too narrow an area and that this contradicted the dictums of tank warfare. Exploiting armoured forces were also supposed to seize opportunities on the battlefield as they emerged, but were hindered in this; in 21st Army Group they were expected to stick to the overall plan with little room for manoeuvre. Monty preferred a tidy and carefully ordered battlefield, one in which he knew what was going on and where commanders had a firm grip on those under their direction.

These traits of 21st Army Group operational technique and their impact on the likely effectiveness of armoured forces, particularly in the exploitation phase, would have mattered less if all staff officers and senior commanders appreciated them or always incorporated them into planning. This did not always occur however, and many plans such as EPSOM, JUPITER and GOODWOOD all suffered because too much was expected, usually of the armoured divisions, or senior commanders employed such forces inappropriately. Monty's operational approach may have served his command well overall, but in some cases and at certain times it choked armoured operations, most obviously in the exploitation phase. Perversely, the greatest weight of historical inquiry, driven by the fascination with *blitzkrieg*, has focused on this, the weakest aspect of British armoured operations and doctrine in Normandy, whilst much less attention has been paid to the much more successful role played by armour in the break-in phase of operations.

Montgomery had at his disposal five regular armoured divisions in the campaign – three British, one Canadian and one Polish – which were theoretically intended to act as weapons of exploitation, once the enemy had been successfully compromised. However, although historians have focused greatest attention on this phase of 21st Army Group operations, it was in fact of lesser importance than the role played by the more numerous independent armoured and tank brigades. These formations, of which there were eight (with extra support provided by the three specialised brigades of 79th Armoured Division), were largely intended to act as firepower support units to the infantry divisions. In all cases however, Montgomery insisted on a degree of flexibility between armoured formations: that they be able to adopt both an infantry support role during the break-in/through phase of an operation, and be able to exploit should an opportunity on the battlefield arise.

In this, however, formations were hindered by equipment. The slow and heavily armoured Churchill tanks of the tank brigades were better suited to infantry support duties, while the Cromwells and Shermans of the armoured brigades and divisions, though less effective in this role, were better able to speed forward quickly and exploit operational opportunities as they emerged in battle. This caused Montgomery to complain that he had been saddled with two distinct types of tank when he would have preferred one standard or 'capital' tank, as he called it. He did not want the Churchill at all, believing it would be unable to keep up with fluid operations due to its low speed. Moreover, he discarded any idea of disseminating separate doctrine for independent brigades equipped with Shermans as opposed to Churchills, even though there was clear and mounting evidence from Italy that different tactics were required. As Lieutenant-General Archie Nye, Vice Chief of Imperial General Staff, stated: 'Are Sherman equipped regiments handled when supporting infantry in exactly the same way as infantry tank battalions? General Montgomery says they are, and everyone else says they are not'.[6] However, Montgomery's approach was not without merit; he desired simplicity for his troops in an effort to minimise confusion on the battlefield. Thus he pressed for a single and straightforward doctrine where possible and viewed different doctrine for the same task dependent on vehicle as unnecessary; consequently, the Churchill was viewed with suspicion and hostility. Nevertheless, in battle in Normandy, Churchills, especially the even more heavily armoured mark VIIs, proved superior in the infantry support role and were well liked because of their thick armour plate.

Matters were further complicated by the structure of the armoured divisions. Each division had two brigades: one infantry, one armoured. Official pre-invasion doctrine stated that the two brigades should operate separately, though in support of each other. The contention was that the armoured brigade within the division would need to be free to move quickly, unencumbered by slower-moving infantry and that any infantry support for the armoured brigade would be supplied by its one motor battalion (transported in half-tracks and tracked universal carriers, rather than lorries). However, this force structure was exposed in Normandy as the armoured brigade was too often short of infantry support at critical moments with a resulting loss of momentum. Guards and 11th Armoured Divisions both suffered in this way, the latter during Operation EPSOM and both during GOODWOOD.

The level of cooperation between infantry divisions and independent armoured and tank brigades is also an area highlighted as a weakness in armoured doctrine in 21st Army Group. Major-General Pip Roberts, GOC 11th Armoured Division, noted that during Operation EPSOM, the level of infantry-armour cooperation between 15th (Scottish) Infantry Division and 31st Tank Brigade was low, and a variety of other actions during WIND-SOR, CHARNWOOD and BLUECOAT all seemed to reinforce this view.

This deficiency has in part been attributed to doctrinal indecision and confusion in 21st Army Group prior to the invasion. There had been little consistency in the methods and approaches to infantry-armour cooperation inculcated into the British army in the 1940–3 period, with an array of difficulties being created by lack of training space, inappropriate equipment and conflicting views being fed back from events in the Mediterranean theatre. By mid-1943 there was still a reliance on squadron-level fire support for infantry assaults, almost in the manner of self-propelled artillery tactics – that is, finding safe positions for the armour and delivering a heavy concentration of high-explosive shells onto the objective from a distance. In part this had been caused by units having to train with outdated or inadequate equipment prior to 1943; often tanks were fitted with 2-pounder guns which could not deliver the required weight of high explosive onto a target without massing them into large static firing groups. Consequently, advancing in close support of infantry or leading infantry onto the target was eschewed as the tanks could not provide sufficient firepower to reach the objective without prohibitive casualties both in infantry and tanks. This conflicted with official doctrine published earlier in 1941, which argued that heavily armoured infantry support tanks should lead ahead of infantry to neutralise enemy strongpoints.[7]

Experience of action in the Mediterranean following the TORCH landings in November 1942, and the increasing likelihood of some of the independent brigades in 21st Army Group having to operate with Shermans rather than Churchills in Normandy, forced a rethink, however. By the autumn of 1943 doctrine was based upon on a revised ATI (Army Training Instruction) No. 2 (May 1943) which pressed for a more flexible approach to infantry-armour cooperation wherein the question of which arm should lead, or whether a grouped attack was desirable, was to be based on the phase of the operation being undertaken, be it initial penetration, development or exploitation. This approach was to be supplemented by a new pamphlet in the autumn of 1943 which provided for separate tactics for Shermans and Churchills in close-support operations.

However, as has been previously noted, soon after his appointment as commander in chief of 21st Army Group, Montgomery blocked the distribution of the new doctrine and attempted to stamp his authority on the situation by issuing the 8th Army method of linking tanks and infantry on the battlefield. In this document, issued in February 1944, following the initial penetration phase of a battle, tanks would lead followed by infantry.[8] Montgomery's approach was to attempt to eliminate any potential confusion by having one straightforward doctrine, though the price of this was to be inflexibility. The impact of Montgomery's 8th Army doctrine came very late however, being issued just four months before the invasion, and consequently had much less impact than he would have wanted.

By the time British armoured formations landed in Normandy, therefore, they were in a state of some confusion as to which approach to infantry-armour doctrine was the official one, let alone the best one. Some conformed to Montgomery's methods, some to the doctrine issued in May 1943, some to the revised May 1943 doctrine issued in December 1943, and some even to the self-propelled artillery tactics developed in the UK between 1941 and 1943. Even in the armoured divisions where a degree of infantry-armour cooperation was still necessary, methods varied from one division to another. It might be argued that such a doctrinal hotchpotch was a recipe for failure and a clear cause of the difficulties encountered in Normandy: the independent brigades had no clear or standard notion of what to do, while the armoured divisions were inappropriately structured and conformed to an inadequate doctrine.

However, what some have argued was a weakness in the Commonwealth armies' approach to doctrine – indiscipline – was to prove a considerable advantage for the armoured units as they attempted to grapple with the operational difficulties thrust upon them by the Normandy campaign. Indeed, the British army's approach to doctrine was to be flexible and non-dogmatic: commanders could not openly contradict official doctrine, but they were encouraged to view it as a starting point and to be willing to adapt and mould practices to operations and battle 'in-theatre' as they saw fit. The disadvantages of this approach were that effective doctrine would not be uniformly practised, resulting in opportunities on the battlefield potentially being lost, and that units would not conform to similar working practices, creating difficulties in units new to each other operating together successfully.

Nevertheless, the advantages of the flexible problem-solving approach to the conduct of operations outweighed the shortcomings in Normandy for the Anglo-Canadian armies, and for the armoured formations. Because the campaign threw up a variety of new tactical problems and issues, some beyond the remit of official doctrinal teachings, the flexible approach allowed battlefield difficulties to be resolved and for different doctrines in the case of infantry-armour cooperation to be tested and jettisoned. Units often found their way quickly, adapting new operating practices to the circumstances in

Normandy, and moulding unit structures to situations as and when necessary. This was not uniformly successful, as might be expected, especially with a largely inexperienced army, but commanders imbued with a flexible approach to doctrine generally identified problems and devised methods to overcome them.

The weaknesses in the force structure of 21st Army Group's armoured formations were exposed in the early stages of the campaign by German strategy adopted in response to the failure of the Allies to achieve all that had been hoped for in D-Day planning. The Allies planned to have pushed deep inland in the opening 72 hours of the landings, capturing Caen and opening up the territory to the south of the city for follow-up operations, in terrain more conducive to fluid armoured battles. This did not happen however, and Commonwealth forces ran out of impetus and were halted outside Caen. The Germans then adopted a strategy of digging in and fighting for every inch of territory rather than falling back onto terrain better suited to conducting a flexible and elastic defence as desired by Rommel, Rundstedt and Geyr von Schweppenburg, though not by Hitler. Thus, the campaign was to become one somewhat different to that originally envisaged by Allied planners, fought across terrain and in circumstances which caught 21st Army Group a little by surprise.

One might argue that Montgomery and his staff should have trained their formations and planned for a number of eventualities and contingencies, but it should be noted that this was a largely inexperienced army and as has been seen there was enough difficulty in finding one mutually acceptable doctrine, let alone a whole variety to be employed in different circumstances dependent on what the Germans did or did not do. Indeed, consideration was given to closer infantry-armour cooperation prior to D-Day but was rejected because 21st Army Group staff expected to be fighting beyond the notorious *bocage* terrain soon after 6 June.[9] It made more sense to plan for the most likely eventuality and use the available time to train accordingly.

The terrain in which British armoured units found themselves in June was quite unsuited to the style of operations for which they had prepared, and was such that it required particularly close infantry-armour cooperation, something in which, as has been noted, the Anglo-Canadians did not yet have a firm grounding. The *bocage* terrain to the west and south-west of Caen consisted of seemingly sunken roads with a patchwork of small fields, often no more than a few tens of yards across, surrounded by steep-banked hedges sometimes 12 feet high and more. Rivers also cut the land at unhelpful angles to the likely axes of 21st Army Group thrusts, often forcing operations to be conducted across steep, wooded valleys with few roads to ease congestion. To the east of Caen the ground was also unsuitable for armoured operations, being partly waterlogged and flanked to the east by wooded high ground still occupied by the Germans. Much of the land in and around Caen was also sprinkled with stout farm buildings, and dotted with woods and orchards, all immensely helpful for the defending Germans and a source of great difficulty for the attacking Allies, particularly the armoured forces.

For the divisions, the early stages of the Normandy campaign were distinctly unsettling. The highly regarded 7th Armoured Division struggled to coordinate its infantry battalions with its armoured regiments during Operation PERCH, the attempt to outflank Panzer *Lehr*, which came to grief at Villers Bocage on 13 June. During EPSOM, 11th Armoured Division's GOC, Major-General Pip Roberts, recorded that he had not combined his infantry and armoured brigades effectively enough, while GOODWOOD again exposed the inherent flaw in the structure of Commonwealth armoured divisions. The separate infantry and armour brigades did not link together effectively on the battlefield, leaving the single motor battalion in the armoured brigade with too much to do. Conversely, the infantry brigade was unsuited to working with the armour as its troops were transported in lorries, which were unable to debus soldiers close enough to the frontline, or mobile enough to work off-raid with the armour.

Yet, the armoured divisions all endeavoured to solve this problem, with considerable success. Senior officers in 7th Armoured quickly identified that closer infantry-armour cooperation would be essential for operations in Normandy and had already operated mixed groups drawn from both the infantry and armour brigades in June. Soon after landing in Normandy units in Guards Armoured Division began experimenting with new infantry-armour tactics, while Roberts and Major-General Allan Adair, GOC Guards Armoured, each pressed for a restructuring of their divisions after GOOD-WOOD.[10] During BLUECOAT both divisions began moving to a mixed brigade organisation, wherein each of the division's four armoured regiments (three from the armoured brigade plus the armoured reconnaissance regiment), worked closely with one of the four infantry battalions (three from the infantry brigade along with the motor battalion). Although the reorganisation sacrificed some manoeuvrability on the part of the armoured brigade, it nonetheless boosted the level of infantry support for the armour and proved both successful and popular in the close and dense terrain in which the armoured divisions found themselves operating, particularly during BLUECOAT.[11]

An obvious difficulty involved transporting the previously lorried infantry with the tanks, but this was partly alleviated by carrying the troops as tank riders, even though this has been previously eschewed in training back in Britain.[12] Infantry commanders would also ride with respective armoured commanders to facilitate greater cooperation. By the time of TOTALIZE the Commonwealth forces had begun converting self-propelled artillery vehicles into large fully tracked personnel carriers, named Kangaroos, to carry the infantry forward into battle alongside the tanks, yet again illustrating flexibility and adaptability. It is worth noting that the Germans also struggled to link armour and infantry on the Normandy battlefield as their half-tracked troop transports did not provide adequate protection against Allied heavy artillery, thus limiting the effectiveness of their panzergrenadiers.

For the Allies, although there was still some increased risk for tank-riding infantry, the mixed brigade group concept worked. Roberts's 11th Armoured employed the new structure most effectively but the Guards also adopted the formation and remained with it for the rest of the war. The Polish 1st Armoured Division employed the mixed structure during TRACTABLE and even the much-criticised 7th Armoured continued to employ a flexible structure, mixing infantry battalions and armoured regiments according to circumstances.

For the independent brigades, revised doctrine was also employed and developed 'in-theatre' in Normandy. Units initially attempted to employ the methods set down and disseminated in training and derived from experiences in the Mediterranean. However, none proved to be universally successful, though some were quickly abandoned after early chastening experiences. Montgomery's 8th Army tactics of leading with tanks once through enemy minefields, perhaps better suited to more open country, were generally found to be unworkable in the close terrain of Normandy. During an attack on Cristot (10–11 June) 4/7 Royal Dragoon Guards found the approach wanting. Dug-in and concealed German troops allowed the leading tanks to pass by, and then shot up the following infantry, before focusing on the now unsupported tanks. Of nine tanks only two withdrew to safety.[13] This and other examples quickly demonstrated that leading with tanks did not work unless the enemy was caught by surprise or was known to be very weak.

Another approach used with more success, though still riddled with shortcomings, was to employ tanks in a self-propelled artillery role, and shoot the infantry onto target with heavy concentrations of high-explosive firepower. Such tactics were on occasion appropriate for Sherman-equipped formations deployed in the infantry support role for, as has been noted, the M4 had limited armour protection which hindered its effectiveness as a close support tank. However, there were weaknesses with this tactic also. With the armour standing off, the infantry risked being exposed without immediate and on-hand fire support to suppress uncovered targets and enemy strongpoints, which could only be provided by closely supporting tanks. Moreover, if the targets became shrouded in smoke or if the weather was poor, the tanks shooting from some distance away proved unable to provide sufficient firepower support. Infantry also felt vulnerable without the comforting and morale boosting presence of tanks close by, however illusory this support was in reality. Tank losses might be reduced by the stand off and shoot approach, but it nevertheless increased the strain on the already overburdened infantry. Finally, in view of the standard German tactic of immediate counter-attack to recapture ground lost to the Allies, it was essential for armour to be on hand to provide direct high-explosive and even anti-tank fire support.[14]

The most sophisticated approach and one that 21st Army Group had been moving towards prior to Montgomery's appointment, was a flexible and fluid doctrine which relied upon infantry and armour generally intermingling to provide immediate and mutual assistance. The infantry would provide the eyes and local protection for the armour, while the armour would deal with identified enemy strongpoints once located. They could also act as mobile rallying and defensive points for the infantry when under small arms fire. Troops of tanks would often employ fire and move tactics, with armour advancing from one position to another while being overwatched by other tanks. In this way, armour could maintain a worthwhile presence with the infantry and provide effective levels of fire support from static positions. Only in the densest terrain, such as *bocage*, would the infantry initially screen the tanks in order to provoke the enemy into giving away their position so that the armour could then be brought up relatively safely to blast the enemy.

These tactics, though more successful than others, did throw up problems and difficulties. Most obviously they relied upon good communications between tanks and infantry and this was not always possible. Tank telephones were useful but easily damaged in action, and the 38-radio set, though technically acceptable, was stretched in action as the communications networks became overburdened; coordinating officers had to communicate with tanks and infantry through the same equipment. Flares and lights were also employed at times for communications purposes, with mixed success. In essence, as the flexible approach was more demanding, it worked best with troops who were experienced and knew how to overcome the various difficulties.[15]

The operating problems were largely dealt with as units began to come to terms with the tactical conditions in Normandy, but the most effective solution was for units to work together regularly. Where they did, better results followed. For example, 6th Guards Tank Brigade trained with 15th Scottish Infantry Division in the UK prior to OVERLORD and a measure of understanding was developed. Alas, 15th Scottish's first major action in Normandy – EPSOM – saw them working with 31st Tank Brigade, a unit with which they had little experience. Partly as a result of this, EPSOM saw a number of problems emerge over infantry-tank cooperation. A few weeks later, when 15th Scottish was able to link up with 6th Guards, much better levels of cooperation were achieved.

It was nevertheless a bone of contention with many middle-ranking and junior commanders that units were moved around far too frequently and that this worked against the development of better understanding and working practices. One report claimed that it took at least two days for infantry and armour units to establish effective lines of communication and interaction. Much of this might have been alleviated by the imposition of a standardised infantry-armour doctrine prior to OVERLORD. However, as has been seen, the only attempt to impose a doctrine – Montgomery's 8th Army method – would have had disastrous consequences if it had been rigorously enforced, because it was largely unworkable in many situations in Northwest Europe. The problem-solving approach allowed the difficulties in Normandy to be overcome but the price to pay for the doctrinal indiscipline or flexibility was that units needed time to communicate to establish respective methods of achieving similar ends.[16] If senior command erred, it was in failing to recognise this and incorporate it fully into planning.

Further problems were encountered in Normandy by British tank formations when dealing with enemy armour. Although a tank's job was still largely centred upon engaging soft targets with high-explosive in Normandy, dealing with German armour was also a key role. The enduring perception of tank-to-tank combat in the summer of 1944 is one based upon the supposed mismatch between Allied and German armoured equipment. British tankcrews had to operate flimsy Shermans and Cromwells against German Tigers and Panthers and therefore were both undergunned and underarmoured.[17]

This view is somewhat misleading, however. Seventy per cent of German armour was little if any better than Allied types; indeed only some 120–30 Tigers, which were in any case dreadfully unreliable, were deployed against the Allies in Normandy. In post-war interrogations German commanders claimed that perhaps some 15 to 30 per cent of their tanks were lost to breakdown.[18] Moreover, weakness in armour protection counted for less in Normandy where the average range at which tanks were knocked out was under 600 metres. At these ranges most German anti-tank guns could penetrate any Allied armour, including the heavy Churchill with its 150mm plus frontal protection, so increases in armour protection would have counted for little.[19]

What mattered much more was the inadequacy of Allied armoured firepower, which consisted predominantly of medium velocity 75mm guns. These were quite unable to penetrate heavy German armour at anything other than very short to point-blank range, if at all. Operational research indicated that it took around 1.5 hits to eliminate a Panzer IV, 1.63 hits to knock out a Sherman, 2.55 to deal with a Panther and 4.2 to disable a Tiger. Perhaps it was as well that Panzer IVs and other weaker models made up the bulk of the German Panzer arm in Normandy. It was clear that increasing numbers of the British 17-pounder anti-tank gun, mounted on Allied vehicles – Shermans, Challengers and M10s – were required to even the firepower score with the Germans.[20]

Although the 'tank gap' was an important issue, it was not the main factor behind the tactical difficulties confronting Commonwealth tank crews as they endeavoured to deal with German Panzers in the summer of 1944. At the short ranges over which lethal anti-tank engagements took place, even the Allied 75mm gun could deal with anything other than Tigers, of which there were few, and Panthers frontally. Furthermore, in the close terrain it was quite possible to gain flanking positions on Panthers where their armour was relatively weak and defeatable at usual battleranges.

Additionally, heavy enemy tanks could also be peppered with artillery stonks and air-strikes to force them to move and risk breakdown, expose themselves to flanking fire, or panic the crew into fleeing.

The tactical environment in Normandy was such that the most important factor in determining the outcome of armoured engagements was who got the first shot from a stable, camouflaged firing position; and more often than not this was the Germans who were for the most part on the defensive. Because of the terrain, Allied advances were forced to work along road networks which could be easily targeted by German guns. The hedges, orchards and woods provided excellent positions for concealing tanks, self-propelled and anti-tank guns which fired upon the cautiously advancing Allied armour, scattering them to cover. It often could take two or more shots before the Allied troops located the firing position, at which point the enemy could be stalked or bombarded. However, increasing numbers of self-propelled guns were being deployed by the Germans and these, like tanks, would often relocate to begin the process again. It had been hoped in pre-OVERLORD planning that artillery would be able to play a major role in suppressing enemy anti-tank gunnery, but in this the Allies were to be somewhat disappointed. Although towed anti-tank guns could often be suppressed in this way, self-propelled weapons proved to be much less vulnerable and thus their increasing presence in 1944 created a further headache for Allied tankcrews.

However, the greatest difficulty in responding came in locating the enemy and then bringing firepower to bear. Technical shortcomings entered the equation, but the process was much more of a combined arms operation involving tanks, artillery, infantry and air power and should not be seen, as is often the case, as a battle between armour plate and tank-mounted firepower alone. It was a difficult and dangerous process which often resulted in Allied casualties. Nevertheless, it proved to be the most effective way of winkling the Germans out of their positions in Normandy; it also indicated that by 1944 the age of *blitzkrieg* was long over.[21]

To the Allies, therefore, fell the burden of having to maintain the offensive with an army still finding its way against an experienced, canny and desperate foe, in difficult terrain. It should be noted however that the Germans found no better solution to the problems of employing armour in a combined arms group on the offensive in Normandy. Indeed, when German forces attempted to launch attacks with armour, they encountered all the same problems as the Allies and suffered heavy losses as a consequence.

Conclusion

British armoured forces, far from being 'disappointing' actually acquitted themselves well during the Normandy campaign. In particular, they played a key supporting role to the infantry – their most important duty – and became increasingly effective in this as the fighting developed. In contrast, when conducting dynamic armoured thrusts in order to exploit battlefield situations, armoured forces performed less effectively. This mirrored the over-all strengths and weaknesses of 21st Army Group's operational methods: it was successfully able to conduct break-in operations and defeat enemy counter-attacks, but was structurally and conceptually found wanting when asked to carry out high-tempo thrusting actions. This did not in itself mean that British armoured forces 'failed' in Normandy; merely that they largely conformed to the preferred operational approach of Montgomery and his staff, even when such techniques actually worked against the successful employment of armour in certain situations.

It is also clear that by the mid-point of the campaign, Commonwealth armoured units had seized upon the methods necessary to combat German forces in the difficult and unhelpful terrain of Normandy. They adapted existing doctrine and integrated new tactics in order to impose themselves upon the terrain, the operational environment and the enemy. In this they were increasingly successful, particularly when viewed as part of a combined arms doctrine which fitted relatively well to the operational techniques employed by 21st Army Group.

There is no doubt that failings and shortcomings in doctrine existed, particularly in the first weeks of OVERLORD, but the British and Cana-dian armoured forces, unlike their German counterparts, were able to abandon failing offensive methods and solve the problems they were con-fronting 'in-theatre'. For a largely inexperienced army, faced with a set of unexpected difficulties, whilst fighting a more experienced and often brutalised enemy, this represents a remarkable achievement. They developed a method of fighting which suited the environment and for the most part comple-mented the manner in which Montgomery and his staff wished to tackle the Germans in 1944. This was not the approach of the Germans in 1940–2 – though the circumstances then were quite different – and not the methods revered by the post-war armies and military analysts. It was, however, an armoured doctrine in keeping with the nature of the Commonwealth forces as they existed in 1944, which suited 21st Army Group's methods, and which demonstrated sufficient flexibility and fighting power to allow us to put aside the criticisms that have been levelled at British and Canadian armoured forces since 1945.

Notes

1 LHCMA (Liddell Hart Centre for Military Archives), Liddell Hart papers, 9/28/84, Tanks in Normandy, Liddell Hart to C.S. Forrester, 18 February 1952; LHCMA, Liddell Hart correspondence with Field Marshal Lord Carver, 8 May 1952; Kurt Meyer, *Grenadiers* (Winnipeg, Manitoba: Federowicz, 1994), pp. 280–98.
2 John Ellis, *Brute Force: Allied Strategy and Tactics in the Second World War* (London: Andre Deutsch, 1990), pp. 373–88; John English, *The Canadian Army and the Normandy Campaign: A Study in the Failure of High Command* (Westport,

CT: Praeger, 1991), p. 312; Russell Hart, *Clash of Arms: How the Allies Won in Normandy* (Boulder, CO: Rienner, 2001), p. 309; Roman Jarymowycz, *Tank Tactics: From Normandy to Lorraine* (Boulder, CO: Rienner, 2001).

3 This view has taken hold in popular military history writing on the Second World War – for example, see Max Hastings's books *Overlord* (London: Simon & Schuster, 1984) and *Armageddon: The Battle for Germany 1944–45* (London: Macmillan, 2004) but has also become the 'official' view of western armed forces, most notably the US and British armies. During the Cold War as NATO sought to develop plans to stop the Soviets, there seemed to be more merit in mirroring the methods employed by the Germans in the later half of the Second World War. Justification was derived from the events of the war to support this position, though in reality this was a highly selective reading of history.

4 See Stephen Hart, *Montgomery and Colossal Cracks: 21st Army Group in North-west Europe 1944–5* (Westport, CT: Praeger, 2000) for a discussion of this; LHCMA Allfrey, 3/1, diary, 17 January 1943, comments by Brigadier Edgar Williams.

5 NAC (National Archives, Canada) RG 24, vol. 10797, G.G. Simonds, 'Operational Policy – 2nd Canadian Corps', 17 February 1944. See also Terry Copp, *Fields of Fire: The Canadians in Normandy* (University of Toronto Press, 2003), pp. 26–7.

6 LHCMA Alanbrooke, 6/2/23, Nye's notes on Montgomery's comments concerning Pyman's pamphlet on infantry-tank cooperation doctrine, 17 December 1943.

7 War Office Army Training Instruction no. 2, *The Employment of Army Tanks in Co-operation with Infantry* (March 1941).

8 See Imperial War Museum (IWM) BLM 52/17, *Eighth Army Notes on the Employment of Tanks in Support of Infantry in Battle* (November 1943) and LHCMA de Guingand, *21st Army Group Notes on the Employment of Tanks in Support of Infantry in Battle* (February 1944).

9 Michael Carver, *Out of Step: The Memoirs of Field Marshal Lord Carver* (London: Hutchinson, 1989), p. 180.

10 LHCMA Liddell Hart, 15/4/85, 22nd Armoured Brigade notes on operations, 6–15 June 1944; WO 171/1257, 3rd Irish Guards War Diary, 13 July 1944.

11 LHCMA O'Connor, 5/3/37, O'Connor to Lt-Gen Allan Harding, CoS, HQ Allied Forces Italy, 19 August 1944; J. Baynes, *The Forgotten Victor: General Sir Richard O'Connor* (London: Brassey's, 1989), pp. 213–14; G.P.B. Roberts, *From the Desert to the Baltic* (London: William Kimber, 1987), pp. 184–5; Allan Adair, *A Guards' General: The Memoirs of Sir Allan Adair* (London: Hamish Hamilton, 1986), pp. 147–52.

12 PRO/National Archives (PRO) WO 171/456, 11th Armoured Division War Diary, intelligence summary, no. 11, 28 June 1944 and notes for August 1944; PRO WO 166/8576, 2nd (Armoured) Irish Guards War Diary, 19 October 1942; PRO WO 166/12687, 8th Rifle Brigade, War Diary, 6 May 1943; Maj John Langdon, 3RTR, interview with author, October 2002.

13 Tpr Austin Baker, 4/7th Dragoons, 27th Armoured Brigade, interview with author, April 2003; L.F. Ellis, *Victory in the West, Vol. I* (London: HMSO, 1962), p. 252; LHCMA Liddell Hart, 15/4/85, 22nd Armoured Brigade notes on operations 6–15 June 1944.

14 WO 171/862, 1st East Riding Yeomanry War Diary, June–July 1944; Similar lessons were being learned in Italy, LHCMA Allfrey, 4/5 XIII Corps conference, 'Need for a common doctrine for infantry-armour co-operation', 8 April 1944.

15 Ian Daglish, *Operation Bluecoat: Battleground Normandy* (Barnsley: Pen & Sword, 2003), p. 69; RAC Archive, Bovington, Minutes of conference held at 34 Tank Brigade HQ to discuss tactics, gunnery and administration, 25 August 1944.

16 LHCMA, Allfrey, 4/5, XIII Corps conference, 'Need for a common doctrine for infantry-tank co-operation', 8 April 1944; Maj-Gen Roy Dixon, 5RTR, interview with author, November 2002.
17 Hastings and others.
18 US National Archives II, RG 331/240E/14, 7th Army Interrogation Center, interviews with Generals Heinz Guderian, Leo Geyr von Schweppenburg, Sepp Dietrich and Paul Hausser, 18 May 1945.
19 US NA II, RG 331/210A/1, 'Intelligence Report of Tanks Rendered Inoperative due to Enemy Action', June to August 1944, First US Army; BRL MR-798, quoted in Jarymowycz, *Tank Tactics*, p. 270.
20 PRO WO 291/1331, 21st Army Group ORS report no. 12, *Analysis of 75mm Sherman tank casualties suffered between 6 June and 10 July 1944.*
21 See John Buckley, *British Armour in the Normandy Campaign 1944* (London: Frank Cass, 2004) Chapters 4 and 5 in particular for a full discussion of these points.

7 Operation BLUECOAT – a victory ignored?

Ian Daglish

It was certainly the toughest battle we had in the campaign.

> Major General G.P.B. 'Pip' Roberts,
> commanding officer, 11th Armoured Division

We experienced battle as we had not met it in previous war years.

> *Unterscharführer* Ernst Streng,
> Tiger tank commander, *schwere SS-Panzer Abteilung* 102

Perhaps the most successful op. of all.

> Major John Kenneth,
> commanding officer, 2nd Argyll and Sutherland Highlanders

Introduction

In the last week of July 1944, Lieutenant-General Sir Miles Dempsey's Second Army moved two entire corps from the Caen sector to the relatively quiet countryside around Caumont. Here, the British XXX Corps prepared to give battle, with VIII Corps advancing in support on the right flank between XXX Corps and the American First Army. The offensive which ensued, Operation BLUECOAT, has not figured prominently in the historiography of the Normandy campaign.

On reaching late July, histories of the campaign understandably tend to focus on Operation COBRA and the American breakout, the story moving on to the encirclement of the German Seventh Army, the débâcle of the 'Falaise Gap', and the rush to the Seine. In such a context, BLUECOAT is memorable for little more than the failure of XXX Corps to keep to its assigned schedule, the final catalyst leading to Dempsey's sacking of the commanders of the corps, its armoured division, that division's armoured brigade and numerous other officers.[1] Indeed, a recent study of the Normandy campaign has represented BLUECOAT as 'a major strategic blunder, perhaps the worst of his [Montgomery's] career'.[2]

This chapter reconsiders the role of Operation BLUECOAT in context of the Normandy campaign, arguing that it was not the failure sometimes

depicted, and that further study of the whole operation can be most rewarding. Not only does BLUECOAT showcase many of the differences
between British and German operational and tactical management of the
Normandy campaign, but in particular we may discern the implementation of important organisational and tactical methods by the British. In
BLUECOAT, we find a major operation which (at least so far as VIII Corps
is concerned) ran to schedule, achieved its objectives, overcame and penet-
rated deep German defences and focused on distress caused to the enemy
rather than on avoiding risk. It is arguable that the refinement of cooperation between tanks and mobile infantry achieved by 11th Armoured
Division in July 1944 and implemented during BLUECOAT heralded an
important step in the metamorphosis of a British citizen army into an effective offensive force.[3]

Why then should BLUECOAT pass (relatively) unnoticed? This chapter
argues that the achievements of BLUECOAT have been not only neglected
but deliberately played down; in particular, that the operation was 'written
out' by Montgomery. No stranger to the benefits of hindsight, Montgomery
chose to represent the Normandy campaign as a 'tidy' sequence of events,
a linear unfolding and homogeneous execution of his own, unchanging
strategy. His presentation left little room for an operation which strayed
from the initial plan, and whose successes were shaped by initiatives taken at
lower – sometimes much lower – levels than the Army Group commander.

A complete account of Operation BLUECOAT would include the story
of many units: both British XXX and VIII Corps, also the various German
formations drawn in to the battle. This chapter necessarily has a tighter
focus and will consider principally the experience – and achievements – of
VIII Corps. After the early hours of the operation it became clear that XXX
Corps' advance was falling seriously behind schedule. Before its momentum
could be regained, VIII Corps had forged ahead. VIII Corps then shed its
intended flank support role to become the principal instrument of breakthrough. In one of several deviations from the plan, BLUECOAT became
primarily an VIII Corps 'show'.

The plan

By the end of July, Allied forces had been fighting in Normandy for seven
long weeks. After the initial achievement of securing a foothold on Hitler's
Fortress Europe, progress had been slow. At least the Americans had
secured most of the Cotentin peninsula, territorial gains and good news head-
lines offsetting some of the high cost in casualties. But on the British side
frustration grew as it became apparent that the front had (in Montgomery's
own words) 'glued up'. British losses mounted and victory seemed to come
no closer.

Montgomery's boss, Supreme Commander Dwight D. Eisenhower, made
clear his frustration. The day after an acrimonious 6 July meeting with

Montgomery, he wrote to clarify his forebodings: 'We must use all possible energy in a determined effort to prevent a stalemate'.[4] The words made little impact. Montgomery carried on with scant regard for criticism, his self-assurance not visibly dented. At the tactical level, he ensured that German advantages in weapons and battle tactics were as far as possible negated by his own forces' superiority in logistics, artillery and air power. At the operational level, his offensives pre-empted German efforts to regain the initiative, forcing the arriving Panzer divisions to be flung into battle piecemeal before they could be concentrated for a strategic counter-thrust.

The British were broadly supportive of the American plan to break out of the Normandy beachhead. Montgomery (still in command of all ground forces) approved Operation COBRA on 18 July. COBRA began inauspiciously. On the afternoon of 24 July, in bad visibility and as frantic efforts were made to recall the bombers, 685 tons of high explosive and fragmentation munitions were dropped through the haze. 'Friendly fire' losses were incurred and the day's operations were called off. Nevertheless, COBRA was reinstated and the following day over 4,000 tons of bombs fell on less than ten square miles. American casualties were again suffered, but whole German units were obliterated. An American breakthrough commenced which, once the crust of German resistance was broken, would lead to Avranches and beyond.

Montgomery's principal support for American operations was unchanged: to 'fix' as many of the enemy's armoured formations as possible in the east, around Caen. But additionally on 25 July he instructed Second Army to recommend more specific actions to minimise German opposition to the American advance. Dempsey responded in characteristic fashion. Less patient than his master, he was keenly seeking opportunities to execute a *British* breakout from the Normandy deadlock. Observing that the British right flank, the boundary with the US First Army, was opposed by only weak enemy forces, his recommendation was a hastily prepared advance southwards from Caumont on a two-corps front.

Though the recommendation was accepted by Montgomery, Operation BLUECOAT was far from being a 'typical' Monty battle. Timing was tight; logistic preparations would be limited and would impose limits on available support. Simply getting the vast numbers of men and vehicles to the battlefield for the morning of Sunday 30 July was a major challenge. Most units did not receive movement orders until late on 28 July. The 43rd Infantry Division was just three days into a rest period after their gruelling ordeal on Hill 112, and the return to action was unpopular. Progress was hardest for the armoured divisions, whose routes took their thousands of vehicles across other units' supply lines. 'Pip' Roberts, commanding 11th Armoured Division, recalled, 'Corps orders arrived at our HQ during the cross-country march, so that our orders to brigades arrived at around 02.00 on 30th July and 'H' hour for the attack was 06.55 hours. It was a scramble, but just worked'.[5]

Sunday 30 July: break-in

The British assault followed a familiar pattern. In the case of VIII Corps' three divisions, the 15th (Scottish) Infantry was to lead the way. Preceded by Royal Air Force bombers, its brigades were as ever supported by their respective Royal Artillery field regiments, its regiments accompanied by squadrons of Churchill 'infantry' tanks. The infantry role was to break into the enemy line. Behind waited 11th Armoured Division, poised to flow through the breach, and behind them Guards Armoured Division awaited its turn to exploit.

The ground to be covered was some of the densest *bocage* in Normandy, and the axis of attack ran directly across some dramatic ridge lines. This was the *Suisse Normande*, the little Switzerland in Normandy, terrain where even depleted and surprised German defenders might sell ground dearly. Correspondingly, 15th Scottish Major-General MacMillan planned a narrow-fronted, multi-phased attack, with just two of his nine infantry battalions in the first wave.

The infantry division was to attack with one brigade 'up'. That is to say, of the division's three brigades, the initial breakthrough was to be led by just 227 Brigade, strengthened by 9th Cameronians for a total of four battalions. In the first phase, just two battalions of the four were to lead the way. And since each infantry battalion advanced on a two-company front, with its two remaining rifle companies to follow, the entire VIII Corps attack was led by four rifle companies: barely 400 men, strung out along a front of about a mile. Moving down off the Caumont ridge, 9th Cameronians on the right would secure the hamlet of Sept Vents, while on the left 2nd Gordon Highlanders would clear the Lutain Wood.[6]

Small groups of seven or eight men advanced at walking pace, well separated, across thickly-hedged fields varying from 100 metres across down to 50 metres or less. Unlike their German counterparts, trained in infiltration, the groups advanced more or less in unison. This was largely to ensure that their progress was closely synchronised with the development of the broader battle, with its complex orchestration of infantry, tanks, artillery and air power. To each company of roughly 100 men was assigned a troop of three Churchill infantry tanks loosely in support, though the ability of the tanks to follow the infantry closely was severely limited by the terrain.

In these circumstances, intimate familiarity between tanks and infantry was called for. Amid the dense Normandy hedgerows, tanks and infantry were mutually dependent yet rarely able to communicate directly. A continuing theme of BLUECOAT (and a relative novelty for the British army in 1944) was the great advantage gained when tank and infantry units were familiar with each other: squadrons with battalions, troops with companies, tank commander with squad leader. In previous Normandy battles, the 15th Scottish had been teamed with an unfamiliar tank brigade. Unfortunate consequences resulted, including 'friendly fire' incidents and failure of infantry adequately to protect tanks in close fighting. By good fortune, 15th Scottish Division had been reunited on the eve of BLUECOAT with 6th Guards Tank Brigade, old friends with whom they had trained in Britain prior to coming to Normandy.[7]

Previous set-piece British offensives in Normandy frequently underestimated the depth of German defensive positions. Time after time, instead of achieving breakthroughs, British and Commonwealth forces were slowed by successive defence lines. Stopping to consolidate, attackers would be thrown back by vigorous local counter-attacks. This time, the forward momentum was supposed to be maintained. But before the morning was out, the advance already risked falling behind schedule. Waiting behind the Cameronians and Gordons were the remaining two battalions of 227 Brigade: 10th Highland Light Infantry and 2nd Argyll and Sutherland Highlanders.

Having displaced forward to their own forming-up places the two battalions waited with growing impatience. The Argylls' acting commander, Major John Kenneth, 'began to wonder about 0820 hrs if we should ever get through to cross our S.L. [start line] on time'. So, on his own initiative and without waiting for the Gordons' struggle in the Lutain Wood to be resolved, he ordered his two leading companies to set off, followed by the supporting tanks of 3rd Scots Guards. Similarly, the 10th Highland Light Infantry set off down the hill towards Sept Vents supported by the tanks of 4th Coldstream Guards. From the outset, command and control were problematic. As usual, the Number 18 infantry wireless sets were either malfunctioning or else their operators were picked off by snipers. The Argylls had difficulty contacting brigade, and 'we found it increasingly difficult for the forward companies of infantry to keep in touch with the tanks, due to the tanks having to jink about and increase speed in order to find crossing places over ditches and hedges. It was not long before we lost sight of the leading squadrons of tanks'.[8]

In fact, the two supporting Guards tank battalions (4th Coldstream and 3rd Scots Guards) were purposefully crashing through the German line ahead of the infantry they were supposed to be supporting. This daring move was highly unorthodox and demands some explanation. Churchill tanks were not expected to press on across country without infantry support. Conferring by the fishing tackle shop in Caumont, the infantry's General MacMillan and the tanks' Brigadier Verney had determined on a gamble which would, if successful, keep the VIII Corps plan on track. As Verney later recalled:

> The situation throughout Phase II had been very confused, and my recollections are of many conversations over the air with the two tank battalions, on the rival themes of hurrying on to the objective or staying close to the infantry whose whereabouts were continually uncertain . . . It was becoming clear that we would never get Phase III off at the rate we were going. It seemed that the only hope was to take a chance and push on alone, and follow up with infantry later as best we could.[9]

Verney and MacMillan agreed to throw away the book of rules and push the tanks on ahead.

A gamble it certainly was. To the British, it seemed incredible good fortune that the enemy lacked heavy anti-tank guns. In fact, the overstretched defenders had few of these to deploy, trusting that the dense hedgerows of the *bocage* country would be impenetrable to vehicles, even fully-tracked tanks. But as was so often the case, from the mountains of Tunisia to the forest of the *Reichswald*, the Churchill tank's extraordinary ability to traverse unfavourable terrain proved equal to the occasion.[10] The Coldstream bade their riding Glasgow Highlanders *au revoir*, leaving them with instructions to 'follow the tank tracks'. The tanks plunged on towards their objective, the distant Hill 309.

The cross-country route was not easy. Some tanks shed tracks as they attempted particularly difficult obstacles. Others simply found the strain too much for their engines. Lieutenant Cazenove's whole troop became bogged; Sergeant Maughan's tank turned over on its side, setting off a grenade inside the turret which severely wounded the three occupants. Yet the objective was reached about 1600 hours. The hill which defending General Straube had said 'must not be allowed to fall into enemy hands' was abandoned by the Germans as the 40-ton monsters clambered towards its summit. Though the hold of the tanks was tenuous – armour unsupported can rarely hold terrain securely – nevertheless the Coldstream remained until the first elements of the 2nd Glasgow Highlanders began to arrive about 2230 hours. By 0230 hours, the last of their rifle companies was on the hill and the guns of the anti-tank platoon had been manhandled into place. From the north, the 7th Seaforth of 46 Brigade were on their way to strengthen the position further. Five miles behind the front at the start of the day, Hill 309 was now firmly in British hands.

Similarly to the east, setting off from the vicinity of the Lutain Wood towards Hill 226, the Scots Guards Churchills experienced a wild ride: crashing over hedgerows like heavy horses in a steeplechase, spraying whole belts of *Besa* and putting high explosive rounds into any knots of resistance. The crews were shaken and bruised, commanders struck by low branches and pelted with small, hard cider apples which accumulated on the floors of the tank turrets. Somewhere behind them, the Argylls were on the move again with a leap-frog advance, alternating fire and movement by companies which carried them rapidly forward in the wake of the tanks. By 1530 hours, the village of Les Loges was secured and B and D Companies of 2nd Argylls joined their armoured friends on the slopes of Hill 226. The infantry dug in on the northern reverse slope while the tanks adopted hull-down positions on the crestline.

Almost uniquely for a major Normandy battle, British forces ended the first day in firm control of ambitious objectives. Success had been achieved with a complex interaction of weaponry: air power and artillery suppressing defenders; specialist armoured vehicles clearing mines and dousing defensive strongpoints with flame. But in analysing the success, the human element must be considered. The commanders of 6th Guards Tank Brigade and 15th Scottish Division risked unorthodox tactics to keep up momentum. The tankers set off alone with every confidence that 'their' infantry would eventually catch them up.

Although achieved by tanks and footsoldiers briefly separated, the break-in south of Caumont was nevertheless an illustration of infantry and 'infantry tanks' working together in harmony. The history of the 15th Scottish records that their success on the first day of BLUECOAT was largely due to the 'previous and intimate cooperation' of 6th Guards Tanks, 'old friends' of the division.[11] The history of the 6th goes further, acknowledging that 'It was an act of providence which ordained that the 6th Guards Tank Brigade should go into their own first battle with their old friends . . . Had the infantry been strangers, the tanks would not have advanced alone so far'.[12]

Monday 31 July: breakthrough

The Scots infantry and their Scots Guards infantry tanks had achieved the break-in, and it now fell to 11th Armoured Division to keep up the momentum. Through the afternoon of 30 July and into the night, tanks and infantry of the division pressed forward, and by nightfall the German defenders of the little town of St Martin-des-Besaces were being hard pressed. But by morning, little further progress had been made. The place was being firmly held.

This was a problem. St-Martin lay squarely astride the axis of the VIII Corps' advance. The Normandy road network of 1944 made few concessions to the needs of a modern army, and traffic jams were an inescapable part of every British offensive there. From Caumont, the only practical artery for the majority of VIII Corps' wheeled vehicles was the single road leading south to St Martin-des-Besaces. From the epicentre of this little town, where bitter fighting continued, armour and infantry fanned out west, seeking points of weaker resistance but finding none. And fanning out even further afield were the troops of armoured cars of the division's reconnaissance regiment, the 2nd Household Cavalry.

Put simply, the job of a reconnaissance unit was to drive beyond the front lines to locate the enemy. In Normandy this usually meant driving until fired upon. Commanders in their thinly armoured cars travelled with eyes peeled for signs of trouble, ready at a moment's notice to trigger the smoke dispensers and engage reverse gear, most often keeping a grenade within easy reach.

One troop of Household Cavalry had already ventured into St Martin from the north, and lost its two leading cars. Another car taking a wrong turning and entering the town from the east was shot to pieces. Probing further west, 1 Troop of C Squadron lost two of its four cars, immobilised in a narrow lane. This left a Daimler Dingo scout car and the troop commander Lieutenant Derek ('Dickie') Powle in his Daimler armoured car.

Passing through a German battery, Powle judged it safer to press on for-
wards than to retrace his way through an alerted enemy. So the two cars
motored on, down dusty minor roads leading through thickly wooded hills,
the Forêt l'Evêque. The road twisted and turned through the dark, eerily-
silent forest. Eventually the cars emerged to pass through the small town of
la Ferrière-Harang, and carried on southwards, still without encountering
any substantial opposition.

Eventually, a bridge appeared ahead of the British cars. The steep sided-
valley of the River Souleuvre was a major obstacle, and the bridge an unexpected prize. The two cars crossed in turn and both vehicles went into cover
in the trees within sight of the bridge. As the crews set about camouflaging
the vehicles, Corporal Staples, the armoured car's gunner/operator, worked
the radio, which in effect was the principal weapon of the troop. Information from behind enemy lines could potentially wreak far more havoc than
a small 37mm cannon. But as with any weapon, range was a factor, and the
combination of distance and rolling wooded terrain made contact very
difficult. Six miles away, 2nd Household Cavalry headquarters was struggling to make contact with cars much closer than Powle's. Staples had to
transmit over and over again before he made contact. Finally, he got off the
vital message: 'At 1030 hours the bridge at 637436 is clear of enemy and still
intact. I say again, at 1030 hours the bridge at 637436 is clear of enemy and
still intact'. When the reference was found to be so far beyond any known
penetration of enemy lines, Colonel Abel Smith was incredulous and demanded an instant repeat. Back came the confirmation. Personal initiative
and extreme good fortune had won a bridge over the Souleuvre, several
miles behind the German front line.[13]

This was not according to plan. Still notionally in a supporting role, VIII
Corps should in theory have been seeking to advance on a south-easterly
axis, not westward, away from XXX Corps. But the commander of 11th
Armoured Division had the imagination to recognise a unique opportunity,
and the initiative to exploit it. Major-General 'Pip' Roberts was a rising
star. Aged 37, he was the youngest British divisional commander. He was
experienced – no British general had spent longer fighting in the turret of a
tank – and he was confident. In leading his division through two major
Normandy battles, Roberts had endured setbacks caused by interference
from above in the management of his division. In both Operations EPSOM
and GOODWOOD, officers of 11th Armoured felt that their division
suffered from misguided directives from Corps. Even General O'Connor's
sympathetic biographer admits that for the Corps commander, EPSOM
'must at times have been a bewildering experience' and that he and his staff
were 'perhaps more concerned with the mechanics of GOODWOOD than
the philosophy of it'.[14] Now, even before seeking O'Connor's approval (which
arrived in due course), Roberts had no hesitation in changing the axis of his
divisional advance. No matter that reinforcing the bridge might involve
trespassing across the army boundary onto roads allocated to American

units. While his division continued to invest St Martin-des-Besaces, all available force was rushed west and south to secure the bridge.

First, six Cromwell tanks of the 2nd Northamptonshire Yeomanry arrived to reinforce the five men and two cars at the bridge; later came more substantial force in the shape of Sherman tanks of the 23rd Hussars carrying infantry of the 3rd Monmouths. By evening, as elements of *21.Panzerdivision* appeared in the wooded heights south of the bridge, the crossing was already secure.

August 1–2: Break out?

Throughout Tuesday 1 August, XXX Corps struggled to make progress southward towards Jurques and Aunay, with Mont Pinçon on the distant horizon. Consequently, instead of covering their sister corps' right flank, VIII Corps' continuing advance increasingly risked exposing its own left flank. And on this flank, German pressure grew with increasing attempts to reduce the VIII Corps salient. 15th Scottish grimly held their line between Hills 309 and 226, first against desperate counter-attacks by *326.Infanteriedivision*, later by Feuchtinger's *21.Panzerdivision*. To the west, 11th Armoured Division poured across 'Dickie's Bridge' and by the end of the day the entire division, with its four armoured and four infantry regiments, was in position south of the Souleuvre, holding the Bény-Bocage ridge and the main road running arrow-straight in the direction of Vire.

From the German perspective, the true front line remained somewhere south of St Martin-des-Besaces, where Guards Armoured Division was struggling to make progress southbound on the originally planned, more direct route to Vire. In this rolling country, pockets of *21.Panzerdivision* resistance succeeded in bringing the Guards to a halt barely halfway to the Vire-Villers-Bocage highway where a combat team on the extreme left flank of 11th Armoured awaited their arrival.

Only late in the day did *Panzergruppe* West awake to the crisis developing north of Vire. The fracture of the German front along the boundary of the two German armies in Normandy posed a threat to Vire, a vital junction and a hinge of the whole defensive line. With *21.Panzerdivision* on the verge of being 'pinched out' between 11th and Guards Armoured Divisions, first *10.SS-Panzerdivision* ('*Frundsberg*') was commanded west and soon after its sister *9.SS-Panzerdivision* ('*Hohenstaufen*') was ordered to proceed directly to confront 11th Armoured. The scene was set for a day of decisive conflict.

Wednesday 2 August was also the day when two months of trial and error culminated in a demonstration of new British infantry and armour tactics. In spite of open flanks, Pip Roberts was looking forward, prepared to strike south. Tactically, his division abandoned the traditional separation of infantry and armoured brigades. Instead, multi-arm regimental task forces were formed, infantry riding on tanks, batteries of the Royal Artillery leap-frogging behind the armoured columns to provide on-call support.[15]

Montgomery had told Dempsey that the operation to assist COBRA would have 'no geographical objective'.[16] Roberts nevertheless had learned in earlier operations the importance of basing tactical objectives on physical features which, once taken, could be securely held. On 1 August, the corps commander had specified the objective of 11th Armoured as the important town of Vire. However, as Roberts finalised his plans for the following day, he received the unexpected and 'somewhat frustrating' news that Montgomery had approved a shift of army boundaries which placed Vire in the American sector.[17] 11th Armoured was explicitly forbidden to enter the place. Roberts' frustration was all the worse given reports that the town was only lightly defended. The reports were correct. The place could have been taken on 2 August with minimal effort. Vire was thereafter hastily reinforced: first by elements of *II.SS-Panzer-Korps* from the east, soon after by elements of *II.Fallschirmjäger-Korps* retreating from the west. Seizing the rubble that had been Vire would later cost the Americans over 3,000 casualties.

The 11th Armoured Division's tactical objective was redetermined, now to be the major ridge running parallel to and just north of the Vire-Vassy road. Three columns radiated out to the south-east, each comprising one infantry battalion and one armoured regiment. The advance was hindered by adverse terrain; few roads ran in the desired direction. Only a lesser force, the Cromwell tanks of the Northamptonshire Yeomanry, probed in the direction of Vire. By day's end, in spite of losses and in the face of increasingly determined counter-attacks, the Perrier ridge was held.

Once again, chance and individual initiatives played their part. One lone tank officer, striding forward at the very apex of the VIII Corps advance, was first to cut the Vire-Vassy road. One lone, angry sergeant-major left his positions wielding a PIAT to destroy a Panther tank and in so doing preserved an outpost which was later to prove a bastion on the open left flank of 11th Armoured. Later, as *II.SS-Panzer-Korps* struggled with increasing desperation to throw the British off the Perrier ridge, one young corporal gave his life – and gained a Victoria Cross – individually throwing back the last assault of the *Frundsberg Panzergrenadiere*.[18]

This fourth day of BLUECOAT was memorable for the new tactics demonstrated by Roberts' 11th Armoured Division, but equally for the operational skill with which the division was conducted. Plunging forward with little regard for flanks could, of course, have ended in disaster. For days to come, the British 'front' would more resemble a series of defensive strongpoints rather than a continuous line. Well might the defenders of Perrier ridge look over their shoulders and wonder if the Royal Army Service Corps convoys bringing forward ammunition and fuel would get through the extensive German penetration of the countryside to the rear. As it happened, the Germans were slow to recognise the enormity of the breakthrough. Even as the *Frundsberg* was pouring out its life blood in increasingly desperate attempts to regain Perrier ridge, the high command persisted in the view that the true 'frontline' remained somewhere to the north around

St Martin-des-Besaces and that the forward elements of the British break-through were liable to isolation. Field commanders dared not contradict the delusions of high command. Even Oberbefehlshaber von Kluge had to maintain the pretence that his élite armoured divisions engaged on the Perrier ridge were still *en route* to participate in the Mortain offensive, when in truth their combat strength was rapidly dwindling.

Assessing BLUECOAT

How should we assess Operation BLUECOAT? As regards Montgomery's challenge to Dempsey (to distract German forces that might otherwise be redeployed against the American breakout), it would be churlish to deny the success of the operation. After the first week of August, *21. Panzerdivision* was a shadow of its former organization. *9.* and *10. SS-Panzerdivision* had each been substantially 'written down' (Montgomery's phrase) with *12. SS* (the *Hitlerjugend*) also weakened. And none of these formations had reached the American sector.

Of course, it may be asked whether similar results might have been achieved by concentrating force further east, even east of the Orne River on the road to Falaise. But it was accepted by Montgomery and Dempsey that alternating hammer blows on widely-spaced parts of the front was preferable to focusing on one single area of operations.[19] And, quite apart from damage inflicted on the field of battle, given Allied command of the skies through the long summer daylight hours, inadequate roads, and the relative weakness of German logistic arrangements, the effort and loss incurred in continually repositioning the German armoured formations must not be underestimated.

Can one go further, speculating that in attempting to 'fix' the German capability for defence, Montgomery unwittingly drew teeth from the coming, and as yet unexpected, enemy attack? Von Kluge certainly had a fair estimation of Operation LÜTTICH's (slim) chances of success. Would the availability of at least part of *II. SS-Panzer-Korps* have made any difference to the fate of the Mortain counter-offensive? As ever, the question of 'what if' is problematic. Historians rightly present alternative possibilities in order to demonstrate that events which transpired were not necessarily inevitable. But the temptation to overreach must be resisted. Battles are frequently won by the side making fewer mistakes; if our speculation excuses the mistakes of one side, must we not allow the other a similar 'break'? A distinguished historian of the German campaign in Russia has warned, 'Which is the more absurd – to allow, with the wisdom of hindsight, an immaculate German campaign against a Russian resistance still plagued by those blunders and follies that arose in the heat and urgency of battle, or to correct both and to reset the board in an atmosphere of complete fantasy?'[20] If we speculate about a reinforced *Lüttich*, perhaps we should also ponder the very real possibility of 11th Armoured Division seizing Vire on 2 August, and the myriad possible outcomes of such a high-stakes venture!

German armour tactics in Normandy is an area still deserving of further study. Several attempts in June and July to apply Eastern Front shock tactics failed dismally as unprepared and poorly coordinated Panzer attacks broke against prepared British and Commonwealth defences. New '*Panzertrupptaktik*' for use on the 'invasion front' from the end of June marked a reversal of policy. Instead of the typical insistence on concentration of armoured force, deployment in 'penny packets' was now sanctioned.[21] While an individual Tiger or Panther tank well emplaced could still represent a formidable obstacle, many British observers criticized German armoured assaults during BLUECOAT for lacking focus and concentration.

The British armour also drew some lessons from disasters of their own in the month of June. Arguably the performance of 11th Armoured Division was influenced as much by inspired leadership as by effective tactics. Nevertheless, the organisational and tactical lessons implemented by 11th Armoured during BLUECOAT stood as a model for other formations. And, in the words of a member of that division, 'There was much unpleasantness to come. But after the crossing of that small bridge over the Souleuvre there was no more retreat for 11th Armoured between Normandy and the Baltic'.[22]

An operation 'written out'

Through nearly two months of bludgeoning by the Allies, the German front had held. Despite high rates of attrition, the defending line showed few signs of being about to shatter. Then on 1 August the British found themselves facing a gap in the defensive wall. The infantry divisions forming the left flank of *Panzergruppe* West and the Panzer divisions sent to buttress them all failed. Fortuitously, this occurred at a time and in a place where a corps commander was giving encouragement to the most creative and energetic divisional commander in the British sector, who in turn led the most effective British armoured division of the war.

The idea that Montgomery then missed a critical opportunity to shorten the war was proposed by Major J.J. How in 1981.[23] Subsequent historians have debated his accusation. Without rehearsing all the arguments, it can safely be said that Montgomery *did* deny O'Connor and Roberts an opportunity which they realised was within their grasp. At a time when a small force could have seized Vire, Roberts recalled later, 'We had strict instructions from Monty that we were not – repeat NOT – to go into Vire. That was the American objective'. One wonders what would have happened if a similar order had been given to American General George Patton, just short of a key strategic goal. Was Montgomery playing a political game? Was he in fact more stung by his enemies' criticism of his perceived failure during GOODWOOD than he liked to make out? Was he seeking to restore his reputation by appeasing Eisenhower?

There is a more likely explanation. By 1 August Operation BLUECOAT was turning into just the sort of fluid encounter which Montgomery abhorred.

In Normandy, Montgomery was keen to avoid any battle which he might lose. Well aware of the shortcomings of the armies he commanded in 1944, he set his sights accordingly. His concern on 1 August was not pushing 11th Armoured Division still further 'into the blue', but rather getting some movement into XXX Corps' stalled offensive. Or as he would have put it: 'ungluing the battle' so that he could 'tidy it up'. Then he could restore a firm front line, bring up the rear elements, and then if the opportunity presented itself have another 'big push'. But on 2 August, he was more concerned with sacking Lieutenant-General Bucknall (of XXX Corps), Major-General Erskine and Brigadier Hinde (of 7th Armoured Division), than with discouraging O'Connor from plunging into the unknown. By 3 August, Montgomery already had half a mind on the forthcoming Canadian assault to the east of Caen, Operation TOTALIZE.

With the benefit of hindsight, Pip Roberts magnanimously conceded that the capture of Vire might have risked 11th Armoured Division becoming stranded beyond the reach of vital supplies and the range of VIII Corps artillery. This is arguable. Perhaps it is most appropriate to end with Montgomery's own memoirs. His only comment on VIII Corps' operations on 2 August was that opposition to its advance 'was now becoming more stubborn',[24] that elements of the division reached the outskirts of Vire, and that patrols cut the Vire-Vassy road. He very much played down the role of BLUECOAT. This operation simply did not fit well into his narrative of a Normandy campaign which went strictly to plan – *his* plan.

Acknowledgement

Ian Daglish is grateful to Pen & Sword Books Limited for permission to use extracts from his work *Operation BLUECOAT, the British Armoured Breakout* and *Operation GOODWOOD, the Great Tank Charge* in the preparation of this chapter.

Notes

1 This topic has been well covered in the literature of the campaign; a good account is found in Stephen Hart, *Montgomery and 'Colossal Cracks', the 21st Army Group in Northwest Europe* (London: Praeger, 2000), pp. 32–3.
2 Terry Copp, *Fields of Fire, The Canadians in Normandy* (Toronto: University of Toronto Press, 2003), pp. 187–9.
3 These and other aspects of BLUECOAT mentioned in this chapter are explored in Ian Daglish, *Operation BLUECOAT, The British Armoured Breakout* (Pen & Sword, 2003).
4 Martin Blumenson, *Breakout and Pursuit* (Washington, DC: US Army Center of Military History, 1989), p. 119.
5 Major-General G.P.B. Roberts, *From the Desert to the Baltic* (London: William Kimber, 1987), p. 185.
6 Brigadier C.N. Barclay, *The History of the Cameronians* (London: Sifton Praed, 1947), pp. 169–70; Wilfred Miles, *The Life of a Regiment, the History of the Gordon Highlanders vol V, 1919–1945* (London: Frederick Warne, 1961), pp. 278–80.

7 The story of Montgomery's attempts to keep 6th Guards Tanks out of Normandy is one involving personal pride and animosities and does him little credit; it is most usefully recounted by Scots Guards officer Charles Farrell, *Reflections, 1939–1945* (Edinburgh: Pentland Press, 2000) pp. 54–8; also Forbes, *6th Guards Tank Brigade, The Story of Guardsmen in Churchill Tanks* (London: Sampson Low Marston, 1946), p. 11.

8 Major John Kenneth, 2A & SH, BAOR Battlefield Tour, 1947.

9 Major-General G.L. Verney, 6 GDS TK BDE, BAOR Battlefield Tour, 1947.

10 Though no single explanation for the Churchill tank's remarkable climbing ability has been identified, an authoritative account of this vehicle's development and performance is to be found in David Fletcher, *Mr Churchill's Tank: The British Infantry Tank Mark IV* (Atglen, PA: Schiffer, 1999).

11 Lieutenant-General H.G. Martin, *The History of the Fifteenth Scottish Division* (London: Blackwood, 1948), p. 81.

12 Forbes, ibid., pp. 14–15.

13 This full story of these events, recounted in Daglish, ibid., pp. 55–61, includes material from several sources, but notably from Roden Orde's delightfully written *Second Household Cavalry Regiment* (Aldershot: Gale & Polden, 1953), pp. 96–107.

14 John Baynes, *The Forgotten Victor* (Exeter: Wheatons, 1989), pp. 194, 201.

15 For details, see Daglish, ibid., Chapter 5.

16 Hart, ibid., p. 139.

17 Roberts, ibid., pp. 191–2.

18 These stories are related in full in Daglish, ibid.

19 Hart, ibid. This is one of the central themes of Dr Stephen Hart's invaluable *Colossal Cracks.*

20 Alan Clark, *Barbarossa, The Russian – German Conflict, 1941–1945* (New York: William Morrow, 1965), p. xxi.

21 Thomas L. Jentz, *Panzer Truppen, Volume 2, 1943–1945* (Atglen, PA: Schiffer, 1996), p. 182.

22 Roger Gray, *Normandy Revisited* (Edinburgh: Blackwood's Magazine, November 1977), p. 397.

23 Major J.J. How, *Normandy: The British Breakout* (London: William Kimber, 1981).

24 Field Marshal The Viscount Montgomery of Alamein, *From Normandy to the Baltic* (London: Hutchinson, 1946) p. 91.

8 'The black day unrealised'

Operation TOTALIZE and the problems of translating tactical success into a decisive breakout

Stephen A. Hart

Many historical analyses of Allied offensives during the 1944 Normandy campaign have focused on operations such as GOODWOOD/ATLANTIC, where the Allies struggled to break-in or through the German defences successfully. Less well understood is Operation TOTALIZE.[1] Lieutenant-General Guy Simonds's II Canadian Corps launched this attack from its positions along the Bourguébus Ridge, striking south-south-east astride the main Caen-Falaise road toward the high ground that dominated Falaise. The relative lack of focus on this operation is surprising given that it utilised sophisticated operational art, and that its initial break-in achieved rapid success. Even more surprising, moreover, is the relative lack of focus on what happened next for, despite this rapid initial success, TOTALIZE did not subsequently secure a decisive operational-level victory. Indeed, Simonds's forces subsequently struggled – in the face of modest opposition – swiftly to complete the second break-in battle, and to transit into rapid exploitation operations. To understand why it proved impossible to exploit this initial success, this chapter will provide an overview of the plan and the successful break-in. It will then examine the problems that dogged the Allied forces during the transition between the first and second phases of the operation, and the Allies' subsequent mounting of the offensive's second phase.[2]

The plan

During late July 1944, the Allies finally managed to shake off the attritional stalemate that had increasingly gripped the Normandy theatre of operations. After the success of the American COBRA offensive around St. Lô, General Patton's ruthless subsequent exploitation translated this into a decisive breakthrough along the western sector of the German front. By early August, therefore, American forces were advancing rapidly through the interior of France in all directions. In contrast to this, however, Montgomery's Anglo-Canadian forces remained bogged down by the determined German defence of the eastern sector, situated between Caumont and the coast at Ouistreham. This strategic context now made it politically imperative that

these forces successfully advanced southwards. It was in this context that
Simonds's II Canadian Corps planned Operation TOTALIZE.[3]

On 1 August, Simonds's corps came under the command of the newly
operational First Canadian Army, led by Lieutenant-General Henry Crerar.
That day Simonds produced a written appreciation of the mission that
Montgomery had recently allocated him; to plan an offensive from the
Bourguébus Ridge toward Falaise to be mounted on 8 August at the latest,
depending on how the American advance influenced the strategic situation.
The attack was designed to facilitate the British and American operations
then unfolding further to the west. Simonds concluded that an attack toward
Falaise would encounter fierce German resistance because the enemy viewed
this sector as the key 'hinge' that supported their forces located further west.
Consequently, they had deployed here elements of the fanatical 1st and 12th
SS Panzer divisions *Leibstandarte* and *Hitlerjugend*. Simonds's appreciation
recognised that to be successful in the face of such opposition, the planned
offensive would have to address four factors.[4]

First, the attack had to reflect the enemy's defensive system, which comprised a forward line that ran west from la Hogue through to May-sur-
Orne, and 7.5km further south a partially prepared reserve position between
St Sylvain and Bretteville-sur-Laize. Simonds concluded that this system
compelled the Allies to mount two separate break-in battles.[5] Second, the
plan also needed to ensure that, unlike previous Allied offensives in Normandy, the attack's forward momentum did not falter just as it reached
the depths of the German defensive zone. If Simonds employed all available
air support to assist the initial break-in battle, the only fire support left
available for the second break-in would be the few artillery pieces that had
managed to move forward. Thus, Simonds decided to mount a daring surprise night assault, backed by all his available artillery, to penetrate rapidly
the first German defence line. This novel approach, he believed, would thus
only require the support of half of his available heavy bomber assets. This
would allow the Allies to keep back half their strategic aerial resources –
the day bombers – to facilitate the second break-in battle that would enjoy
only limited artillery support. Simonds believed that with this approach the
offensive would swiftly penetrate the entire depth of the German defences,
thus permitting rapid exploitation toward Falaise.[6]

Third, the appreciation stated that any plan would have to accept that the
terrain favoured the defenders. The open terrain was dominated by enemy-
controlled high ground, and thus Allied forces would enjoy little protection
from the long-range killing power of well-concealed German tanks and anti-
tank guns. To obtain initial success, therefore, the offensive had to curtail
these capabilities by attacking at night, when enemy German observation
would be handicapped. Moreover, as the attack's objectives and axis of
advance were obvious, a night attack was the only way of gaining tactical
surprise.[7] Last, Simonds recognised that the offensive would have to destroy
the enemy's deep-lying anti-tank positions. Consequently, he employed night

infiltration tactics; all-arms mobile columns would bypass the enemy's forward defended localities (FDLs), race through the depth of the initial German position, and overrun the enemy's deep anti-tank positions. To ensure that the columns' infantry could keep up with the tanks, and once on the objective help the latter repel enemy ripostes, Simonds insisted they be embussed in armoured vehicles.[8]

Four days later, on 5 August, Crerar briefed his subordinates on the forthcoming offensive – now called TOTALIZE. He stressed that if success-ful, the operation might lead to 'a quick termination of the war'. Observing that TOTALIZE was to start on the same date as the Amiens offensive of 1918, he expressed his hope that the offensive would make 8 August 1944 'an even blacker day for the German Armies than is recorded against that same date twenty-six years ago'.[9] Next, Simonds outlined his corps plan to the assembled officers. This plan envisaged that after strategic night bombers had struck targets on the flanks of the attack, two infantry divisions would mount the initial night break-in. Then, around 1300 hours the next day, a second strategic bombing run would strike the reserve Ger-man defensive position. Subsequently, in the offensive's second phase, an armoured division would then break through this second enemy line, before two armoured divisions advanced 14km during the final phase to seize the key high ground situated north of Falaise.

Reflecting the high hopes expressed by Crerar on 5 August, the critical potential significance of TOTALIZE only gradually became apparent as events developed apace elsewhere in Normandy. Indeed, it was only by the end of the now abortive offensive on 10 August that its real significance had become evident for, if Simonds's corps had only managed to advance to Falaise, it could have cut the key lateral road that ran through the town. In so doing, Simonds's forces might well have prevented the German Seventh Army from escaping eastward from the looming encirclement it now faced. If Simonds's forces could have subsequently advanced further south, they might have been able to seal the pocket in the Falaise-Argentan area by linking up with the northward advance of Patton's spearheads. Such a success might have ensured the destruction of an entire German army and thus have realised the re-creation of the enemy's 'black day' that Crerar had envisaged back on 5 August. Sadly, it was not to be.

The day after Crerar's briefing, Simonds had to issue a modified corps plan. The Allies had gained intelligence that indicated the withdrawal of the *Leibstandarte* from the front opposite II Corps. Simonds interpreted this (erroneously) as indicating a weakening of the first German defensive position and the bolstering of their second line.[10] His new scheme now committed two armoured divisions simultaneously to the second break-in across a widened frontage. It also amalgamated the operation's original second and third phases into a new consolidated second phase, this change being designed to drive the Allied armour forward so that it secured the high ground north of Falaise by 9 August. In so doing, Simonds also hoped to exploit any tactical advantage that would accrue in the immediate aftermath of the second Allied bombing run.[11]

Night break-in

By 7 August, Simonds's corps had assembled 85,000 troops backed by 2,000 aircraft and 720 artillery guns. The main force deployed against it was the 89th Infantry Division, part of I-SS Panzer Corps, while located to the rear were the fanatical teenagers of the *Hitlerjugend*.[12] Simonds's plan envisaged that from 2300 hours on 7 August, two infantry divisions would execute the initial night break-in. On the Allied left (east) the British 51st (Highland) Division grouping was to operate, while west of the road the 2nd Canadian Infantry Division grouping was to attack. Seven mobile columns spear-headed the initial break-in, with each typically fielding an embussed infantry battalion, armoured forces and supporting arms. These columns would rapidly infiltrate between the German FDLs to seize key objectives up to 6.3km behind the enemy frontline. As the column assault unfolded, five Allied infantry battalions would advance on foot to secure the FDLs that the columns had bypassed. These foot missions were just as important as the more spectacular column assaults. If these bypassed FDLs continued to hold out, their fire could interdict the forward movement of Allied forces and supplies up the routes cleared by the columns, and thus slow the offensive's momentum.[13]

Even though the columns, predictably, experienced severe problems with maintaining command and control in the confusing shroud of darkness, Simonds's novel night infiltration attack nevertheless secured resound-ing success. By noon on 8 August, five of the seven columns had secured their objectives, while the remaining two had dug in not too far away from these locations.[14] In addition, two of the five marching infantry attacks had secured their objectives, while the remaining three would subsequently complete their missions later that afternoon.[15] For the tolerable cost of 380 casualties, Simonds's night break-in had secured a 7km-wide penetration of the entire, 6.3km deep, first German defensive position.[16]

Dilemmas of phase transition

With the rosy benefit of hindsight available to the historian, it seems that if the Allies had mounted an improvised continuation of the break-in offens-ive that morning, they may have achieved considerable success, for their night attack had shattered the initial German defensive zone, and the latter's second defence line remained largely unmanned. Simonds's plan, however, understandably assumed that a successful assault on the supposedly potent second German line was only feasible after a second bombing strike had occurred. Unfortunately, as this second bomb run was not due to commence until soon after noon, the Allies were apparently left with an undesirable three-hour operational pause, during which the enemy could recover from the shock action already inflicted by the Allied offensive. After the war, *Hitlerjugend* commander SS-Colonel Kurt Meyer lambasted Simonds's approach because it 'transferred the initiative' from 'leading combat elements to timetable acrobats [back at] Headquarters'.[17] Irrespective of the perceptiveness (or not) of Meyer's verdict, this lull in the offensive's forward momentum no doubt helped contribute to the subsequent failure of TOTALIZE to translate its early promise into a decisive success.

In all probability, such a loss of offensive momentum was, however, unavoidable. First, at this late hour, Simonds could not have brought these complex air support arrangements forward in time. Nor was it easy simply to cancel them at this late stage. It would have taken Crerar's authority to do so, and even then it would have been an extremely controversial decision. After all, Crerar had lobbied the reluctant bomber barons long and hard to secure this support. It might also have proven impossible to recall all of the bombers then approaching the Normandy coast successfully: this left Simonds with little choice but to follow the original plan. But these arguments miss the point. At that time Simonds did not know what we now know: that the German second line was largely undefended. So there was no compelling reason to abandon his plan, even if waiting for the bombers meant a lull in forward momentum. Even cancelling the aerial strike might not have solved this loss of momentum, for that morning the armoured divisions were struggling forward through traffic congestion to their assembly points. A passage of lines is always a difficult task to accomplish, but given the troop densities in this area, this was an extremely difficult one.

Nor would scrapping the bombing run and continuing the initial break-in have solved the problem. Such a decision may have kept momentum going during the middle part of the day, but at some point the armoured echelon would have to pass through the spearhead break-in forces. This would merely have postponed the loss of momentum, not made it go away. Of course, if the passage of lines had been delayed to after the second break-in battle had been completed, say late on the 8 August, this lull in momentum may not have been so significant. On the other hand, the break-in forces were tired and disorganised after the night infiltration and an impromptu continuation of the assault, without properly arranged fire support, was probably asking too much of them. Some loss of forward momentum was therefore unavoidable. The key points to consider are: when would it occur, how long would it last, and what would be the consequences of it occurring?

The second break-in

During the late morning of 8 August, therefore, Simonds's break-in forces completed their missions or consolidated their recent gains. Meanwhile, the 1st Polish and 4th Canadian Armoured Divisions struggled forward to their assembly areas, ready to spearhead the offensive's second phase once the B-17s had unleashed their cargoes of destruction. Subsequently, between 1226 and 1355 hours, 497 B-17s successfully struck six targets, with the remaining bombers having to abort their runs. To prevent the risk of 'blue-on-blue' casualties, the Allies had established a 1.3km-wide safety area between their positions and the bombing zone. Despite these provisions, tragic friendly-fire incidents still occurred which left 315 Canadian and Polish troops killed or wounded. These accidents caused widespread confusion within the affected units, and sapped troop morale. The Polish division was particularly heavily hit, and the subsequent lack of dash evident that afternoon among some of its sub-units may in part be explained by the damage inflicted by these accidents.[18]

It was now that I-SS Panzer Corps – whose response to TOTALIZE had hitherto been lethargic – struck back with a vengeance. This local riposte contributed to the Allied failure to translate the early success gained in TOTALIZE into a decisive breakthrough. Shortly before noon, Kurt Meyer and SS-Major Hans Waldmüller were observing the battlefield from an observation point situated on the gentle rise northeast of Gaumesnil. Meyer now feared that the Allies, having sundered the first German position, would swiftly pass through massed armour, smash through the as yet largely unmanned German reserve line and race south to Falaise. Surveying the battlefield, the officers apparently observed the vanguard of two Allied armoured divisions ready to strike south – a sight that, according to Meyer, took their breath away![19]

Initially, Meyer could not fathom why this mass of armour had not commenced its attack south, but he knew that his forces had to stall the Allied attack before it developed forward momentum. Consequently, he ordered all *Hitlerjugend* units located nearby to launch an immediate counter-attack. These forces amounted to ten tank destroyers, 20 tanks, and 500 *panzer-grenadiers* from Battle Group Waldmüller, plus the four Tigers of SS-Captain Michael Wittmann's staff troop of the 2nd Company, SS Heavy Tank Battalion 101. Despite facing numerically superior forces, Meyer's audacious riposte might surprise the Allies and delay the impending Allied onslaught, thus buying precious time for other German reserves to man the second defensive line.[20]

Meyer then allegedly witnessed a solitary American bomber flying over his location several times, sending out coloured flares – a Pathfinder aircraft marking the aim points for an impending heavy bomber strike that was just minutes away! Now Meyer knew why the Allied armour had not commenced its assault south. If his forces remained in their present positions, they would soon be obliterated. Immediately after such a strike, Meyer calculated, the Allied armour would pour south, overrun his still dazed forces, swiftly shatter the second German defensive line, and charge south to Falaise. Meyer immediately ordered his forces to counter-attack north into the relative sanctuary of the 'safety area' that the Allies typically left between their own forces and the bombing zone.[21]

In fulfilment of these orders, Wittmann's Tigers rumbled forward in line ahead. Wittmann had anticipated enemy fire from the main road to the north-north-west, but this rendered the Tigers vulnerable to fire from the north-east. In this latter location, elements of the 1st Northants Yeomanry had – unbeknown to Wittmann – only recently secured the orchards south of St Aignan. At 1240 hours, a Yeomanry Sherman Firefly engaged the Tigers from the edge of the orchard, while simultaneously, Sherwood Forester and 144th RAC Fireflies engaged Wittmann's tanks from west of the main road and Hill 122, respectively. Ten minutes later, with the range shortened, a hail of standard Yeomanry Sherman fire fell upon Wittmann's Tiger. While these rounds failed to penetrate the tank's thick frontal armour, they caused the vehicle to veer out of control. At 1252 hours, additional hits caused Wittmann's tank to burst into flame, by which time his other three Tigers had also been knocked out. As befitted his legendary reputation, Wittmann had met a warrior's death attempting to stem the TOTALIZE offensive.[22]

Meanwhile, 20 tanks and 200 *panzergrenadiers* from Battle Group Waldmüller had struck north to capture the high ground south of St Aignan. By 1255 hours, the force had reached the hedge-lines around Daumesnil, which they used as cover to advance to the eastern end of the le Petit Ravin defile. The force then infiltrated south-west through the defile to engage the Yeomanry from the flank. Although Waldmüller's forces had accounted for 20 Shermans, by 1340 hours, intense Allied fire had forced them to retreat south in some disarray after losing six panzers. By 1400 hours, Waldmüller's forces were digging themselves in back at their original starting positions – just as the Allied armour rolled south.[23]

Even though Meyer's bold attempt to disrupt the Allied advance had been rebuffed, it seemed to him that it had stalled the Allied onslaught for a precious 90 minutes during which German forces could frantically dig in along their second defensive line. In reality, however, the Allied armoured attack was only due to commence at 1355 hours, well after the bombing had ended. Thus, Meyer's counter-strike had gained the Germans no additional time. Yet Meyer's riposte was far from being a futile and costly exercise. Rather, this display of audacity in the face of overwhelming odds sapped Allied offensive determination. It was this that helped make the afternoon of 8 August a fleeting battlefield opportunity that the Allies could not seize.

The Allied drive south that afternoon, moreover, was hampered by a number of problems. At 1355 hours, Simonds's corps commenced the second phase of TOTALIZE – the (second) break-in battle against the (second) German defensive position. The 1st Polish and 4th Canadian Armoured Divisions thrust south along axes located either side of the main Caen-Falaise road. In the western sector, as the Canadian division advanced, some of its units – including Halpenny Force – experienced communication problems. In some cases, these difficulties hindered them in calling down prearranged artillery support. At certain times, moreover, this fire support was less extensive than had been anticipated, as some artillery units had been disrupted by the recent 'friendly-fire' accidents.

The 4th Division, moreover, was a 'green' formation – it had not fought before in Normandy and had only recently joined Simonds's command. These circumstances no doubt reinforced the grave concerns that many of the division's armoured unit commanders had about the enemy's potent anti-tank capabilities. Most had heard about the costly encounters that other Normandy 'veterans' had experienced in recent weeks. Their recent witnessing of Meyer's daring riposte, moreover, only fuelled these fears. Consequently, 4th Division's unit commanders conducted their operations that afternoon in a cautious manner. When the advancing spearheads encountered various copses or hedges that might conceal German anti-tank or tank assets, for example, they paused until their unreliable communications had called down artillery to suppress these potential positions. South Alberta tank troop leader Lieutenant Gerry Adams, for instance, concluded that his regiment's inexperienced soldiers had mounted the attack on the lightly-defended locality of Cintheaux with excessive caution and an amateurish lack of coordination.[24]

The large number of troops operating in a modest battle space that contained few quality routes, moreover, created congestion that further slowed Allied offensive momentum. Now, another retarding factor on Allied progress emerged – problems with command and control. It is alleged, for example, that 4th Division commander George Kitching found the exhausted 4th Armoured Brigade commander, Brigadier Booth, asleep in his command tank. Simonds was by no means an experienced armoured commander, but he nevertheless believed that greater forward momentum ought to have been generated that afternoon. This perception led him to become increasingly irritated by the lack of progress. Soon, repeated exhortations were coming down the chain of command urging the spearhead units to get a move on – but to little avail. The frontline units failed to generate the momentum expected – whether appropriately or not – by the higher commander. At 1900 hours, for example, Booth ordered Halpenny Force to capture Bretteville-le-Rabet before daylight faded. But the battle group could only manage to form up by dusk; in these circumstances, Lieutenant-Colonel Halpenny decided a night attack was too risky. Postponing the mission until dawn, his tanks instead obeyed current doctrine by withdrawing back to harbour that night in Cintheaux.[25]

If these problems were not enough with which to contend, some advancing Canadian units encountered ad hoc enemy forces that nevertheless offered fierce resistance. These encounters helped restrict what little forward momentum the Allies had managed to generate. Between 1500 and 1900 hours, for example, one Canadian battle group did push 2.1km south to secure Cintheaux and the northern part of Haut Mesnil. Here, however, the intense resistance offered by the improvised Group Klein – formed from an SS *panzergrenadier* battalion's staff company and 89th Division stragglers –

stalled the Canadian advance. When some Shermans attempted to outflank Klein's position they suffered heavily when caught in the open by accurate 88mm fire. Meyer, sensibly, had moved his two 88mm-equipped flak batteries to near Potigny, where they dominated the Caen-Falaise road. As twilight fell, the Canadians had no choice other than to abandon the advance and consolidate their gains. By dusk, therefore, 4th Division had managed a maximum advance of just 3.8km.[26]

That same afternoon, similar problems dogged the advance undertaken by 1st Polish Division to the east of the main road. Like the 4th Division, the Polish formation had never fought as a division, and possessed no experience of either combat in Normandy or of working within Simonds's corps. From 1355 hours, two Polish armoured regiments probed their way south from St Aignan, only to stumble into an enemy killing zone. In just 15 minutes, German anti-tank fire left 40 wrecked Polish tanks burning furiously. This appalling introduction to the brutal realities of warfare in Normandy forced the Polish armour to withdraw back into the shelter of the nearby orchards. After two hours of reorganisation the Poles courageously resumed their thrust south. As the Polish armoured columns rumbled cautiously forward they passed the still-burning wrecks of their tanks destroyed in the earlier battle. The combination of this painful reminder of the enemy's potent capabilities and the serious damage done to morale, staff procedures and effective fire support by the earlier 'friendly-fire' accidents, accounts for the cautious manner in which the division executed its subsequent operations. Consequently, by dusk the Poles had only managed to advance a disappointing distance of 1.8km.[27]

Although the Poles could make a more convincing defence of their limited progress that afternoon than could the 4th Division, none of this special pleading cut much ice with their increasingly frustrated corps commander. Simonds had expected his armour to exploit the second bombing strike by swiftly breaking through the second German line and then race south to secure the hills north of Falaise by evening. Dogged periodically by problems of unreliable communications, unsatisfactory command and control and inadequate fire support, the cautious operations mounted by Simonds's inexperienced forces failed to overcome the numerically inferior forces deployed against them. The instances of fierce resistance offered by the latter, and their skilful exploitation of favourable defensive terrain, moreover, further retarded Allied offensive momentum. The combination of these factors ensured that Simonds's forces could not grasp the golden opportunity that existed during the afternoon of 8 August: to translate the significant success achieved in the initial break-in assault into a decisive breakthrough.

Turning point

At this point, the II Canadian Corps still might have resurrected the flagging prospects of the TOTALIZE offensive. However, over the next 18 hours the risks inherent in Simonds's attempts to restore offensive momentum ultimately led to the demise of the ill-fated offensive. At 2100 hours on 8 August, Simonds cast aside standard Allied doctrine by ordering his armour to continue their attacks relentlessly throughout the night. Halpenny Force was tasked with a 7.4km night advance to secure Bretteville-le-Rabet, while Worthington Force was to secure by dawn the vital Hill 195 north of Fontaine-le-Pin. From this latter location, the Allies could observe the western exits of Falaise, located 9.9km further south.[28]

At 0400 hours on 9 August, Worthington Force – formed from British Columbia Regiment tanks, two embussed Algonquin infantry companies and supporting arms – set off from Gaumesnil. The battle group headed down the Caen-Falaise road until at Haut Mesnil it encountered the stalled Halpenny Force. Worthington Force detoured south-east along an ancient raised grass track – the Chemin Haussé du Duc Guillaume – to avoid Halpenny's engagement. The task force intended subsequently to swing south-west to rejoin the main road and from there continue the advance to Hill 195 as planned. Unfortunately, during the next hour Worthington Force became lost and inadvertently continued south-east along the Chemin Haussé. Eventually, Worthington's disorientated soldiers sighted through the gloomy half-light some high ground in front of them. With much relief, the task force uncritically assumed that this must be their objective, Hill 195. Continuing along the Chemin Haussé, the battle group secured the high ground without a fight at 0655 hours, and then radioed back to 4th Brigade Headquarters that it had secured its objective. Sadly, by then the seeds of the disaster that was to engulf Worthington Force had already been sown. The high ground the task force had secured was not Hill 195, but rather the les Trentes Acres area, part of the Hill 140 ridge feature. Worthington Force was positioned west of the main road, a staggering 6.6km north-north-east of their objective, Hill 195! The fact that both the battle group and the Allied higher command wrongly believed the force to be on Hill 195 helped seal its fate.[29]

Unfortunately, SS officers located at the la Brèche observation point and at the divisional Headquarters (situated by the adjacent Tombeau de Marie Joly) had already detected the battle group as it approached les Trentes Acres.[30] Over the next 14 hours the 'lost' Worthington Force courageously repelled repeated SS armoured onslaughts. Sadly, during this time the task force lacked significant assistance from friendly forces: the Allies directed some of their relief efforts – including accurate artillery support – onto Hill 195. Consequently, the heroic defenders of les Trentes Acres could do no more than delay until evening their inevitable destruction at the hands of numerically superior SS forces. This ill-fated 18-hour odyssey represented the most heroic yet most tragic action of the entire TOTALIZE offensive. The Allied failure to locate Worthington Force, and then reinforce its success, allowed the offensive's most promising tactical advance to degenerate into disaster. This painful experience also reminded Simonds's forces of the terrible dangers they might face when mounting a daring advance that might leave the unit without adequate fire support.[31]

As this tragedy unfolded, the other advances that Simonds's forces mounted that day again demonstrated that the open terrain favoured the long-range killing power of German tank and anti-tank assets. During the afternoon of 9 August, for example, the Canadian Grenadier Guards struck south-east from Cauvicourt toward Hill 140 to locate and assist Worthington Force. At about 1615 hours, however, the regiment was caught in the open by accurate German fire, which speedily accounted for 26 Shermans. Disregarding such losses, Simonds viewed the progress secured that day by his forces as no more satisfactory than it had been the previous afternoon. By now, however, the chances of translating the initial success of TOTALIZE into a decisive breakthrough had dwindled substantially.[32]

During 10 August a disappointed Simonds attempted to kick-start his corps' flagging advance. At 1600 hours, 3rd Canadian Division and 2nd Canadian Armoured Brigade were to mount an improvised attack. Backed by substantial artillery support, they were to thrust south-east from Langannerie through Quesnay Wood, across the Laison River, to secure the high ground north of Falaise. The attackers fought their way into the wood, but after extremely bitter fighting that raged all night, the survivors had to withdraw. Simonds's hastily-arranged attempt to kick-start the stalled momentum of TOTALIZE had been a dismal failure. During the night of 10–11 August, therefore, the corps commander terminated his stalled offensive. Although TOTALIZE had secured major territorial gains – a 15km advance across a 13km frontage – it had not entirely realised Simonds's aim of seizing the high ground that dominated the road that ran through Falaise.[33]

Summation

The ultimate failure of TOTALIZE is surprising given the significant success achieved during the offensive's initial night break-in operation. This failure can be attributed to two periods of the subsequent operation: first, the transition from Phase One to Phase Two; and second, the manner in which Phase Two was conducted. With regard to the first period, Simonds has been criticised for allowing a loss of momentum during the morning of 8 August, when his forces had to sit patiently for three hours until the second bomber armada unleashed its cargo of destruction. Some loss of momentum, however, was inevitable that day during the period when Simonds's second echelon – his armoured divisions – passed through his spearhead break-in forces. The key issue was how far could the enemy recover during this brief respite.

The real reasons for the failure of TOTALIZE, however, can be traced to the way in which Simonds's forces conducted Phase Two of the offensive. In particular, during the afternoon of 8 August, they forces could not grasp the golden opportunity that existed to translate the significant success already achieved into a decisive breakthrough. Periodically hampered by unsatis-factory command and control, unreliable communications and restricted fire support, the cautious operations mounted by these inexperienced forces failed to overcome the numerically inferior forces deployed against them. The fierce improvised resistance offered by the latter in certain locations, and the enemy's skilful exploitation of favourable defensive terrain, further impeded the generation of Allied offensive momentum.

By dusk on 8 August, however, it was far from the case that TOTALIZE now stood no chance of realising the decisive potential Crerar had voiced on 5 August. True, the chances were much slimmer than they had been at noon that day, but it was the events of 9 August that doomed the offens-ive to failure. The risks inherent in mounting daring night-time armoured assaults came to haunt TOTALIZE that day. The Allied failure to know where Worthington Force was allowed the enemy's energetic responses to transform the most threatening tactical advance achieved during TOTALIZE into its greatest disaster. This setback reinforced the dangers inherent when Allied units daringly charged off into the enemy rear and rendered themselves lacking effective artillery support. The other actions mounted that day, 9 August, again demonstrated some of the problems that had haunted the operations of the previous day. With the failure of Simonds's last-gasp attempted to breathe life into the offensive on 10 August, it was all but over.

The fate of Worthington Force, moreover, sheds much light on the ambi-guities of Allied operational art that haunted the TOTALIZE offensive. For it was only through such audacity that Simonds's forces would overwhelm the improvised German defensive measures they encountered. It may well only have been possible for the Allies to translate the early tactical success of TOTALIZE into a decisive victory by embracing such a high-risk approach. Yet, this flew in the face of the instincts of many armoured unit commanders, who understandably feared the deadliness of enemy anti-tank capabilities. As TOTALIZE unfolded, indeed, some of these officers person-ally experienced the terrible price that the enemy could exact from Allied units that embraced such risk-taking. This remained the intractable paradox that dogged Allied offensives in Normandy.[34]

The tactically-justified cautious manner in which many Allied tactical actions were executed, however, had an obvious price. This approach restricted the generation of Allied offensive momentum, and consequently allowed the enemy valuable time during which they could recover the battle-field cohesion that the immediately preceding Allied actions had degraded. Perhaps unsurprisingly, Allied offensive technique in Normandy never fully surmounted the many tensions that arose as a result of the interplay of these various factors. Consequently, during the second phase of TOTALIZE, Simonds's forces could not translate the offensive's initial success into the significant breakthrough that, at various times, remained so tantalisingly close to being realised.

Notes

1 The latest analysis of TOTALIZE is Stephen A. Hart, *The Road to Falaise* (Battlezone Normandy series) (Stroud: Alan Sutton, 2004).
2 Other analyses include: Terry Copp, *Fields of Fire: The Canadians in Normandy* (Toronto: University of Toronto Press, 2003), pp. 187–204; John A. English, *The Canadian Army and the Normandy Campaign: a Study in the Failure of High Command* (London: Praeger, 1991), pp. 263–94; R.J. Jarymowycz, 'Canadian Armour in Normandy: Operation TOTALIZE and the Quest for Operational Maneuver', *Canadian Military History*, 7(2): 19–40, and *Tank Tactics* (London: Lynne Reinner, 2001), pp. 163–83; C.P. Stacey, *Official History of the Canadian Army in the Second World War, Vol. 3, The Victory Campaign* (Ottawa: The Queen's Printer, 1960), pp. 203–31.
3 For Simonds's career, see Dominick Graham, *The Price of Command: The Biography of Gen. Guy G. Simonds* (Toronto: Stoddart, 1993).
4 National Archives of Canada, Ottawa (henceforth NAC), Papers of General Crerar, Vol. 2 (CP/2), File 1-0-7/1, folios (fs) 2–3, Operation TOTALIZE: Appreciation by Simonds, 1 August 1944.
5 Ibid.
6 Ibid.
7 Ibid.
8 Major-General George Kitching, *Mud and Green Fields: The Memoirs of Major Gen. Kitching* (Langley, BC: Battleline, 1986), p. 207. See Lieutent-General O'Connor's earlier efforts, Liddell Hart Centre for Military Archives, London (LHCMA), O'Connor Papers, 1/5.
9 NAC, CP/2, 1-0-7/1, fs. 17–18, Remarks to Senior Officers, 5 August 1944.
10 NAC, CP/2, 1-0-7/1, f. 11, Notes of Telephone Conversation, 4 Aug 1944; Jarymowycz, 'Canadian Armour', pp. 19–20.
11 NAC, CP/2, 1-0-7/1, fs. 34–5, Memorandum, Simonds to Crerar, 2100 hours 6 August 1944.
12 See Stephen A. Hart, 'The Fanaticism of the 12th SS Panzer Division *Hitlerjugend* in Normandy', in Matthew Hughes and Gaynor Johnson, *Fanaticism in Modern Conflict* (London: Frank Cass, 2004).
13 The National Archives, Kew, London (TNA), WO179/2964, War Diary (WD) II Canadian Corps (2CC), August 1944, Operation Instruction 4, 5 August 1944.
14 TNA, WO171/640, WD 33rd Armoured Brigade; /859, WD 1st Northants Yeomanry (1NY); /878, WD 144th Regt RAC; /880, WD 148th Regt RAC; WO179/2859, WD 4th Canadian Infantry Brigade; /2964, WD Royal Regt of Canada; /2931, WD 1st Essex Scottish; /3010, WD Sherbrooke Fusiliers; J.B. Salmond, *The History of the 51st Highland Division* (Edinburgh: Blackwood & Sons, 1953), pp. 154–9.
15 TNA, WO171/674, WD 152nd Brigade; TNA, WO171/877, WD 141st RAC; WO171/1369, WD 2nd Seaforth Highlanders; WO179/2944, WD Les Fusiliers Mont Royal; Alastair Borthwick, *Battalion: A British Infantry Unit's actions from El Alamein to the Elbe, 1942–1945* (London: Bâton Wicks, 1994), pp. 142–4; Ken Tout, *The Bloody Battle for Tilly* (Stroud: Alan Sutton, 2000).
16 TNA, CAB106/1047, BAOR Battlefield Tour (BFT) TOTALIZE, pp. 21–2.
17 Meyer Interview, cited English, *Canadian*, p. 292, n. 9.
18 Hubert Meyer, *History of the 12SS-Panzerdivision 'Hitlerjugend'* (Winnipeg: J.J. Fedorowicz, 1994), p. 173.
19 Kurt Meyer, *Grenadiers* (Winnipeg: J.J. Fedorowicz, 1994), p. 259.
20 For Wittmann's career see E.G. Krätschmer, *Die Ritterkreuzträger der Waffen-SS* (Preußisch Oldendorf: Verlag K.W. Schütze, 1982), p. 622.
21 Meyer, *History*, p. 172.

22 TNA, WO171/859, WD 1NY; The Tank Museum, Bovington (TTM), R.F. Neville, *The 1st and 2nd Northamptonshire Yeomanry, 1939–46* (Brunswick: Johan Heinrich Meyer, 1946), pp. 22–36; John Abbott, '1st Northamptonshire Yeomanry, St Aignan', *Military Illustrated*, 69 (February 1994): pp. 12–18; Les Taylor, 'Wittmann's Last Battle', *After the Battle*, 85 (1995): pp. 46–53; Eric Lefevre, *Panzers in Normandy: Then and Now* (London: Battleline Books, 1984), pp. 181–3.

23 The Yeomanry's maps showed the defile as flat ground; see, for example, the maps in CAB106/1047, BAOR BFT TOTALIZE.

24 Donald E. Graves, *S. Albertas: A Canadian Regiment at War* (Toronto: Robin Brass, 1998), p. 113.

25 Kitching, *Mud*, p. 213.

26 TNA, WO179/2924, WD Argyll and Sutherland Highlanders; WO179/3012, WD South Albertas.

27 Jarymowycz, *Tank*, p. 172.

28 TNA, WO179/3011, WD British Columbia Regiment (BCR); /2923, WD Algonquin Regt (AR); /2900, 10th Cdn Infantry Brigade; English, *Canadian*, pp. 279–82; Graves, *Albertas*, p. 113; Meyer, *History*, pp. 177–9; Stacey, *Victory*, pp. 225–7.

29 NTA, WO179/2923, WD AR; /3011, WD BCR.

30 Trees obscured observation from these locations, except for the direction where Worthington Force was; Hart, *Falaise*, pp. 165–8.

31 The task force suffered 250 personnel casualties and lost 47 tanks; TNA, WO179/3011, WD BCR; Stacey, *Victory*, p. 228.

32 Meyer, *History*, p. 178.

33 Will R. Bird, *The North Shore (New Brunswick) Regiment* (Fredericton, NB: Brunswick Press, 1963), pp. 410–11; Stacey, *Victory*, pp. 230–1.

34 For Anglo-Canadian operational art in Normandy, see Stephen Hart, *Montgomery and 'Colossal Cracks': the 21st Army Group in Northwest Europe, 1944–45*, (Westport, CT: Praeger, 2000).

9 Dead cows and Tigers

Some aspects of the experience of the British soldier in Normandy, 1944

Gary Sheffield

> In my experience, the glory and thrill of battle were missing, to me the most important things in life were – When would I see my wife again? Where was my next meal coming from? What would it consist of? Would I have a dry and warm bed that night? Would I still be alive to see the next dawn? All of these things were of vital importance to me, and these, together with long periods of extreme boredom and others when I was scared out of my wits, made up my life.[1]

This comment, made by Gunner Jack Vivian, who fought with 185 Field Regiment Royal Artillery, encapsulates much of the British soldier's experience in the Normandy campaign. It was a period composed of tedium and fear, bereft of glamour. His mental horizons, restricted by the uncertainty of whether he would be alive or dead in a few hours, rarely lifted beyond the basics of life: the desire for food, shelter and a modicum of comfort. British soldiers were, to quote the Shakespearean title of a novel of the campaign written by a Normandy veteran, *Warriors for the Working Day*, not professional soldiers, and certainly shared little of the fanaticism of some of their opponents.[2] Nevertheless, their performance in a bloody, attritional operation was impressive. It was characterised by stoicism, determination and some skill. Above all, they, along with forces from the USA, Canada and other Allied nations, were ultimately victorious in a hard-fought campaign against a determined and skilful enemy.

This chapter examines a few aspects of the experience of the British soldier in Normandy. It is based on a work in progress, a full-scale 'bottom-up' study of the experience of the British soldier and regimental officer in the Second World War, provisionally entitled *Citizen Army*.

The British soldiers that fought in Normandy were members of an army that had already endured five years of war. A depressing series of defeats in 1940–2 reinforced a pre-existing cynicism – the initials BEF (for British Expeditionary Force) were reinterpreted as meaning 'Back Every Friday'. Montgomery's victory at Alamein had reversed the trend, although the subsequent conduct of the war in Italy by British generals scarcely engendered optimism. Cynicism was rife. The British army that was sent to Normandy was originally named the British Western European Force, and the acronym BWEF was interpreted as 'Burma When Europe Finished'. When the name changed to British Liberation Army, BLA was said to stand for 'Burma Looms Ahead'.[3] Many of the men of 1944 were children of the Depression, who had seen that their fathers and uncles had returned from the First World War to a land that was not, despite the promises of politicians, 'fit for heroes'. In the 1930s there had been a period of widespread, although shallowly rooted, pacifism. Many men carried a streak of anti-militarism – 'anti-Blimpism' might be a better term – into the army. Left-leaning and less deferential than their fathers' generation, they were apt to write to their MP, or the *Daily Mirror*, if they felt themselves ill-used. They were, after all, citizens of a democratic state at war.[4]

One should not push this line too far, however. The men of 1944 were drawn from a class-based society, in which many individuals were brought up to 'know their place'. The army was structured upon hierarchical lines instantly recognisable to products of that society. This could cause outrage among middle-class men who found themselves at the bottom of the military pile rather than in the officers' mess. One grammar school boy complained that at his training unit 'There was no apparent understanding . . . that it was a *citizens'* army they were dealing with'.[5] But for working-class men used to industrial and social discipline, the army provided more of the same. 'The wartime Army was *tough*' recalled a man who joined the Royal Welch Fusiliers in 1943. 'Few men were happy with their lot, especially upon being first called-up . . . None of this bothered me. I hadn't been accustomed to anything better and was, at least, being well-fed, with solid and regular meals, for the first time in my life'.[6]

It is possible to talk, in a general sense, of a collective British experience in Normandy. In their writings, many soldiers of all arms described the taste of Calvados; the heat of Normandy summer; cider apples; and Camembert cheese, once compared to the stench of dead cows, 'of which there were many'.[7] However, there are obvious differences between infantry, gunners and armour, between making an assault beach landing and fighting in *bocage*, and so on and so forth. Above all, an invisible wall separated the experience of the 'teeth arm' troops – infantry, armour and artillery – from the 44 per cent of British soldiers who served on the lines of communication, and indeed some other troops. The historian of a unit of medium and heavy artillery alluded to this when he commented that the hedgerows of the *bocage* provided excellent cover for gun positions but 'made for very difficult tank country . . . so were only a blessing to some branches of the service'.[8] In campaigns earlier in the war, the threat from the Luftwaffe had made logistic work a hazardous business.[9] The almost complete domination of the skies over Normandy by the Allied air forces transformed the situation. This is not to suggest that service in the Royal Army Service Corps (RASC) or Royal Army Ordnance Corps (RAOC) in Normandy was devoid of danger;

rather, that the substantial diminution of the air threat widened the gulf between the rear area and the frontline, especially the rifle companies.[10] These caveats notwithstanding, some valid generalisations can be drawn, at least about the armour and infantry.

The official historian rather optimistically called the British army in Normandy a force of 'seasoned soldiers', in the sense that all were well trained.[11] In reality, it was a mixture of green and veteran soldiers. While three divisions (50th, 51st and 7th Armoured) were brought back from the Mediterranean, not all members of these formations were combat veterans. Many British soldiers, however, saw their first action in Normandy after having undergone up to four years of training in the UK.

From Dunkirk to D-Day, the British army fought its major battles in alien terrain: desert, jungle, and Mediterranean scrub. Normandy was different. The countryside looked very familiar, very English. It is not surprising to find, for example, soldiers making comparisons with Box Hill, a beauty spot in Surrey and a popular excursion for south Londoners.[12] This perhaps helps to explain why soldiers found the Normandy countryside so disconcerting. Even more jarring was the phenomenon of the so-called 'empty battlefield'. An apparently peaceful area could conceal an enemy machine gun or tank – and the tank was likely to be described as a Tiger, whatever it was in reality. One experience must stand for many similar ones: 8th Rifle Brigade, the Motor Battalion of 11th Armoured Division, fought its first action at Hill 112 in late June:

> This operation combined the worst features of the fighting at this time . . . Most of the Riflemen were subjected to shelling and mortaring without ever seeing a German, and our tanks were picked off by an enemy whose better armament and skill in concealment gave him an advantage over our troops who were advancing across the open. The thick, wooded, leafy bocage country handicapped our Gunner observation posts as well as the armoured regiments . . .[13]

In Normandy, the terrain favoured the defender, and added to the quality of some of the German troops and Montgomery's strategy, which drew enemy forces on to the eastern flank, the inevitable consequence was attrition. When two British veterans of Normandy quoted Evelyn Waugh's aphorism 'All wars are infantry wars' in their study of the battle, they did so with good reason.[14] British infantry battalions in Normandy suffered a minimum of 100 casualties per month, but 175 per month were not uncommon – the figures for North Africa and Italy were about 70 per month.[15] The British style of warfighting in Normandy depended on massive firepower. One German soldier involved in the fighting for Hill 112 commented that the British used a volume of 'fire such as we Eastern Fronters had never known; the Russians had never as many guns as this'.[16] Eighteen per cent of British troops in Normandy were gunners, while infantry amounted to 14 per cent.[17]

Of the roughly 18,000 strong standard infantry division in Normandy, the 36 rifle companies totalled only some 4,500 soldiers. Yet 70 per cent of casualties were sustained by what Terry Copp has rightly called this 'tiny minority' in the rifle companies.[18] In comparison to the First World War, Britain had a gentle introduction to heavy battle casualties in the early years of Hitler's war. Only towards the end of 1942 did casualties in the armed forces exceed those of civilians. Normandy was a brutal reminder of how bloody modern industrialised warfare could be. Overall, the casualty rate for the Allied armies in Normandy was higher than for the British army (including the Royal Flying Corps) at Passchendaele in 1917.[19] More than half of the deaths in the British armed forces during the Second World War occurred in the final 18 months of the conflict. For the army, the proportion would have been even higher.[20]

The units that took the bulk of the casualties in Normandy were battalions of county infantry regiments. The county regimental system was an invention of the Victorians, who imposed order and a degree of logic on an existing system. Like another Victorian invention, the Dickensian Christmas, it soon became so familiar that it became difficult to remember a time when it had not existed. The variety of regimental badges on the headstones in war cemeteries in Normandy bear mute testimony to the fact that this campaign saw a late flowering of the system. In 1948, a process of amalgamation and disbandment began that has continued unabated to the present day. One incident is instructive. In 1943, the War Office ordered that regimental shoulder titles should be replaced by a standardised form. The Oxfordshire and Buckinghamshire Light Infantry was denied permission to use the wording 'Oxf & Bucks Lt Infty'. Instead, the War Office suggested 'two anathemas which made some vomit indignation'. The eventual compromise, which 'please[d] no one' was 'Oxf & Bucks'.[21] The criticism that it was ludicrous to expend energy on such trivialities would be hard to refute, were it not for the importance that British regiments attach to such things, and the formidable record of the regiment in developing cohesion and *esprit de corps*.

However, this was a regimental system under pressure. From 1942, soldiers were initially enlisted into the General Service Corps (GSC), before being assigned to the branch of the army that they were – in theory – best suited.[22] While this and other reforms to the selection of other ranks instigated by Sir Ronald Adam, the reforming adjutant-general, improved the efficiency of the army's use of manpower, this system was subjected to considerable criticism from officers who saw it as weakening the regimental system.[23] A survey of February 1945 showed that only just over half (53 per cent) of recruits 'were posted to the regiment to which they were most closely connected'.[24] Moreover, being assigned to anonymous general service was very different from being embraced by the regimental family, for such it was at least in theory. Some indication of attitudes can be gauged from the fact that officers commissioned into the General List, who wore the royal coat of arms as a cap-badge, as did members of the GSC, nicknamed themselves 'the Crosse and Blackwell Hussars', from the royal warrant displayed on jars of pickle.[25]

By 1944, the shortage of British infantry had become serious. 'Latest drafts of men . . . very good' reported the commander of British 1st Division in the Anzio beachhead in April 1944, '[but] Not enough of them and infantry bns still short. "No rifle coys – no nothing" – this simple truth has escaped emphasis the whole war'.[26] In reality, British higher commanders and the War Office were all too aware of the severe restrictions on Britain's infantry manpower budget. As Stephen Hart has demonstrated, Montgomery went into the Normandy campaign aware that he could not afford to be profligate with the lives of his infantrymen. His operational design was based on the linked concepts of 'casualty conservation' and maintaining morale. Hart has demonstrated that before the campaign the War Office underestimated the rate of infantry wastage in Normandy by about 17 per cent. This exacerbated the problem, but it did not create it.[27]

There was a particular shortage of infantry officers. A report from late 1944 on the Italian campaign stated that 'The platoon commander influences his command in a greater degree than a commander at any other level, and a platoon reflects the character of its commander to a remarkable degree'. Although NCOs could and did serve as platoon commanders, a commissioned officer was seen as being vastly preferable. Unfortunately, 'The supply of platoon cdrs does not meet the demand, and it is unusual for a battalion to go in to battle with twelve really good rifle platoon commanders'.[28] Expedients included transferring officers from other arms to the infantry, and seconding 623 infantry officers (and a further 50 ordnance officers) from the Canadian army. These 'Canloan' officers, wearing 'Canada' flashes on their battledress, proved an invaluable accretion to British strength, wining nearly 100 gallantry awards, and sustaining 75 per cent casualties.[29]

Increasingly, officers and men were posted to where they were needed, rather than to a battalion of their own regiment. Major Martin Lindsay of the Royal Scots Fusiliers, posted to Normandy in mid-July, was initially offered to the 9th Durham Light Infantry in 50th (Northumbrian) Division before being posted to 1st Gordon Highlanders in 51st (Highland) Division. Although he was proud to join such a distinguished formation, he noted in his diary that he would 'have to read up the history' of the regiment.[30] Replacements tended to be either youthful or 'old sweats' who had been wounded or somehow had been excluded from front line infantry service hitherto. Into the former category came the 'large number of young soldiers of nineteen years of age brought forward to replace the casualties of the past fortnight' in the 4th and 5th battalions of the Wiltshire Regiment (43rd (Wessex) Division) who attacked at Maltot on 19 July.[31] The latter included the 2nd Scots Guards, which while in training in the UK in June 1944 received 400 men from the RAF Regiment. The resulting clash of cultures took some time to resolve. The newly-reinforced battalion joined Guards Armoured Division in Belgium in early 1945.[32] Of course, it was not just the infantry that suffered from the manpower shortage. Lacking adequate rein-forcements, two experienced armoured units, 3rd and 4th County of London Yeomanry, were forced to amalgamate in Normandy on 29 July 1944.[33]

It is one thing to recite facts and figures, quite another assess the impact of attrition on units, formations and individuals. Units did not have to attack to suffer heavy casualties. In the understated but revealing words of the Black Watch's historian, 'The entire period in the Bois de Bavent . . . was most trying. There was little to be done but sit and endure the shelling and mortaring, and to seek to keep up morale in these most difficult of all conditions'.[34] Private Richard Harris landed on D-Day as an 18-year-old in 1st Suffolks, a green soldier in a largely green battalion. His platoon was 33 strong. By 29 June there were just six originals left. He was wounded on 18 August, along with the other remaining original – 'so our casualty rate in Normandy was 100 per cent'.[35]

As Lord Moran suggested in 1945, soldiers cannot go on indefinitely in battle: like clothes, they wear out. A Royal Army Medical Corps report from the end of June 1944 noted that 'battle exhaustion' was running at about 15 per cent of all casualties, and much of it was 'exhaustion in the everyday sense of the word'.[36] An officer of 4/7 Dragoon Guards recorded that simply being in a tank for days on end was exhausting, and the oppor-tunity of sleeping outside, on hay, for nine hours was 'pure nectar'.[37] For some, it went much further than mere tiredness, however extreme. A tank gunner of the Sherwood Rangers refused to emerge from his tank.[38] A sig-naller of 43rd (Wessex) Division was found hiding under a scout car, crying and trembling uncontrollably. The latter had been subjected to mortaring and artillery fire for seven weeks.[39]

The length of time in action was important. While psychiatric casualties in June were manageable, the duration as well as the intensity of the fighting led to men becoming 'bomb happy': a euphemism for becoming a psychiat-ric casualty. As Copp and McAndrew have argued, there was a 'battle exhaustion crisis' in 21st Army Group in July 1944. About a quarter of the infantry casualties were due to this cause – in 3rd Division, a green forma-tion that had shown plenty of enthusiasm for fighting in the initial stages of the campaign, the figure was one in three.[40] As we have seen, a dispropor-tionate number of casualties fell on a small part of the army, the infantry rifle companies, which amounted to less than a quarter of divisional strength. The 15th (Scottish) Division suffered 18 per cent casualties during Opera-tion EPSOM, in late June, but 80 per cent of the losses were borne by rifle companies. As one veteran commented, 'Regimental esprit [*sic*], the mutual trust of men in the fighting platoons, carefully built up in years of training, would have a struggle to survive'.[41]

Two interesting examples demonstrate low-level institutional responses to heavy losses. The casualties sustained by 53rd (Welsh) Division in July led to a readjustment of the divisional order of battle. Two of the three battal-ions of the Royal Welch Fusiliers in 158 Brigade were exchanged for other units, and likewise the two Welch Regiment battalions in 160 Brigade were split up, because, as the divisional historian explained, 'Difficulties were experienced in providing reinforcements in the event of heavy casualties. This was particularly so with Officer reinforcements . . . By this means it was likely that a more even spread of casualties among regiments would result in the event of any part of the Division suffering severe losses'.[42]

By the end of the fighting at Rauray on 1 July, the 1st Tyneside Scottish had lost roughly 50 per cent of personnel that had arrived in Normandy only three weeks earlier. On 2 July the battalion received as replacements 200 South Wales Borderers and 100 men from the Herefordshires. The battalion was restructured to minimise the disruption to sub-unit cohesion. The remaining Tyneside Scots were formed into B and C Companies, while the newcomers formed A and D Companies.[43]

Against this backdrop it is not surprising that 'morale [which] pertains to [the individual's] efforts to enhance the effectiveness of the group in accomplishing the task in hand'[44] has sometimes been identified as being low. Certainly, cynicism was rife:

> When one's battalion has a period of rest in war[,] delight in washing and sleeping, in drinking, perhaps, Calvados, and in buying eggs and butter, is tempered by the realization that this respite does not spring from the altruistic motives of the Higher Command, but that you are simply being fattened up, like pheasants in pre-war Septembers, for a particularly important occasion.[45]

These words, from the history of the Rifle Brigade, would have been echoed by many other soldiers. When 1st Black Watch (51st (Highland) Division) received news that the battalion was going into action it was greeted with a shout of 'Monty, you bastard! Give us a bloody break!' – although Private Stan Whitehouse, who told this story, noted that Montgomery was 'generally popular' with the rank and file. However it is one thing to grumble and carry out orders, quite another to refuse to do so; and grumbling can be a valuable safety valve. Whitehouse told another story, indicating that he was aware that other units had undergone worse experiences. 1st Black Watch received reinforcements from the Tyneside Scottish in October 1944. Whitehouse recalled that the Tynesiders were 'Bitter and angry towards the hierarchy, maintaining that they had been used needlessly as cannon fodder in Normandy' and wondered whether this unit had been deliberately split up, its morale and cohesion broken beyond repair.[46]

As Marcus Cunliffe, who served in an armoured regiment, noted frankly, to the ordinary soldier in the second half of June and July, it appeared as if their efforts were achieving little. Despite the hopes invested in Operation GOODWOOD, 'progress seemed to be as difficult as ever . . . Whether in the "bocage" or in the open, rolling countryside south of Caen, the Germans, if not masters of the situation, at any rate appeared to adapt themselves to it only too well'. However, Cunliffe went on to argue that what the troops on the ground could not know, any more than the purveyors of 'armchair criticisms' from home, was how well Montgomery's attritional strategy was working, and he traced the growing optimism when, after Operation COBRA, it became clear that the Allies were indeed winning.[47] Cunliffe's perspective, as a Normandy veteran who served in Operations EPSOM and TOTALIZE, and who went on to become a distinguished historian, is one that demands respect.

The constituents of morale, and the relationship between morale, combat effectiveness and psychiatric casualties is a complex topic. Fear was ever present, but that should not necessarily be confused with low morale or poor combat cohesion, and most soldiers mastered fear to a greater or lesser degree. The ultimate test of morale is the willingness to engage in combat,[48] and judged by this criterion, British morale in Normandy was good enough. In the actual conduct of battles, British troops demonstrated much the same stoicism and endurance as on the Somme in 1916 – a battle that Normandy resembled in many ways.

The morale of units of individuals depended on a vast number of variables. The age of the soldier could influence attitudes. Ray Bottrill of 1 Coldstream Guards (Guards Armoured Division), who fought in Normandy as a 19-year-old, recalled it as 'a great adventure'. Older men with families thought somewhat differently.[49] Just before leaving England to join 1st Gordon Highlanders, Major Martin Lindsay wrote a letter, the sentiments of which were echoed in those written by hundreds of thousands of other soldiers: 'Darling wife . . . if I do not return I want you please to remember that the boys . . .'[50]

Members of armoured units had a particular challenge to their morale, when it became painfully clear that some enemy tanks (although not all) were superior to their Shermans and Cromwells. Allied tanks were particularly vulnerable to the German 88mm anti-tank gun. The Panzer VI 'Tiger' was particularly feared, with the less effective Panzer IV frequently being misidentified as its fearsome cousin. Montgomery, ever conscious of the importance of morale, was evidently perturbed, writing when the campaign was three weeks old to Brooke: 'I have had to stamp very heavily on reports that began to be circulated about the inadequate quality of our tanks, equipment etc., as compared with the Germans'. Montgomery blamed reports written by a staff officer: 'he is a very unbalanced officer and his views are of no value. Furthermore his experience is confined to the "bocage" country – which is not tank country – it is infantry country . . . If our armour is used properly we have nothing to fear from enemy tanks; in close country we have had cases of infantry "doing in" the Panther with a Piat mortar (sic)'.[51] Montgomery might have suppressed official criticism, but he could not remove the feelings of many that their equipment was inferior to that of the enemy, especially – and this is a point often forgotten – given that the Germans were able to use defensive tactics 'so that', a Sherman commander of the Sherwood Rangers wrote, 'their lack of mobility counted for less. Once the pursuit began, however, the Sherman's greater speed and endurance came into its own and our tanks overwhelmed the German defences in a mobile battle'.[52]

For the tank crew, death could be particularly random. A tank of the Fife and Forfar Yeomanry was hit during Operation EPSOM. Two crewmen escaped, but the tank commander and gunner did not. The men who crewed the armoured cars of the 11th Hussars, used for reconnaissance, soon came to terms with 'one grim fact . . . that . . . their first contact with the enemy was most likely to come from an armour-piercing shell fired point-blank at the leading car'. The crew realised 'full well their chance of survival . . . rested on the aim of the first German gun or tank they might encounter'. 'Providentially', wrote the historian of the 11th Hussars, 'soldiers are not given to dwelling too much on the fate which they may meet in war'. This is perhaps as good an explanation of the survival of morale under severe stress as one is likely to find.[53]

The morale of an individual was subject to fluctuations as circumstances changed. The diary of Private N. Bretherton, a member of a glider-borne air landing battalion, 2nd Oxfordshire and Buckinghamshire Light Infantry (or the 52nd, as they referred to themselves) is an interesting case study. He was a member of 6th Airborne Division, a self-consciously elite formation. On 15 June he implicitly contrasted low German morale with the high morale in this division. On 22 June he is wondering when the division will be relieved. By 3 July, after a spell of trench-digging as 'Glorified Pioneers', in the rain and being attacked by mosquitoes, his diary recorded that 'Everybody [was] fed up to the teeth'. Apart from the unpleasant conditions, Bretherton's main complaint was that his battalion and division, trained as a *coup de main* formation, found itself holding the line as standard infantry (moreover, without the equipment of a standard division). He laid stress on the unfairness of 'crack troops [b]eing used like children'.[54] This sense of fair and unfair play was not just a public school trait: it went to the very heart of the paternal/deferential relationship between the leader and the led.

In the battle conditions of Normandy, the role of the leader – both NCO and officer – was vitally important. This naturally placed a huge burden on the leader. Nineteen-year-old Lieutenant Michael Bendix of 5th Coldstream Guards recalled 'the dread of showing fear and not doing your best for your Platoon'.[55] Many led in a literal sense. Private Harris of 1st Suffolks wrote of the vicious battle at Chateau de la Londe on 28 June. Following a creeping barrage, the line of infantry was thinned by German fire but 'the Major was still in front, bellowing words of encouragement to those remaining, a leader of men if there ever was one; I followed like a dog at his master's heel'.[56]

In war, the leader's role is Janus-faced: to exercise paternal care for his men; but also to ensure that they risk their lives by fighting. These two roles are in direct conflict with each other, and it is a tribute to the effectiveness of leadership in Normandy that there were relatively few combat refusals or breakdowns in unit cohesion. The importance of good leadership to defy logic and human instinct and go forward into battle is captured by these two quotations, one from the infantry, one from the Royal Armoured Corps (RAC). Private Ron Ludgater (1st Manchesters, 53rd (Welsh) Division), wrote:

> [W]e always seemed to be moving on our own; it was a small platoon world. On some days nothing happened and on others you dug like mad with mortar bombs dropping all around and steel splinters everywhere. The worst thing of all was not being kept in the picture, not being told of the state of things and the reason for failed attacks.[57]

Trooper Steve Dyson, 107 Regiment RAC (King's Own) recalled:

> [A]n individual's part in a battle seems infinitesimally insignificant . . . The private or trooper doesn't know much about the part he is playing . . . in the wider context of the battle. He just does what he is ordered, and that's it . . . I recall the tank commanders returning from briefings and synchronising watches. They would briefly tell the crew that we were going to attack a certain target; we would mount up; and, in liaison with the infantry, fight our way to the objective.

Dyson got to the heart of the matter when he went on to say that 'it is the amount of sacrifice, tenacity and courage the individual can display under great pressure, welded together hundreds of times in a unit, that determines defeat or victory on the battlefield'.[58]

The officers and NCOs did the welding; but an important part of building and maintaining operational effectiveness lay in individuals becoming 'battlewise'. Jack Vivian wrote of learning 'an instinct for survival . . . it was a reflex action when moving about to automatically register in your mind the nearest slit trench . . . this reflex was linked with an automatic listening for shells coming inward', while by the afternoon of D-Day, an subaltern of 45 Royal Marine Commando had come to realise 'the value of digging', having realised the truth of the military aphorism that all a soldier needed in a battle was 'a bloody good rifle and a bloody good shovel'.[59]

The British army contributed mightily to the Allied victory in Normandy. As Stephen Hart has demonstrated, Montgomery's operational methods played to British strengths and minimised weaknesses, delivering success at a manageable cost in casualties and with morale intact. It was a citizen army that achieved this victory. Most soldiers would never have joined the army had it not been for the war. Some were deeply cynical. Most treated the war simply as a job that had to be done before they could go home to their families and jobs. This was not an army of crusaders or fanatics. In the land of dead cows and Tigers, under conditions of extreme fear and appalling stress, they did their job well.

Marcus Cunliffe's comments about the Royal Warwickshires, although occasionally exaggerated, can be applied to the experience of the entire British Liberation Army:

> In comparison with their comrades of earlier wars, the men [who fought in Normandy] had many advantages. They were well fed and equipped; medical services were excellent; they were never thrown away in ill-conceived battles, but benefited from thorough and expert generalship. Even so, they faced a very capable enemy; they were required to attack often and usually by night; by day they remained in close contact. The physical and mental ordeal of a week of such activity was prodigious . . . in courage, stamina and battlecraft the British soldier could challenge any in the world. Months and years of training and preparation at every level had preceded the Normandy landings. The campaign that ensued proved how profitably the time had been spent. Like those in other units, the officers and men of The Regiment emerged from Normandy as veterans deservedly victorious and anxious to clinch the matter.[60]

Acknowledgement

I would like to thank the following for permission to make use of material for which they hold the copyright: the Trustees of Oxfordshire and Buckinghamshire Light Infantry Museum; the Trustees of the Liddell Hart Centre for Military Archives; Mr M. Bendix; Mr B. Evans; the National Archives. I would also like to thank Mrs Pam Cooper for her assistance with research.

Notes

1 Jack Vivian, unpublished memoir, p. 1. Oxfordshire and Buckinghamshire Light Infantry Museum, Slade barracks, Oxford.
2 Peter Elstob, *Warriors for the Working Day* (London: Corgi, 1974 edn).
3 Martin Lindsay, *So Few Got Through* (London: Collins, 1946), p. 16.
4 G.D. Sheffield, 'The Shadow of the Somme: The Influence of the First World War on British Soldiers' Perceptions and Behaviour in the Second World War', in Paul Addison and Angus Calder (eds) *Time to Kill: The Soldier's Experience of War in the West 1939–1945* (London: Pimlico, 1997), pp. 29–39.
5 Norman Smith, *Tank Soldier* (Lewes: Book Guild, 1989), p. 26.
6 D. Evans, unpublished account, p. 9, Imperial War Museum, Department of Documents (hereafter IWM Docs) 92/37/1.
7 L. Chrimes, *Five Agra: The story of the 5th Army Group Royal Artillery* (Dannenburg: privately published, 1945), p. 74.
8 *Ibid.*, p. 73.
9 For the problems of operating in conditions of enemy air supremacy in Greece and Crete 1941, see (no editor given) *The Story of the Royal Army Service Corps* (London: Bell & Sons, 1955), pp. 164, 166, 168.
10 It should not be forgotten that the term 'logistic troops' covers a wide variety of service. 6th Airborne Division's 90-strong light company RASC landed by air on D-Day and suffered 36 casualties. *Ibid.*, p. 394.

11 L.F. Ellis, *Victory in the West, Vol. I The Battle of Normandy* (London: HMSO, 1962), p. 132.

12 E.g., Stuart Hills, *By Tank into Normandy* (London: Cassell, 2002), p. 137.

13 R.H.W.S. Hastings, *The Rifle Brigade in the Second World War, 1939–1945* (Aldershot: Gale & Polden, 1950), p. 358.

14 Eversley Belfield and Hubert Essame, *The Battle for Normandy* (London: Pan, 1967 edn), p. 182.

15 Jeffrey Williams, *The Long Left Flank* (London: Stoddart, 1988), p. 318.

16 J.J. How, *Hill 112* (London: William Kimber, 1984), p. 185.

17 Ellis, *Victory in the West*, I, p. 536.

18 Terry Copp, ' "If this war isn't over, And pretty damn soon, There'll be nobody left, In this old platoon": First Canadian Army, February–March 1945' in Addison and Calder, *Time to Kill*: pp. 148–9.

19 Williams, *Long Left Flank*, pp. 318–20; Julian Thompson, *The Imperial War Museum Book of Victory in Europe* (London: Sidgewick & Jackson, 1994), p. 138.

20 Malcolm Smith, *Britain in 1940* (London: Routledge, 2000), p. 70; Adrian Gregory, *The Silence of Memory* (Oxford: Berg, 1994), p. 213. I am grateful to Dr Gregory for his guidance on this matter.

21 J.E.H. Neville (ed.) *The Oxfordshire and Buckinghamshire Light Infantry War Chronicle, Vol. IV, 1944–1945* (Aldershot: Gale & Polden, 1954), p. 468.

22 'Notes for S. of S. Estimates Speech – Feb 1943. A.G.'s Dept', Sir Ronald Adam papers, ADAM 3/3, Liddell Hart Centre for Military Archives (hereafter LHCMA), King's College London.

23 Jeremy A. Crang, *The British army and the People's War 1939–1945* (Manchester: Manchester University Press, 2000), pp. 11–17.

24 *Ibid.*, p. 17.

25 Denis Healey, *The Time of My Life* (London: Michael Joseph, 1989), p. 51.

26 'Notes by Comd 1 Div', 21 Apr 44, PENNEY 8/33, W.R.C. Penney papers, LHCMA. 'Bn' and 'Coy' were standard abbreviations of 'Battalion' and 'Company'.

27 Stephen Hart, *Montgomery and 'Colossal Cracks': The 21st Army Group in North-west Europe, 1944–45* (Westport, CT: Praeger, 2000), pp. 50–61.

28 'Lessons from the Italian Campaign' (Dec. 1944), pp. 77–8. WO 231/8, The National Archives/Public Record Office (hereafter TNA/PRO).

29 Wilfred I. Smith, *Codeword CANLOAN* (Toronto: Dundurn, 1992), p. xi.

30 Lindsay, *So Few Got Through*, pp. 9, 13, 16.

31 H. Essame, *The 43rd Wessex Division at War 1944–1945* (London: William Clowes, 1952), pp. 47–8.

32 W.A. Elliott, *Esprit de Corps* (Norwich: Michael Russell, 1997), pp. 104–6.

33 G.L. Verney, *The Desert Rats: the History of the 7th Armoured Division* (London: Hutchinson, 1954), p. 210.

34 Bernard Fergusson, *The Black Watch and the King's Enemies* (London: Collins, 1950), p. 270.

35 R. Neillands, *The Battle of Normandy 1944* (London: Cassell, 2003 edn), pp. 49, 193, 389.

36 'Note on surgery . . .' Appx D, WO 222/176, TNA/PRO.

37 John Stirling, *D-Day to VE-Day from my Tank Turret* (privately published, nd), p. 25.

38 Hills, *By Tank*, p. 130.

39 Stan Procter, *A Quiet Little Boy Goes to War* (Tadworth: Dillons, 1997), p. 72.

40 Terry Copp and Bill McAndrew, *Battle Exhaustion: Soldiers and Psychiatrists in the Canadian Army, 1939–1945* (Montreal: McGill-Queen's University Press, 1990), pp. 114–15.

41 How, *Hill 112*, pp. 125, 140.
42 C.N. Barclay, *The History of the 53rd (Welsh) Division in the Second World War* (London: Willian Clowes, 1956), pp. 66–7.
43 Kevin Baverstock, *Breaking the Panzers: The Bloody Battle for Rauray, Normandy, 1 July 1944* (Stroud: Sutton, 2002), p. 162.
44 Definition by Irvin L. Child, quoted by G.D. Sheffield, *Leadership in the Trenches* (London: Macmillan, 2000), p. 180.
45 Hastings, *Rifle Brigade*, p. 359.
46 S. Whitehouse and G.B. Bennett, *Fear is the Foe* (London: Robert Hale, 1995), pp. 87–8. Conversely, another ex-Tyneside Scot, Private L. Baverstock, although sad at the break-up of his battalion, was proud to serve with 1st Black Watch. E-mail, K. Baverstock to author, 6 July 2004.
47 Marcus Cunliffe, *History of the Royal Warwickshire Regiment 1919–1955* (London: William Clowes, 1956), pp, 105, 118, 20. I am grateful to Professor Brian Holden Reid for details of Cunliffe's military career; see also the introduction to Brian Holden Reid and John White (eds) *American Studies: Essays in Honour of Marcus Cunliffe* (Basingstoke: Macmillan, 1991), pp. 3–5.
48 For a dissenting view, see Gerard Oram, *Military Executions during World War I* (Basingstoke: Macmillan, 2003).
49 Interview with author, 20 July 2004.
50 Lindsay, *So Few Got Through*, p. 8.
51 Montgomery to Brooke, 27 June 1944, Alanbrooke 6/2/25, Alanbrooke papers, LHCMA.
52 Hills, *By Tank*, pp. 96–7.
53 Dudley Clarke, *The Eleventh at War* (London: Michael Joseph, 1952), pp. 342–3.
54 Private N. Bretherton, diary, Oxfordshire and Buckinghamshire Light Infantry Museum, Slade Barracks, Oxford.
55 Michael Bendix, unpublished memoir, p. 27, 98/3/1, IWM Docs.
56 Neillands, *Battle of Normandy*, p. 192.
57 *Ibid.*, p. 377.
58 Stephen Dyson, *Tank Twins* (London: Leo Cooper, 1994), p. 51.
59 Vivian, unpublished memoir, p. 36; Bryan Samain, *Commando Men* (London: Greenhill, 1988 edn), p. 11.
60 Cunliffe, *Royal Warwickshires*, p. 121.

10 The Luftwaffe in Normandy

James S. Corum

The air side of the Normandy campaign can be easily summarised as: Allies, – 1, Germans – 0. Given the enormous disparity of the respective air forces in mid-1944 the outcome of the air campaign was never in doubt. However, although the German side of the Normandy air battle is usually ignored in all the major histories of the war it was still one of the decisive moments of the air war. Just as the Normandy battles ruthlessly attritted the German army on the ground, the air campaign saw the destruction of the last fighter and bomber reserves of the Luftwaffe. After Normandy the Luftwaffe was a broken force, able to carry out nuisance raids over the front and occasionally able to inflict serious damage on Allied bomber units, but it was no longer a force that could achieve operational results.

If any single campaign of the war can be termed 'decisive', the Normandy campaign is it. In the first half of 1944 the German high command held out the hope that somehow the Eastern Front could be stabilised and the relentless Russian advance halted. But if the Allies managed to land and establish a second front in the West then the strategic position became hopeless for Germany. Already hard-pressed in Russia, the Mediterranean and by the Allied bombing offensive, the Germans simply did not have the manpower or resources to successfully hold on if Allied army groups began advancing in the West. Unlike Italy, where the army and the Luftwaffe had the option of retreating and fighting again from better defensive positions with only a slight weakening of their strategic position, in France the only realistic option was to defeat any Allied landing attempt quickly and decisively.

The Wehrmacht High Command in the spring of 1944 was well aware of the weakness of the Luftwaffe in comparison to the Allied air forces and little was expected of *Luftflotte* 3 (Air Fleet 3). The *Oberkommando der Wehrmacht* placed its trust in the fighting ability of the German soldier and was still confident that the army could hold and repel the Anglo-American invasion.[1] Still, almost as a matter of pride, the Luftwaffe planned to carry out a maximum effort against the expected Allied landings with the understanding that even if it could not sink the Allied fleets, even a moderate rate of attrition of the Allied shipping or disruption of Allied port operations would work to the benefit of the hard-pressed ground forces.

In Italy the Luftwaffe had inflicted relatively light damage to Allied shipping.[2] When the battle of the Channel coast began, the Luftwaffe would have to do much better.

The Luftwaffe's forces in the West in the spring of 1944

Luftflotte 3, under the highly experienced Field Marshal Hugo Sperrle, commanded all the Luftwaffe forces in France and the Low Countries in 1944. On paper, it was an impressive organisation. As of 6 June 1944, the Third Air Fleet had 384,579 troops under its command, including 16,109 Luftwaffe *Helferinnen* (uniformed women assigned to the Luftwaffe); 45,331 German and foreign workers; 24,019 labourers of the Reichs Work Service; and 323,139 officers and men of the regular Luftwaffe.[3] The air commands of *Luftflotte* 3 consisted of: X Air Corps, a force of heavy bombers and specialist naval attack aircraft; IX Air Corps, a force of conventional bombers (mostly JU 88s); II Fighter Corps, headquarters for the fighter wings stationed in Belgium and France; and II Air Corps, organised as a command headquarters for fighter-bomber and ground attack aircraft. The largest command was III Flak Corps with tens of thousands of personnel manning radar and flak positions in the Low Countries and France.

In reality, the air units of the Luftwaffe were hopelessly inadequate for the task. At the beginning of June in 1944, II Fighter Corps was down to a mere six fighter groups, with 160 operational Me 109 and F-W 190 fighter planes. *Luftflotte* 3 had had only 272 bombers of all types including the virtually unusable He 177 heavy bombers, Dornier 217s, F-W 200 long-range bombers and 136 Ju 88 torpedo bombers of X Air Corps and 144 Ju 88/Ju 188 aircraft of IX Air Corps. II Air Corps had four groups of twin engine Ju 88 fighters and F-W 190 fighters, for a total of 67 aircraft, plus one tactical reconnaissance group of 42 Me 109s. Of a total 693 aircraft, the serviceability rates were low, normally no more than 60 per cent of aircraft operational (in contrast to the 70–80 per cent operational rates of the RAF and AAF) so that when the Allies landed in Normandy *Luftflotte* 3 would have no more than 500 operational aircraft to oppose over 7,000 Allied aircraft supporting the invasion.[4]

The Luftwaffe's air forces on the Western Front were in a state of rapid decline by the spring of 1944. Air superiority over Germany had been lost in February and March, during the massive Allied bombing offensives against Germany. Several books describe in detail how the Luftwaffe lost the command of the air in early 1944.[5] The Allied bomber offensive, now supported by long-range escort fighters, quickly decimated the ranks of German pilots. From February 1944 on, the Luftwaffe lost more trained pilots than it could replace. In March, losses reached 22 per cent of Reich Air Defence pilots. In April, losses were 38 per cent of Reich Air Defence pilots and 24 per cent of *Luftflotte* 3 pilots. In April 1944 the Luftwaffe lost 489 fighter pilots, but trained only 396.[6] The replacement pilots were barely trained in comparison with the airmen of 1940–2. Until September 1942, all Luftwaffe fighter and bomber pilots received a thorough flight training and a course in the latest aircraft models before being sent into combat.[7] In 1942 shortages of fuel and instructors forced the Luftwaffe High Command to shorten aircrew training courses and in 1944 Luftwaffe fighter pilots went into action with little more than 130 hours total flight time and usually no more than 25 hours in operational aircraft. In contrast, the US fighter pilots entered combat during this same period with well over 400 hours of flying time, including over 100 hours in operational aircraft.[8] Since the beginning of 1944, II Fighter Corps had been taking a consistent battering while opposing the Allied bomber offensive and for several months it was unable to replace trained airmen lost in combat.

The combat effectiveness of the German flak force was another story. As the air units of the Luftwaffe declined, the flak force had become increasingly larger. The Germans used their mobile flak units as multi-purpose weapons and the mobile 88mm flak guns in particular had been designed to engage enemy tanks as well as aeroplanes. On the Russian front, the Luftwaffe flak corps and divisions had racked up an impressive tally of Soviet tanks, in many cases Luftwaffe flak regiments destroying more Russian tanks than planes. Through the Normandy campaign, the flak would not only be the most effective weapon against the Allied air forces, it would play a major role in the ground battles.

In preparation for the anticipated invasion of the Channel coast, the Luftwaffe created III Flak Corp in February 1944. It was designed as a mobile force to be rushed to the most threatened part of the front and deployed over 3,500 light (20mm and 37mm) and medium (88mm) flak guns.[9] The 88mm medium flak guns as well as the rapid firing 20 and 37mm light flak guns, many of them in multiple mounts, were among the most effective anti-aircraft weapons of World War II. By the time the Allies landed, Flak Corps III was carefully dispersed in reserve positions near the coast and ready for immediate deployment.[10] The commander of III Flak Corps was General der Flakartillerie Wolfgang Pickert. As commander of the 9th Flak Division on the Russian Front in 1942–3 Pickert had established an outstanding combat record. He insisted that his force be trained for mobile field operation and be proficient in destroying tanks as well as planes. In the weeks before the Allied landing, he put his flak regiments, which had gone a bit soft on occupation duty in France, through a series of exercises to bring up their tactical skills to the level of the flak forces in Russia.[11]

In addition to the flak guns of Flak Corps III, each army and SS division had its own flak battalion and sometimes additional flak batteries were attached. The number of flak guns assigned to an army division ranged from 12 guns for an infantry division to 74 light and heavy flak guns in a Panzer Grenadier division.[12] German naval units were stationed in all of the French and Low Country ports and the *Kriegsmarine* had its own flak force. By 1944, the German navy had 88 flak battalions with four to six batteries per battalion (and usually four guns to a battery). In addition to all this, many of the static coastal defence divisions had been equipped with a wide array of extra weaponry, including numerous captured anti-aircraft guns taken from the French in 1940. An exact accounting is difficult, but one can reasonably estimate that all the branches of the Wehrmacht had 7,000–8,000 flak guns in France and southern Belgium by mid-1944.[13]

Anticipating the invasion: the strategy in early 1944

With an Allied invasion threatening, the Luftwaffe considered several strategies to deal with it. Since the Luftwaffe had little realistic chance of regaining air superiority over France, operational thinking had to be geared to the best means of hampering Allied efforts and attriting Allied forces, especially Allied shipping. In 1943, Field Marshal Sperrle proposed that the Luftwaffe build up its last reserves of bombers and retrain and re-equip them as an anti-shipping strike force. He urged that the Luftwaffe increase the effort to conduct anti-shipping strikes and long-range reconnaissance over the Atlantic. In this he was strongly supported by the German navy, as this strategy could assist the U-boat campaign.

Sperrle was well aware of the weakness of the Luftwaffe's bomber force which had been steadily decimated since the Stalingrad disaster of 1942–3, when the equivalent of three experienced bomber wings were destroyed in an attempt to use bombers to lift supplies to the doomed 6th Army. In Italy the bomber wings assigned to *Luftflotte* 2 had suffered heavy attrition in trying to stop the Allied landings. However, in late 1943 and early 1944 IX Air Corps, *Luftflotte* 3's main bomber force, saw a rise in aircraft numbers as bomber groups were pulled out of Italy and the Mediterranean and brought to France for re-equipping and training. By early 1944 the last reserve of Luftwaffe bombers had been concentrated in France.

In one of his most impressive strategic blunders, Hitler insisted on using these last bomber reserves in attacks against British cities to crush British civilian morale. Sperrle was strongly opposed to Hitler's strategy. In 1943, Sperrle proposed that the Luftwaffe's bomber units in the West not be used in attacks on British cities which he saw as potentially costly yet strategically meaningless.[14] Sperrle argued that the bombers could best be used in a naval air campaign to attack shipping in and out of Britain, outside of the RAF Fighter Command's effective defensive range.[15] Hitler, supported by Goering, saw Sperrle's air strategy as too passive. Ever since the bombing of Hamburg in the summer of 1943, the Nazi leadership had turned more and more toward terror-bombing campaigns as a strategic solution and Hitler and his entourage believed that terror-bombing would break British morale. Hitler insisted, 'I can only win the war if I destroy the enemy more than he destroys us – therefore, I will bring the terror war to him . . .'.[16] So in late 1943 IX Air Corps was taken away from the operational control of *Luftflotte* 3 and placed under the direct control of Hermann Goering, who would select the targets for the bomber force, presumably after consultation with Hitler. Bomber expert Major General Dietrich Peltz was placed in command of IX Air Corps and continued to receive additional reinforcements of aircraft and aircrew. By December 1943, IX Air Corps contained 524 bombers, mostly Ju 88s and Do 217s as well as a few He 177 heavy bombers. Although this force looked impressive on paper, Luftwaffe aircrew training was very deficient and extra training was paramount as the bombing campaign could only be conducted at night due to the huge superiority of the Allies in day fighters.

The German night bombing techniques of 1944 were similar to those of the British. For there to be any reasonable chance of the bombers to hitting the target at night they needed to be guided by a highly experienced and specially trained bomber pathfinder force. Unfortunately for IX Air Corps, they were given no time to develop pathfinders.[17] Indeed, the training levels for the Luftwaffe bomber force in basic skills were exceptionally weak. Due to the heavy attrition of 1942–3, the flight hours in the Luftwaffe bomber training programme had been cut to the bone and the Luftwaffe was unable to replace trained airmen with pilots of even minimal competence.[18]

Peltz was ordered by Goering to begin a major bombing offensive against the British in January 1944 and Goering selected London as the major target – at that time the city with Britain's largest concentration of flak and night fighter defences.[19] In the first Blitz of 1940 the British night defences had been extremely weak and the Luftwaffe could attack British cities with minimal losses. However, in 1944 the British were fully prepared to repel night bomber attacks. The first big German raid was carried out against London on 21 January 1944 with a force of 447 bombers. German bomber losses were heavy and little was accomplished. It set a pattern for future Luftwaffe bombing operations. Because of the poor level of aircrew training few bombs even came near the assigned targets.[20] In 29 night attacks from January to May, IX Air Corps flew 4,251 sorties. The Luftwaffe loss rate averaged 7.7 per cent per raid and by May 1944 329 bombers had been lost over England, along with their aircrews.[21] In short, the Luftwaffe destroyed its last reserve of bombers in pointless attacks and eliminated its best hope of inflicting a heavy attrition upon the Allied shipping when the invasion came. By D-Day, IX Air Corps possessed only 261 twin-engine bombers and the bomber units were clearly worn out. In fact, the operational rate of the force had dropped to below 50 per cent.[22]

The other bomber force of *Luftflotte* 3, X Air Corps, was in no better shape than IX Air Corps. X Air Corps specialised in anti-shipping attacks by torpedoes and by radio-guided dive bombs, the Fritz X and the Henschel Hs 293. To make these revolutionary but cranky weapons effective, the precision-guided bombs of World War II called for considerable specialised aircrew training. As potentially dangerous as these weapons were, the Luftwaffe never had more than 40 crews at any time who were fully trained to use them.[23]

X Air Corp's most serious problem was lack of personnel, not aircraft. As of 30 May 1944, Group III of Bomber Wing 100 in Toulouse, France, was equipped with 30 Dornier 217 bombers, but had only 17 trained crews. II Air Corps, intended as the specialised ground-attack force for the Western Front, had virtually no planes or trained pilots available to meet the Allied invasion as nearly all the Luftwaffe's ground attack aircraft had been thrown into combat against the Russian offensive on the Eastern Front. Due to a general shortage of trained ground-attack pilots, there would be no reserve available to meet the Allied invasion in June 1944.

Because of the weakness of *Luftflotte* 3, any hope for an effective Luftwaffe contribution to the Wehrmacht defence of the French coast would require strong reinforcements from the Reich air defence. In December 1943, detailed Luftwaffe plans were published under the code name *Drohende Gefahr West* ('Immediate Danger West'), also known as 'Operation Doktor Gustav'.[24] The Luftwaffe planned to shift the major proportion of the home defence fighter forces to airfields near the invasion area as soon as the Allies landed. In the first days of the invasion, 31 fighter units were to be transferred from Germany to France with 700–800 aircraft.[25] Stripping the Reich air defence meant that Germany was left with only eight night fighter groups and three replacement fighter groups, all of limited effectiveness.[26] However, the battle for France was considered so important that the risk was regarded as worth it.

D-Day and the first days of the campaign

The Luftwaffe made a considerable effort to attack the D-Day landings on 6 June 1944 with the very limited forces at hand yet, on that day, *Luftflotte* 3 was able to fly only 319 sorties against the Allies.[27] On the first day, the primary effort of the Third Air Fleet was made by General Peltz's IX Air Corps, which sent 130 bomber sorties against the invasion fleet on the evening of 6–7 June.[28] X Air Corps sent 40 guided bomb and torpedo planes against the Allies on the night of D-Day, but failed to sink any Allied ships. The Luftwaffe's counter-offensive intensified over the next few days. On 8 June, 500 sorties were flown against the Allied forces off Normandy.[29] Despite the increased effort, there were few results to show for it.

In the days immediately after D-Day, the Luftwaffe attempted to conduct the kind of air campaign it had conducted against the British and American fleets a few months before during the Salerno landings in Italy. The two groups of X Air Corps equipped to drop the radio-guided bombs attacked shipping with the Fritz X guided bomb and other bombers dropped torpedoes. IX Air Corps' bomber force, with an operational strength of scarcely more than a wing (100 aircraft), dropped torpedoes and conventional bombs. In the air campaign over Salerno, the Luftwaffe had been able to inflict considerable damage against Allied shipping during night attacks. For example, in September 1943 German radio-guided bombs disabled the British battleship, HMS *Warspite*, badly damaged the British cruiser HMS *Uganda* and sank the US cruiser *Savannah*. An Allied hospital ship, two merchant vessels and 20 other craft were also sunk, mostly by radio-controlled bomb attacks.[30] Yet in the two weeks after the landing in Normandy, the radio controlled bombs sank only two Allied vessels and damaged seven. Torpedoes sank three ships and damaged two more. In contrast to the Mediterranean, where large Allied ships had been disabled or sunk, the largest Allied vessel to be lost from air attack off the Normandy coast was a destroyer.

One reason behind the poor showing of X Air Corps' radio-controlled bombs during OVERLORD was the increased effectiveness of Allied electronic warfare capability that had been developed after the Salerno campaign. In late 1943 parts of an unexploded radio-guided bomb had been recovered in the Mediterranean and carefully examined by Allied intelligence. The likely bomb guidance radio frequencies were determined from recovered radio crystals and when the same weapons were used over the Normandy beaches the Allies were ready for them. Aircraft that broke through the Allied night defences faced an impressive electronic barrage by several vessels ready to jam the signals.[31]

The conventional bombers of IX Air Corps fared worse than the units of X Air Corps. Poorly-trained German bomber crews flying at night were especially dependent on assistance from German ground radar and navigation aids to get to the target. However, the thorough Allied pre-invasion air offensive had effectively knocked out over 80 per cent of the German coastal radar sites before the invasion.[32] In case the Luftwaffe managed to get their radars working and use their communications effectively, the RAF had prepared a strong force with effective counter-measures to oppose them – an entire group of 100 bombers equipped to conduct electronic warfare. On top of the electronic warfare defences the Allied fleet and ground forces were well defended by anti-aircraft guns and several squadrons of night fighters that kept up a constant patrol over the embarkation sites. On D-Day, anti-aircraft units of the US 9th Air Force, the IXth Air Defence Command, a two-brigade strong anti-aircraft command, started moving ashore and the Allied defences were constantly reinforced just as the Luftwaffe's attack capabilities decreased.

IX Air Corps pilots sent back hair-raising reports on the strength of the Allied night fighter opposition. One Luftwaffe bomber officer commented: 'Every raid we made, four attacks by night fighters!'[33] From the start, the Luftwaffe's bomber forces suffered a heavy loss rate in every attempt to attack Allied shipping. At dusk on D-Day there was the famous incident of Spitfires of 410 Squadron shooting down six Ju 88s over Sword Beach. Ulf Balke's story of Luftwaffe Bomber Wing 2 (*Kampfgeschwader* 2) (KG 2) tells the story of the steady attrition faced by the Luftwaffe's conventional bomber units over Normandy. On the night of 6–7 June KG 2 lost three planes. On 8/9 June one aircraft was lost and on 10/11 June three planes were lost. Between 6 and 29 June this one wing lost a total of 31 bombers –

most of its operational aircraft.[34] Interestingly, fully half of the German bomber losses were not from Allied flak or fighters but from landing accidents or damage from German flak. The poorly-trained bomber crews were not proficient in the always tricky procedure of night landings and poor navigation skills led the bomber units over areas where the Luftwaffe's flak units had not been warned of the presence of Luftwaffe bomber operations.

Other factors that limited the effectiveness of *Luftflotte* 3's bomber force were the lack of aerial reconnaissance units to find targets for the bombers and the generally poor intelligence provided by the Luftwaffe staff on Allied forces and shipping. The few reconnaissance planes of *Luftflotte* 3 were able to provide only the most perfunctory information concerning the Allied dispositions. In the absence of hard information on Allied shipping and locations of Allied ground troops, the German bomber and fighter-bomber units were simply told to attack the beachhead in the hope that, with luck, they might hit something. German intelligence failed in other ways as well. For example, on the night of 6 June, German E-boats of the 4th Motor Torpedo Boat Flotilla were ordered to make torpedo attacks against Allied shipping. However, German intelligence was unable to provide the requested information on the draft of the Allied vessels. This knowledge was vital because in lieu of accurate data the *Kriegsmarine* would have to arm the torpedoes with the less effective contact fuses rather than the more effective and more lethal magnetic fuses because magnetic fuses could only be used at preset depths.[35] Such lapses in basic tactical and operational intelligence explain how, even when the bombers got through, they had trouble finding worthwhile targets.

Of course, the primary reason for the Luftwaffe's performance over Normandy was the enormous degree of Allied air superiority. On D-Day alone, the Allies together flew 14,674 sorties; the German could only mount a few hundred to oppose them.[36]

The campaign continues: Operation Doktor Gustav activated

On D-Day the Luftwaffe activated its plan to counter the Allied invasion: 'Operation Dr Gustav'. Luftwaffe fighter and ground attack units that had been pushed out of Northern France by the relentless Allied attacks on airfields in the months before the invasion were now ordered to stage forward to airfields in Northern France. The plan started to unravel as soon as it was activated. Some fighter units were actually shot to pieces while flying in transit. On 6 June Group III of Ground Attack Wing (*Schlachtgeschwader*) 4 with 50 FW 190s was ordered to fly from Southern France to the St Quentin airfield where it would be better placed to attack the Allied landings. One of the squadrons, the 9th, was intercepted en route by Allied fighters with five of the Luftwaffe fighters falling in flames.[37] Throughout the campaign the Allies had a tremendous operational advantage in the Luftwaffe message traffic intercepted by *Ultra*. Decrypted Luftwaffe Enigma messages gave the RAF and AAF complete information on major German air movements and the Allies just 'happened' to have fighters ready to intercept *en route* or were ready to target their forward airfields as soon as the Luftwaffe units landed. Since Allied air power and reconnaissance was so ubiquitous over Northern and Central France, and since the German airfields within 150 miles of the Normandy coast were under fairly constant attack, the Germans failed to notice that airfields receiving Luftwaffe reinforcements came in for a bit of extra punishment.

The German airfield system in France was extensive, well-camouflaged and hardened with aircraft placed in revetments, bunkers or in carefully concealed positions far from the runway. While all of these measures ensured that the Allied campaign against the Luftwaffe airfields destroyed relatively few aircraft on the ground (many of the aircraft claimed by the Allied fighter planes were dummies or worthless obsolete aircraft expressly set out to attract the attention of British and American fighters), repair facilities and fuel storage took a constant beating. With the airfield facilities under regular punishment, the Luftwaffe units deployed to France had a very low operational rate during the whole Normandy campaign.

Within days of the Allied landing, over 800 fighter planes were sent to France from the Reich Air Defence force. The Luftwaffe also scraped up its last available bombers to go to France. X Air Corps received 45 JU 88 torpedo bombers as reinforcements and IX Air Corps received an additional 90 bombers.[38] Half of the fighter planes deployed to France were immediately allocated to the II Air Corps for ground attack missions. Although the FW 190 was a superb ground attack aircraft, all of the pilots deployed from the Reich were trained (minimally) as interceptor pilots and none had received any training in ground attack. Ground attack missions were also regularly intercepted by Allied fighters and German units were forced to drop their bombs prematurely and abort their missions. Allied air superiority was so overwhelming and the ground attack missions of the Luftwaffe so ineffectual that on 12 June II Air Corps ceased ground attack missions and all of its surviving FW 190s reverted to a pure interceptor role.

In an extraordinary effort, by 9 June the Luftwaffe was able to fly more than 500 sorties a day against the Allied forces in Normandy, though even this effort achieved minimal results. German fighter aircraft had little effective ground control thanks to the Allies' destruction of most of the radar sites in France. Moreover, because of little air reconnaissance or accurate intelligence, *Luftflotte* 3's fighter units were reduced to flying fighter sweeps in the general direction of the Allied beachhead. This was fine for the RAF and AAF as they could regularly intercept the Luftwaffe sweeps and inflict a high daily attrition on the Germans.

A major part of the Luftwaffe's anti-shipping offensive was to carry out extensive aerial mining of the sea approaches to the invasion beaches. Aerial mining had been used against the Allied landings in Salerno and Anzio – but the Luftwaffe planned for a much larger campaign when the Allies landed in France. The Germans had a superb, new naval mine in production in

1944, the 'oyster mine', which reflected a major advance in technology and would cause the Allies a good many headaches in the campaign. The oyster mines worked on hydrostatic pressure and were thus much more difficult to detect and sweep than other mines. The change in water pressure by the movement of a large vessel armed the mine, which was then detonated by a conventional acoustic or magnetic trigger. There was, in fact, no method to safely sweep the mines once they were delivered. The Luftwaffe decided it was too risky to use the mines against Allied shipping before the invasion in case the Allies should manage to acquire an intact mine and develop countermeasures. Instead, the Luftwaffe built up a large stockpile of the mines and prepared to launch a mining campaign the moment the invasion began.[39] A mining campaign also made a good deal of sense, given the state of training of the German bomber force. It was a lot easier for the poorly trained pilots of *Luftflotte* 3 to find an area of water near the beachhead, drop the mines and run for home than it was to carry out an accurate night-time bomb run against an allied ship.

Because IX and X Air Corps' valiant effort to drop torpedoes and bombs on the Allied fleet showed few results, the German bomber force was relegated to less risky minelaying missions after 12 June. The Luftwaffe's minelaying operations went on almost nightly through the whole campaign. By 6 July, more than 600 of these mines had been dropped.[40] The oyster mines sank five warships and four other ships off the British beaches between 22 and 29 June. In the American Utah Beach sector, four destroyers and two minesweepers were sunk and 25 other vessels were damaged in the first ten days of the mining campaign.[41] The mere presence of oyster mines hampered Allied shipping operations as ships could not safely travel faster than four or five knots in areas where mines had been sown or where mining was suspected. By August, the Luftwaffe had sown over 4,000 mines on the sea approaches of Normandy.

In June–July 1944 the Third Air Fleet's mining campaign was far more successful than its bombing attacks. However, the price was high and every mission had to fight its way through Allied night fighters and anti-aircraft capability. If the Germans came in high, they would certainly be spotted by the radars of the Allied night fighters; if they came in very low they were vulnerable to Allied anti-aircraft fire. To avoid the Allied air and ground defences the Luftwaffe bombers could try to get over the Allied shipping lanes in poor weather – but this greatly increased the possibility of a crash or landing accident by the mostly inexperienced pilots. In any case, attrition of the bomber force was constant and at the end of the Normandy campaign several bomber wings were simply disbanded as there were not enough replacement bombers or crews to man what had once been the primary force of the Luftwaffe.

Through the summer of 1944 the Luftwaffe carried out a maximum effort. In June 1944 over 1,100 aircraft were sent from the Reich to reinforce *Luftflotte* 3 and most were quickly lost with few results to show from the effort. From 6 to 30 June, *Luftflotte* 3 and Air Fleet Reich flew 13,829 sorties and lost 1,181 aircraft from all causes. Indeed, June was the bloodiest month for the Luftwaffe in all of 1944.[42]

German flak operations

In contrast to the aerial actions the ground-based Luftwaffe flak operations in the spring and summer of 1944 were fairly effective and inflicted serious losses on the RAF and USAAF. During the Allied pre-invasion bombing campaign the Luftwaffe, fully aware of the Allied targeting strategies, emplaced heavy flak defences around the obvious targets such as vital bridges, railyards, major airfields and military command centres. Luftwaffe airfield units were also equipped with extra flak guns for defence. In the spring of 1944 the Germans, knowing the propensity of Allied fighter bombers to make low-level attacks on Luftwaffe airfields, set up numerous 'flak traps' on French airfields equipped with decoy or derelict aircraft sitting on runways in order to bring Allied fighters straight into the fire of several rapid-firing 20 or 37mm flak guns.[43] The US 9th Air Force's accounts of the Normandy air campaign indicate that it was a rare for American air units to even see a Luftwaffe fighter but that flak opposition was extremely heavy and led to constant attrition of aircraft and crew. Between April and July of 1944, the medium bombers of the 9th Air Force took a monthly attrition rate of 10–15 per cent – virtually all losses caused by flak.[44] By June and July 1944, 9th Air Force medical officers commented on the relatively large number of psychological casualties caused by the high intensity of the 9th Air Force bomber operations and by the stress of constantly flying in a highly lethal flak environment.[45]

During June 1944, the RAF and USAAF lost 1,564 aircraft over France and Germany, with the majority of losses over France caused by flak. Indeed, June was the month of maximum effort by both the German and American air forces in 1944. The attrition rate imposed by the German flak forces in the spring and in June finally led to a reduction of Allied air activity in July and August. Because losses were heavier than planned for, the air units that had borne the brunt of the pre-invasion air campaign needed a rest. So in July, with air superiority assured and the interdiction campaign working well, the British and Americans were able to reduce the number of air sorties over France by 20 to 25 per cent. The US 9th Air Force reduced its daily bomber sortie rate from a figure of 400 in May and June to 270 in July, while from June to July the daily fighter-bomber sortie rate fell from 1,000 to 750.[46]

German 'wonder weapons' in the campaign

The Luftwaffe employed several of its newest 'wonder weapons' in the Normandy campaign. New and high-tech weapons usually look wonderful in theory and sometimes look very good in tests. However, real operations often show up the flaws in the concepts and this was certainly the case for the Luftwaffe's special weapons in Normandy. The first to be employed was the *Mistel*, an obsolete Ju 88 bomber armed with an 8,400 lb warhead and equipped to fly by remote control. The crewless Ju 88 was mated with a manned Me 109, which was attached above it. The Me 109 pilot flew both aircraft off the ground and, upon reaching attack altitude and position, released the Ju 88 and guided the bomber into an Allied warship using a simple joystick remote-control device. Theoretically, the *Mistel* should have been quite lethal. In actuality, the concept worked poorly. The *Mistel* was slow, not very manoeuvrable and was not survivable in a high-threat environment. The Luftwaffe carried out a few *Mistel* sorties against the Allied shipping in June and July, all of which failed.

The first sortie was typical of the *Mistel* programme's performance. On 24 June a flight of five *Mistel*s guided by pilots of the 4th Group of *Kampfgeschwader* 101 were on their way to attack Allied shipping off the British sector. They were intercepted by Allied night fighters long before they reached effective release range and the *Mistel* controllers quickly released their lumbering bombers to crash in the countryside early and retreated to their bases.[47]

Another wonder weapon upon which the Germans placed considerable hope was the Me 262 jet fighter. This aircraft had just come into mass production but, by the time of the invasion, the Luftwaffe had few pilots who were even minimally qualified to fly the jet. There were also difficulties with deploying the Me 262 to France. The Me 262 needed much longer runways than conventional fighters due to much higher landing and take-off speeds. The short range of the Me 262 also required that it be deployed to forward airfields, but by this time all of the improved runways in France and the Low Countries were under constant attack by the Allied air forces. Despite these problems, nine Me 262s of KG51 were ordered to France on 20 July 1944 – even though the unit reported only four pilots were even moderately competent in the aircraft.[48] A few aircraft of this unit did take to the skies over France, flying patrols and apparently missing the notice of any of Allied air units. In any case, just getting the early jets into the air was a big problem for the Luftwaffe. In the summer of 1944 the average lifespan of a jet turbine engine was about eight hours and the Luftwaffe repair and supply services were too hard-pressed to effectively support the jet maintenance. Since the Luftwaffe's airfields were under constant attack, the Me 262 detachment was forced to change airfields constantly. This left the mechanics and motor convoys of spare engines and parts to drive all over France in order to keep up with their unit – all the while being constantly bombed and strafed by Allied fighter-bombers. After a month of intermittent operations in France the Me 262s were evacuated to Belgium and then to Germany, but not before one of the ground support convoys of KG 51 got lost, took a wrong turn and was captured by Allied forces, thus delivering a new jet turbine engine to the Allies.[49]

Conclusion

While the Luftwaffe had no hope of winning even local or temporary air superiority over the Normandy beachhead it still could have waged a much more effective campaign against the Allied landings. The greatest German mistake, and one that saved the lives of many Allied troops and sailors, was Hitler's decision to throw away his last reserve of bombers in meaningless attacks on British morale. Had the more than 300 Luftwaffe bombers lost over England in early 1944 been available to drop mines off the Normandy coast, Allied shipping losses would have been dramatically increased.

The Luftwaffe's operations also demonstrate the mistake of relying too much on unproven 'wonder weapons' to redress an imbalance in numbers. Between September 1943, when the weapons were first employed, and June 1944 the British and Americans learned to adapt to the German radio-controlled bombs and developed effective counter-measures, and these weapons therefore proved much less effective than they had been in the Mediterranean campaigns. The first use of jets in combat operations was a complete washout. The Luftwaffe's Me 262s claimed not one Allied plane while deployed to France. The *Mistel* programme, which looked awfully good in the concept phase, proved a waste of effort as the weapon could only be effectively used in a benign air environment – something that the air over Normandy wasn't in 1944. It is notable that the most effective and lethal technology employed by the Luftwaffe was a small improvement in a weapon that had been around for a long time – the naval mine. The difficulty of sweeping the oyster mines with their hydrostatic pressure arming device made life difficult for the RAF and USAAF in the summer of 1944 and potentially could have seriously hindered Allied shipping operations if more had been employed.

In the end, the most effective contribution by the Luftwaffe to the German defence of Normandy was the flak force. While German air units were ineffective, the Luftwaffe proved that flak forces could, by themselves, inflict a heavy attrition rate upon enemy aircraft. Perhaps more importantly, the Luftwaffe's flak units, especially the 88mm medium guns with their exceptional tank-killing capability, played an important role in making the German defence of Normandy such a tough nut to crack. When the campaign began, the Luftwaffe ordered extra flak units to the front in France and an additional 140 heavy and 50 light flak batteries were dispatched.[50] The effectiveness of the German flak units in the ground battles is mentioned in most of the major histories of the Normandy campaign. In mid-June the 88mm guns of Flak Corps II helped hold British armour back from the approaches to Caen.[51] In the July battles, Luftwaffe flak regiments played a prominent role in support of the 1st SS Panzer Division and other German divisions deployed to halt the British offensives.[52] There is much more to say about the employment of the Luftwaffe's flak units in the Normandy campaign, their important role in the German defence and their eventual destruction as the Allies drove the Germans in disorder across the Seine. If there is a major issue in the Normandy campaign that merits a fresh look and its own book, the role of III Flak Corps in the ground battle is certainly it.

Notes

1 General Walter Warlimont, *Inside Hitler's Headquarters 1939–1945* (Novato: Presidio Press, 1964), p. 424.
2 For an overview of the Luftwaffe's campaign against the Allied landings in Sicily see James Corum, 'To Stop Them on the Beaches: Luftwaffe Operations Against the Allied Landings in Italy', *RAF Air Power Review*, 7(2), summer 2004, pp. 47–68.
3 USAF HRA Monograph: Karl Gundlach, *Die Einfluss der allierten Luftangriffe der Bodenorganisation der deutsche Luftwaffe im Westen*, 1944, pp. 14–18. Edward Westermann, *Flak: German Anti-Aircraft Defenses 1914–1945* (Lawrence: University Press of Kansas, 2001), p. 259.
4 For a good summary of the Luftwaffe campaign in Normandy see Horst Boog, 'Strategischer Luftkrieg in Europa und Reichsluftverteidigung 1943–1944', in Horst Boog, Gerhard Krebs, Detlef Vogel (eds) *Das Deutsche Reich und der Zweite Weltkrieg* (Stuttgart: Deutsche VerlagsAnstalt, 2001), pp. 3–418. On Normandy operations see pp. 288–97.
5 See Steven McFarland and Wesley Newton, *To Command the Sky* (Washington, DC: Smithsonian Institution Press, 1991) and Donald Caldwell, *JG 26-Top Guns of the Luftwaffe* (New York: Orion Books, 1991).
6 Caldwell, JG 26, pp. 231, 241.
7 *The United States Strategic Bombing Survey, The Defeat of the German Air Force* (1946), pp. 19–20.
8 Ibid.
9 Westermann, pp. 259–61.
10 General Hans von Rohden, *Die deutsche Luftwaffe im Angesicht der Invasion 1944*, Unpublished MS in Air University Library, Maxwell AFB (1947).
11 Information obtained from copies of service records in Karl Friedrich Hildebrandt (ed.) *Die Generäle der deutschen Luftwaffe 1935–1945*, vols. 1–3 (Biblio Verlag Osnabruck, 1992).
12 von Rohden, *Die deutsche Luftwaffe im Angesicht der Invasion 1944*.
13 Ibid.
14 Rolf Schabel, *Die Illusion der Wunderwaffen* (Munich: Oldenburg Verlag, 1994), p. 141. Also see Basil Collier, *The Defence of the United Kingdom* (London: HMSO, 1957), p. 512.
15 von Rohden, *Die deutsche Luftwaffe im Angesicht der Invasion 1944*.
16 Helmut Hieber (ed.) *Hitler's Lagebesprechungen. Die Protokollfragmente seiner militaerischen Konferenzen 1942/1945* (Stuttgart: Deutscher Verlag, 1962), p. 296.
17 See Matthew Cooper, *The German Air Force 1933–1945* (London: Janes, 1981), pp. 332–3, and General Hans von Rohden, *Die deutsche Luftwaffe im Angesicht der Invasion 1944*.
18 Interview with Hansgeorg Wilberg, September 1993. Wilberg received his pilot training in multi-engine aircraft in 1943. He entered combat as a Ju 188 pilot in late 1943, with a little over 100 hours' total flight time. He maintains the only reason he survived is that he was deployed as a reconnaissance pilot to the Eastern Front, where the air opposition was not nearly as effective as on the Western Front.

19 Interview by the author with Major General a.D. Dietrich Peltz, 14 June 1994.
20 For example, only 30 tons of bombs, out of 500 tons dropped, actually hit the target city of London in the first raid on 21 January 1944. See Rolf Schabel, *Die Illusion der Wunderwaffen*, p. 172.
21 Matthew Cooper, *The German Air Force*, pp. 332–3.
22 Alfred Price, 'The IX Air Corps', in *The D-Day Encyclopedia* (New York: Simon & Schuster, 1994), pp. 390–1.
23 Interview with Major General Dietrich Peltz, 14 June 1994.
24 Karl Gundelach, *Effect of the Allied Air Attacks on the Ground Echelon of the Luftwaffe in Western Europe in 1944* (USAF HRA Monograph, 1956), pp. 18–29.
25 Hans Ring and Werner Girbig, *Jagdgeschwader 27* (Stuttgart: Motorbuchverlag, 1991), p. 295.
26 General Beppo Schmid, *The Employment of the German Luftwaffe Against the Allies in the West 1943–1945*, USAF HRA Doc. K113.107-58. pp. 11–12. Matthew Cooper, *The German Air Force 1933–1945*, p. 335.
27 Matthew Cooper, *The German Air Force 1933–1945*, p. 335.
28 *The D-Day Encyclopedia*, pp. 390–1.
29 Ibid., p. 459.
30 See Martin Blumenson, *Salerno to Cassino* (Washington, DC: US Army Center for Military History, 1993), pp. 147–8, and Brigadier C.J. Maloney, *The Mediterranean and Middle East*, vol. 5 (London: Her Majesty's Stationery Office, 1973), pp. 312, 322, 325.
31 Alfred Price, *The Last Year of the Luftwaffe* (London W.J. Williams, 1991), p. 58.
32 W.A. Jacobs, 'Operation Overlord', in B.J. Cooling (ed.) *Case Studies in the Achievement of Air Superiority* (Washington, DC: Center for Air Force History, 1990), p. 305.
33 Alexander McKee, *Last Round Against Rommel: Battle for the Normandy Beachhead* (New York: Signet Books, 1964), p. 276.
34 For a detailed view of the campaign from the German side see Ulf Balke, *Der Luftkrieg in Europa*, vol. 2 (Bechtermuenz Verlag: Augsburg, 1997). On losses see pp. 492–3.
35 Interview with Lieutenant Dietrich Bludau, 8 June 1990. Bludau was with the 4th MTB Flotilla, based in Le Havre, and took part in the naval engagements of 6–7 June as an e-boat commander.
36 Matthew Cooper, *The German Air Force 1933–1945*, p. 335.
37 Alfred Price, *The Last Year of the Luftwaffe*, p. 57.
38 Von Rohden, *Die deutsche Luftwaffe im Angesicht der Invasion 1944*.
39 Hans Ring and Werner Girbig, *Jagdgeschwader 27*, p. 295.
40 Theodore Wilson (ed.) *D-Day 1944* (Kansas: University Press of Kansas, 1994), pp. 107, 116.
41 Hans Ring and Werner Girbig, *Jagdgeschwader 27*, p. 156.
42 Major Stangl, 'Operationsfuehrung und Taktik der Englisch/Amerikanische Luftwaffe vom Absprungbasis'. 8th Section (Luftwaffe General Staff, Study of Allied Operations Against the Germans in France), 24 September 1944, in USAF HRA doc. K113.60.
43 When the Americans attacked the German airfield at Valence, France on 6 June, a derelict old Italian Caproni 3-motor bomber had been set out as a target for them. See Karl Gundelach, *Effect of the Allied Air Attacks*, p. 52.
44 USAF HRA. Report of 323 Medium Bomb Group. Office of the Surgeon. Report on Casualties 29 Jan. 1945. Doc. 5-1946-28.
45 Ibid.
46 USAF HRA, *Historical Summary of Ninth Air Force Operations 1944–1945*.

47 William Green, *Warplanes of the Third Reich* (New York: Doubleday, 1971), p. 478.
48 Wolfgang Dierich, *Kampfgeschwader 51 'Edelweiss'* (Stuttgart: Motorbuch Verlag, 1991), p. 230.
49 Ibid., pp. 230–4.
50 Westermann, p. 260.
51 Major L.F. Ellis, *Victory in the West – The Battle of Normandy*, vol. 1 (London: HMSO, 1962), p. 265.
52 Ibid., pp. 311, 332.

11 Arthur Tedder and the transportation plans

Vincent Orange

When Air Chief Marshal Sir Arthur Tedder landed in England on 20 January 1944, to take up his appointment as Deputy Supreme Allied Commander to General Dwight D. Eisenhower, he ended 38 months of service in the Mediterranean theatre, broken only by two visits to London that lasted a total of 18 days. He therefore had plenty of sand in his shoes. So, too, had Eisenhower, Lieutenant General Carl A. Spaatz and those colleagues they brought with them to England. The future would show that this gritty sign of experience at the sharp end of war justified them in imposing their opinions on those who were 'sandless' and, consequently, 'not one of us'.[1]

Tedder was 'an anomaly among RAF senior leaders', thought Williamson Murray, in that he was 'consistently willing to take a joint service perspective rather than follow the narrow prejudices of his own service'.[2] He had created in the Mediterranean a balanced air force that was skilled at interrupting enemy supply lines in addition to winning air superiority and offering close support to soldiers. John Terraine agreed. His handling of that air force, together with his achievements before and after D-Day, made him 'the outstanding airman of the war'. In Terraine's opinion, 'We dwell too much on D-Day and the Normandy beaches. We should think more about what made D-Day possible': air superiority and Tedder's first transportation plan.[3]

We also dwell too much, I believe, on the Luftwaffe's weakness by 1944, as if that made life cushy for airmen while poor old brownjobs slugged it out against poor old greyjobs in the real war down below. Aircraft were vulnerable to ground fire, bad weather and, only too often, the courage of their crews, determined to press home attacks at all costs. During the first eight months of 1944, no fewer than 6,000 aircraft and nearly 29,000 airmen were lost.[4]

In addition to advocating his plan, against persistent opposition from many quarters, service and civilian, Tedder had learned in Cairo, even before Pearl Harbor, that this was a *coalition* war. More exactly, a war in which the British Empire and the USA gradually became effective allies, with the Soviet Union as an uncooperative co-belligerent. By 1944, he was more acutely aware than many British officers in all three services, quite apart from xenophobic politicians, journalists, broadcasters and civilians, that the USA was the *senior* partner in the alliance. That awareness enabled him to win support, however grudging, from those of his American friends who were thoroughly 'sanded'.

Like the rest of us, Tedder at times wanted to be someone else: in his case, a scientist, which helps to explain what drew him to Solly Zuckerman.[5] This particular scientist shared his malicious delight in waspish one-liners, delivered deadpan. But Tedder also had a gift for manipulating dogged opponents (and they come no more dogged than Spaatz, commanding the American heavy day bombers, and Air Chief Marshal Sir Arthur Harris, commanding the British heavy night bombers) into reluctantly conceding that his arguments in favour of impeding German access to Normandy's beaches before D-Day might possibly have some merit.

Zuckerman, already an eminent zoologist by 1939, got into war work in England by studying the effects of exploding bombs on humans, animals and structures. He arrived in Algiers in March 1943, where he began to frame a bombing strategy. Tedder invented for him in May an impressive title – 'Chief Scientific Officer' – and graded him as a Group Captain. In July, when the Allies were safely ashore in Sicily, Tedder arranged for Zuckerman to examine the damage done by bombing in order to use air power more efficiently in the forthcoming invasion of Italy. He concluded, from a study of railway records, that concentrated attacks on certain key points – those regulating major traffic routes, servicing and repairing loco-motives and wagons – would impede large-scale movement of troops with heavy equipment. Tedder and Zuckerman then formulated, and refined in the light of experience, a coherent bombing strategy that proved of great value during the rest of the war. Yet it generated opposition from officers and civilians, British and American, of such bitter intensity that neither man ever forgot or forgave those responsible. Operation OVERLORD could not succeed unless the Allies ruled the skies above the landing areas and inhibited enemy movement toward those areas, but Tedder had noticed the ability of German soldiers in the Western Desert, Tunisia, Sicily and Italy to fight fiercely without either air support or reliable lines of supply and reinforcement. These were unpromising omens for OVERLORD, where much larger enemy forces would be encountered, with access to a much denser rail, road, river and canal network. Moreover, Tedder had no hope of unstinting support from the heavy bomber commanders for his first assault upon that network.

Spaatz grossly exaggerated the bomber's capacity for destruction. On 20 November 1943, for instance, he assured Harry Hopkins (President Roosevelt's special adviser) that once the weather cleared over Germany next spring, thus allowing continuous operations from England and Italy, Germany would surrender in three months. Neither the transportation plan, nor OVERLORD itself, need ever be mounted. These opinions were seconded by Harris in even more extravagant language: 'to divert Bomber Command from its true function', he asserted, 'would lead directly to disaster'.[6] In order to win from these strong, stubborn men (supported by large, devoted staffs) a measure of cooperation, Tedder would need all those qualities that Zuckerman saw in him of 'patience, tact, cunning and political sense', together with Eisenhower's backing, who had 'infinite faith in the judgment that he quietly exercised in the background'.[7]

Advised by Tedder, Air Chief Marshal Sir Charles Portal (Chief of the Air Staff) drafted a directive on 5 March that reconciled Eisenhower's demand for complete control of the strategic air forces with Churchill's desire, backed by many airmen, that Operation POINTBLANK (Anglo-American raids on Germany) should continue. Although these air forces would remain under the command of Spaatz and Harris, Eisenhower was able to rule on 14 April that they would 'receive their general directives' from Tedder: 'an historic event by which a supreme air command was at last created'.[8] As Harris later wrote, 'I recall only one period of calm sailing [in all his time at Bomber Command] when all went well, when all pulled together . . . and that was during the all too short period when Eisenhower was Admiral and Tedder the Captain on the bridge'.[9] I must emphasise here that Tedder and Harris were not friends and had never served together. They had disagreed very sharply in 1942–3 when Tedder retained Bomber Command crews in the Mediterranean, and just as sharply over the transportation plan. Yet Tedder won him over. The Royal Air Force has had few officers more difficult to move than Harris, and few more capable of managing that feat than Tedder.

Admiral Eisenhower's 'Captain' worked hard to implement a plan which, he later wrote, 'was to run like a thread through all the operations up to the end of the war': a thread sometimes tangled by 'deliberate intrigue and sometimes by ignorance and misunderstanding'.[10] On Zuckerman's advice, he proposed a systematic attack on the numerous railways, roads, bridges, rivers and canals which the enemy could use to move reinforcements into the invasion area. Railways were particularly vulnerable because nearly a third of the pre-war locomotives had been transferred to the Eastern Front, 'including most of the more powerful types, suitable for heavy hauling. Also, there had been little or no repair work during the war'. The tactical air forces would certainly play their part, but the main servicing and repair centres could only be disrupted by heavy bombing.[11]

The attack should be prolonged for as many weeks as possible, in order to exhaust repair squads and use up their materials. If the Allies were not to be swept back into the sea shortly after D-Day, the German build-up must be delayed and disorganised. The plan was so arranged that Calais, rather than Normandy, seemed to be its focus.[12] It was all the more essential in the light of the British army's weakness in training, leadership, equipment, numbers and the fears so often expressed by Churchill and his top soldier (Field Marshal Sir Alan Brooke) of a massacre on the beaches.[13]

A number of fluent civilian pundits, American and British, many of them academics over-stimulated by their first brush with the real world, examined Tedder's plan and condemned it. Although ignorant of the actual workings of transport systems (to say nothing of military operations), they argued that the systems available to the Germans in France and Belgium were too large and complex to be seriously wrecked in time to help the field armies.[14]

Encouraged by Spaatz, they advocated an 'oil plan', without realising the difficulty day bombers, lightly loaded because they were operating far from their English or Italian bases, would face in attempting to destroy widely-dispersed, well-defended and carefully-camouflaged oil targets.[15] Scepticism about the destructive power of American 'precision' bombing was justified. On 10 January 1944, for example, Spaatz advised General Henry H. Arnold (head of the USAAF) to avoid the accurate term 'blind bombing' in press handouts and speak instead of 'overcast bombing technique' or 'bombing with navigational devices over cloud'.[16]

On 25 March, Portal summoned everyone who mattered to a grand meeting which was intended to settle the argument, once and for all. Spaatz admitted that his oil plan could have no *immediate* effect, certainly not in time to help soldiers establish themselves ashore. Eisenhower therefore backed Tedder because victory, he believed, depended on 'the plodding doughfoot' taking and holding ground. Spaatz left the meeting apparently defeated, but actually 'jubilant and overjoyed'[17] on being assured that Tedder (whom he respected) would be 'directing' the heavy bombers and not Air Chief Marshal Sir Trafford Leigh-Mallory (whom he did not).

Leigh-Mallory, appointed in 1943 to command the newly-formed Allied Expeditionary Air Force, held an important position in what Spaatz called the 'lousy organisation' devised to employ air power in OVERLORD.[18] It was an unwise appointment. His record over the past five years as a fighter commander was poor; he lacked experience in handling aircraft other than fighters; he knew nothing about inter-Allied relations; his opinion that air superiority might not be won *until* D-Day alarmed officers who had sweated through the campaigns in Sicily and Italy; his assertion that the heavy bomber should be regularly employed as a battlefield weapon was rejected by many, especially Spaatz and Harris; he was 'sandless, not one of us'; and he had an abrasive, pompous manner. Tedder had disliked him since their under-graduate days in Cambridge, he distrusted his judgement, and had grown wary of his ambition since 1940. Leigh-Mallory did not formally leave his command until October, but by then Tedder, Harris and their American friends had long since marginalised him.[19]

Spaatz was also pleased by the decision of 25 March because he knew that whatever Harris might assert or write (in his colourful way), he too respected Tedder and obeyed specific orders. In fact, British night bombers, carrying far heavier loads than American day bombers, did most of the work, while Spaatz had enough bombers on hand both to appease Tedder and satisfy his own determination to hit targets in Germany.

After that meeting, Portal informed Churchill that 'very heavy' civilian casualties would be 'unavoidable' when Tedder's plan was implemented. Churchill, who had overlooked this obvious consequence of a major assault on occupied Europe, asked Lord Cherwell, his scientific and technical adviser, to comment. The noble lord asserted, with his usual confidence, that as many as 40,000 civilians might be killed, a further 120,000 were likely to be gravely injured, and the plan would fail anyway. Bomber Command experts agreed, claiming that 80–100,000 casualties might result.[20]

Churchill thereupon arranged a string of meetings, 'midnight follies' as Zuckerman called them, in April to reconsider a plan which airmen were already carrying out. It soon became clear that the assertions of Cherwell and Bomber Command were grossly exaggerated and that most French and Belgian civilians understood that their transport networks must be attacked. But Churchill's opposition did not weaken, nor did Tedder waver in the face of the great man's hostility. 'You are piling up an awful lot of hatred', he snapped at Tedder on 3 May. 'You will smear the good name of the Royal Air Force across the world'.[21]

Advised by Tedder, Eisenhower responded to Churchill the next day, 2 May. The entire campaign, he said, was based on the assumption that the Allies' overwhelming air power would be fully used. Otherwise, an already hazardous enterprise must fail. French and Belgian people were now 'slaves' and it would be 'sheer folly' to abandon a carefully-considered plan to help free them because of 'grossly exaggerated' casualty estimates.[22] Disregarding the Supreme Commander's unusually blunt words, Churchill invited Roosevelt on 7 May to order the plan's cancellation. His letter used the word 'slaughter' (of civilians) four times and quoted casualty estimates that he then knew to be false. Roosevelt, neither impressed nor deceived, replied coldly on 11 May: he refused to intervene and Churchill grudgingly accepted defeat on 16 May, but nearly three months later, on 10 July, one of his nastier minutes arrived on Tedder's desk: 'how many Frenchmen did you kill' before D-Day?

Civilian casualties from attacks on rail centres *before* D-Day cannot now be separated from the horrendous suffering of those helpless victims of powerful armies and the destruction of their homes, fields, crops and livestock *after* that day, but it seems that fewer than 6,000 French civilians were certainly killed and an unknown number injured; no figures for Belgian losses survive.[23] Every raid had tragic consequences, for airmen as well as those on the ground.[24] Could more use have been made of agents working in France for the Special Operations Executive (SOE) and members of the Resistance movements to achieve Tedder's goals at less cost? M.R.D. Foot, SOE's official historian, claimed that too much credit was given to what he called 'the photogenic allied air forces'; more was due to 'obscure, devoted French saboteurs',[25] but their gallant actions were too widely spread to be immediately helpful to Allied troops bound for Normandy, and Tedder could not reveal to SOE agents or French and Belgian resisters the focus of his plan.[26]

The Transport Ministry in Berlin reported on 15 May that 'large-scale strategic movement of German troops by rail' in western Europe 'is practically impossible at the present time'. A week later, on 23 May, the German-controlled radio station in Paris admitted 'complete chaos' throughout the rail network, made worse by 'experienced squads of saboteurs'. By 25 August, Tedder and Zuckerman were in Paris and came into possession of daily traffic-flow charts which confirmed the success of their plan and convinced them that a second plan should be made to wreck the transport network in western Germany and, more ambitiously, to strangle the enemy's entire war economy.

There were, inevitably, failings in the first plan.[27] For example, a month after D-Day, when a million men and 190,000 vehicles were ashore, and air control was total, the Germans were still able to get enough men and material forward to prevent a breakout for another three weeks. Bombs do not always hit their targets, even nowadays, nor do they always explode; darkness and bad weather have always been good friends to defenders; and many Germans were skilful, determined and brave. 'Crucial to their logistic support was barge traffic on the Seine – inexplicably not a major target of Allied interdiction efforts.'[28] Tedder also took too long to recognise that the tactical air forces could shatter bridges over the Seine, Meuse and Loire. And although he understood the importance of marshalling yards, he overrated attacks on locomotives and the sheds where they were serviced and repaired.

Despite such criticisms, the plan was an overall success, although neither in conception nor execution did it require more than common sense. It was, in fact, a perfectly obvious method of helping those landing in Normandy, and the Allies had the air power needed to implement it, even without wholehearted backing from the heavy bomber commanders.

The Germans, however, had in their grasp two equally obvious methods of defeating those hoping to land in Normandy. One was the unpiloted flying bomb. Cheap to produce and difficult to destroy, this weapon could have been available in quantity long before D-Day. Fortunately, the lack of sensible direction at the top of the Reich's chaotic structure meant that a fortune was wasted on the V-2 (a complex rocket carrying the same explosive load) and the V-1 appeared too late to be a *disaster* for the Allies, rather than a *serious problem*. If hundreds of flying bombs had been launched against soldiers, trucks and tanks tightly packed into roads and fields near England's south-eastern coasts during April and May, it seems likely that the invasion force would have been dispersed, D-Day postponed, and the attack on communications halted until missile-launching sites were destroyed.[29]

The second German means of defeating OVERLORD seems equally obvious. Fewer than 60 German divisions were based in the west, whereas 322 lay elsewhere. Even a dozen more divisions in France and Belgium would have cost the hard-pressed Allies much heavier losses, despite Tedder's best efforts. As Pete Quesada, a great American tactical air commander, later reflected: 'one's imagination boggled at what the German army might have done to us without Hitler working so effectively for our side'.[30]

Tedder made such a thorough job of wrecking the north's transport system that by August there was a clear need for access to the system, and capacious ports, of southern France. He therefore supported Eisenhower against Churchill and many senior British officers in his determination to activate Operation ANVIL/DRAGOON. Marseille and Toulon were, in fact, essential to supply Allied forces after the Normandy breakout; there was a need to feed into France those French divisions being formed in Italy and North Africa; Resistance forces were numerous in the south and could easily be supplied from the Mediterranean; finally, German forces there were weak and poorly trained. Landings began on 15 August, Napoleon's birthday, and by late October the southern French ports were handling nearly 40 per cent of all American supplies reaching Europe, and transporting them along a rail network deliberately left intact by Tedder.

The British belief that the alternative to ANVIL/DRAGOON, 'a push into northern Italy and into the Alps toward Austria would have gotten anywhere, is beyond belief', thought Gerhard Weinberg. 'As Stalin tried to point out to Churchill at Teheran, there were some very high mountains barring that route into Central Europe.' In their opposition to ANVIL/DRAGOON, the British showed 'a complete disregard of logistics', an essential factor in military operations which inspired both Tedder's transportation plans. He would have echoed Weinberg's cry: 'how did they expect the huge armies of the Allies to be supplied without the French Mediterranean ports?'[31] Marseille was 'a logistical godsend', agreed Williamson Murray and Allan Millett, 'especially since the Allies could not use the port of Antwerp until December . . . while the French rail network up the Rhone River valley remained intact because Allied air forces had concentrated mostly on destruction of the French railroad network in northern, western, and central France'. The Allies had to supply not only their own men, but also to feed thousands of French and Belgian civilians, whose livestock and crops had been stolen or destroyed by retreating Germans or incinerated by 'friendly fire'.[32]

After the Normandy breakout, Allied armies found themselves on the far side of a 'supply desert' created by Tedder's plan. Consequently, 'No matter how fast or how hard engineers worked to rebuild bridges and marshalling yards', Allied commanders faced grave difficulties in moving large forces forward quickly.[33] These difficulties meant that 'The great arguments over a narrow versus a broad front in the West were largely academic', in Weinberg's opinion: 'Until major ports, especially Antwerp, were operational and the railway system was functioning at a high level of efficiency, there was no prospect of a major advance against the stiffening German resistance on either a broad or a narrow front'.[34] All the more reason, then, for backing Tedder's second plan.

His first plan had not isolated the Normandy battlefield, but it had significantly impeded access to it. His second plan proved even more successful, leading to a gradual collapse of the German transport system over the winter of 1944–5. The second plan, recalled Air Chief Marshal Sir Norman Bottomley (Deputy CAS), was 'completely successful' in isolating the Rhineland: 'Coal piled up at the pit-heads of the Ruhr and could not be distributed. Electricity plants and gas plants began to close down; and so did industries all over Germany'.[35]

That happy state took too long to achieve: 'I feel our efforts are rather patchwork', Tedder complained to Portal on 25 October. 'The various targets (oil, cities, depots, marshalling yards, canals, factories, etc.) do not together build up into a really comprehensive pattern'; we need 'a common denominator', which is communications.[36] During the war's last winter the effectiveness of transport bombing was consistently undervalued until February 1945, when Oliver Lawrence (Ministry of Economic Warfare) was obliged to admit that 20,000 commercial intercepts made weekly were left undecrypted because he considered them worthless. 'In effect', his actions 'prevented the full fury of Allied air capabilities from destroying the German transportation network before winter began, and thus they may have extended the war by several months'.[37]

The Enemy Objectives Unit (a group of articulate and confident Americans based in the London embassy) declared on 11 September 1944 that the European war would be over in October and a second transportation plan was therefore a waste of time and effort. This 'Happy Hypothesis' of imminent victory was widespread before Antwerp, Arnhem and the Ardennes jointly dispelled it, and gradually obliged reluctant minds to listen to Tedder.[38]

All intelligence agencies were guilty of shaping their appreciations to suit a strong preference for oil targets, but oil was not essential to German industry and a concentration on communications, especially marshalling yards, might have ended the European war months sooner. The German rail network, aided by the inland waterway system, was vital for moving the economy's lifeblood: coal – 'Six tons of coal stood behind every ton of synthetic gasoline', calculated Alfred Mierzejewski; 'A heavy tank could rumble from the factory only after 115 tons of coal had been burned by a myriad of companies to produce it'. Fortunately, this intelligence failure was offset by the immense power of the Red Army on the Eastern Front and, in the West, the 'crushing superiority' of the Allied air forces and, Mierzejewksi argued, 'the successful bureaucratic game played by Sir Arthur Tedder'.[39]

Here you may protest: did not that nice Nazi, Albert Speer, Hitler's Armaments Minister, state after the war that attacks on oil posed his most serious problem? Indeed he did. Like the Bible, Albert has words of comfort for everyone. Area bombing on the scale achieved over Hamburg in July–August 1943, he said, would soon have compelled surrender; so, too, would attacks on ball-bearing factories; and so, too, attacks on the transport network.[40]

American pundits flocked to Germany on the heels of the Allied armies, desperate to confirm their faith in precision attacks by day bombers and equally desperate to denounce the heresy of area attacks by night bombers. Their admirable energy, their unreliable methods, their contradictions of one another and their inability to offer general conclusions produced 'a set of documents more often quoted than read, and more often read than understood'.[41] But John Kenneth Galbraith (later to become one of the most distinguished economic gurus of the age) upset many pundits by finding that 'the attack on transportation, beginning in September 1944, was the most important single cause of Germany's ultimate economic collapse'.[42]

British pundits were also keen to assess the value of attacking various targets. Tedder invited Portal's support in March 1945 for a field research team, under a senior officer and an experienced scientist. Portal needed no persuasion. He had already told his fellow Chiefs of Staff that without such an inquiry, 'we shall face the grave danger of Government opinion on the lessons of this war being based largely on propaganda, personal recollection, or on the results of investigation by other nations'.[43] Sadly, the proposal came before Churchill in one of his perverse moods. He refused his support and did his best to scupper it. According to Sir Michael Howard, the Prime Minister probably referred the proposal to create a 'Bombing Research Mission' to Cherwell, who would certainly have advised blocking an inquiry that was likely to invalidate his own 'grandiose claims' for area bombing.[44]

Despite Churchill's opposition, there *was* a British inquiry. It reflected the opinions of Tedder and Zuckerman and, thanks to the meticulous critique of Sebastian Cox, its failure to give fair weight to the oil and area offensives is now clear.[45] But Cox accepted as 'sound' the conclusion that Germany's economic collapse followed from the destruction of her transport systems.[46] And 'sound' is the finest tribute an official historian can pay to any measure.

On 6 June 1964, 20 years after Eisenhower launched what he called 'this great and noble undertaking',[47] he wrote to Tedder: 'I suspect your memory goes back, as mine does, to live over again the gnawing anxieties, the realisation of unavoidable sacrifices and the bright hopes that filled us on D-Day 1944'. The former Supreme Commander then paid this magnificent tribute to his former deputy: 'Your professional skill and selfless dedication to the cause in which we all served will be noted by the historians of those dramatic months, but no historian could possibly be aware of the depth of my obligation to you'.[48]

Notes

1 This chapter is partly based on my biography, *Tedder: Quietly in Command* (London: Frank Cass, 2004), pp. 249–99.
2 Williamson Murray and Allan R. Millett, *A War to be Won: Fighting the Second World War* (Cambridge, MA: Harvard University Press, 2000), p. 326.
3 John Terraine, 'World War II – The Balance Sheet', *Proceedings of the Royal Air Force Historical Society*, 2 (August 1987): 26–7.

4 John Terraine, *The Right of the Line: The Royal Air Force in the European War* (London: Hodder & Stoughton, 1985), pp. 662–3.

5 Solly Zuckerman, *From Apes to Warlords: The Autobiography of Solly Zuckerman 1904–1946* (London: Hamish Hamilton, 1978), *passim*; Lord Zuckerman, *Six Men Out of the Ordinary* (London: Peter Owen, 1992), pp. 65–97.

6 Ralph Bennett, *Behind the Battle: Intelligence in the War with Germany, 1939–1945* (London: Pimlico, 1999), p. 157.

7 Zuckerman, *Six Men*, pp. 79, 65.

8 Sir Charles Webster and Noble Frankland, *The Strategic Air Offensive Against Germany, 1939–1945* (London: HMSO, 1961), vol. iii, pp. 20–1.

9 Henry Probert, *Bomber Harris: His Life and Times* (London: Greenhill Books, 2001), p. 303.

10 Lord Tedder, *With Prejudice: The War Memoirs of Marshal of the Royal Air Force Lord Tedder, GCB* (London: Cassell, 1966), p. 506.

11 Air Vice-Marshal E.J. Kingston-McCloughry, 'The Transportation Plan', Item 16, paras 19–22, 26–8 of *Air Ministry Exercise Thunderbolt, Old Sarum, August 1947*, two vols, British National Archives (BNA), formerly Public Record Office, AIR 8/1536.

12 Tami Davis Biddle, *Rhetoric and Reality in Air Warfare: The Evolution of British and American Ideas About Strategic Bombing, 1914–1945* (Princeton, NJ: Princeton University Press, 2002), pp. 236, 242–4, 253.

13 Noel Annan, *Changing Enemies: The Defeat and Regeneration of Germany* (London: Norton, 1995), pp. 54–7.

14 Alfred C. Mierzejewski, 'Wheels Must Roll for Victory: Allied Air Power and the German War Economy, 1944–45' (D.Phil dissertation, University of North Carolina at Chapel Hill, 1985) and his subsequent book, *The Collapse of the German War Economy, 1944–1945* (Chapel Hill, NC: University of North Carolina Press, 1988), *passim*.

15 The transport versus oil debate is well summarised by Robert C. Ehrhart, 'The European Theater of Operations, 1943–1945', in John F. Kreis (ed.) *Piercing the Fog: Intelligence and Army Air Forces Operations in World War II* (Bolling AFB, Washington, DC: Air Force History and Museums Program, 1996), pp. 208–15, 225–6 (with a clear map of Normandy's transport network on p. 227).

16 W.W. Rostow, *Pre-Invasion Bombing Strategy: General Eisenhower's Decision of March 25, 1944* (Austin, TX: University of Texas Press, 1981); Spaatz Papers, Box 14, Library of Congress, Washington, DC.

17 Richard G. Davis, *Carl A. Spaatz and the Air War in Europe* (Washington, DC: Center for Air Force History, 1993), pp. 352–3.

18 Responses to Dr Bruce Hopper, USSTAF historian, 20 May and 27 June 1945, Spaatz Papers, Box 136, Library of Congress, Washington, DC.

19 Richard G. Davis, 'Pointblank vs Overlord: Strategic Bombing and the Normandy Invasion', *Air Power History*, 41(2): 4–6.

20 Davis, 'Pointblank vs Overlord', p. 10.

21 Zuckerman, *Six Men*, pp. 82–3; Zuckerman, *Apes to Warlords*, pp. 25, 246–56; Defence Committee Minutes for April and May, BNA PREM 3/334/2–3; Tedder, *With Prejudice*, pp. 521–33.

22 BNA AIR 37/1030; Alfred D. Chandler, Jr. and Stephen E. Ambrose (eds) *The Papers of Dwight David Eisenhower: The War Years* (Baltimore, MD: Johns Hopkins University Press, 1970), vol. III, p. 1892.

23 Sir Charles Webster and Noble Frankland, *The Strategic Air Offensive Against Germany, 1939–1945* (London: HMSO, 1961), vol. III, pp. 37–8; 'Effectiveness of Air Attack against Rail Transportation in the Battle of France', 1 June 1945: Maxwell AFB 138.4–37; A.L. Funk, 'Caught in the Middle: The French Population in Normandy' in T. Wilson (ed.) *D-Day, 1944* (Abilene, KS: University Press of Kansas, 1971, 1994), pp. 238–57.

24 Martin Middlebrook and Chris Everitt, *The Bomber Command War Diaries: An Operational Reference Book, 1939–1945* (London: Viking Penguin, 1985), pp. 489–520.
25 M.R.D. Foot, *SOE: An Outline History of the Special Operations Executive, 1940–46* (London: BBC, 1984), p. 225.
26 Tedder Diary (in author's possession), 12 & 25 May, 13 & 16 June 1944.
27 The issues are well summarised by John E. Fagg, 'Pre-Invasion Operations' in Wesley Frank Craven and James Lea Cate (eds) *The Army Air Forces in World War II* (Chicago: University of Chicago Press, 1951, new imprint, Office of Air Force History, Washington, DC, 1983), vol. III, pp. 138–81.
28 Murray and Millet, *War to be Won*, p. 425.
29 Basil Collier, *The Defence of the United Kingdom* (London: HMSO, 1957), pp. 338–9, 354–6, 386–8; F.H. Hinsley *et al. British Intelligence in the Second World War*, vol. 3, part 1 (London: HMSO, 1984), pp. 357–9; Jozef Garlinski, *Hitler's Last Weapons: The Underground War against the V-1 and V-2* (London: Methuen, 1978), pp. 78–80; David Irving, *The Mare's Nest* (London: Granada, 1985), *passim*.
30 Max Hastings, *Overlord: D-Day and the Battle for Normandy, 1944* (London: Michael Joseph, 1984), p. 179; Ronald Lewin, *Hitler's Mistakes* (London: Book Club Associates, 1984), pp. 150–1; Peter Calvocoressi *et al. Total War: The Causes and Courses of the Second World War* (London: Viking Penguin, 2nd edn, 1989), p. 510; Gerhard L. Weinberg, *A World at Arms: A Global History of World War II* (Cambridge: Cambridge University Press, 1994), pp. 676, 685.
31 Weinberg, *World at Arms*, pp. 677, 725; Matthew Jones, *Britain, the United States and the Mediterranean War, 1942–4* (London: Macmillan, 1996), pp. 138–9; Alan F. Wilt, 'The Summer of 1944: A Comparison of Overlord and Anvil/Dragoon', *Journal of Strategic Studies*, 4(2): 187–95.
32 Murray and Millet, *War to be Won*, pp. 433, 444.
33 Ibid., p. 456.
34 Weinberg, *World at Arms*, p. 762.
35 ACM Sir Norman R. Bottomley, 'The Course of the Combined Strategic Bomber Offensive from 14th April 1944 to the End of the European War', item 18, para. 29 of *Air Ministry Exercise Thunderbolt, Old Sarum, August 1947*, 2 vols, BNA AIR 8/1536.
36 Mierzejewski, 'Wheels Must Roll', pp. 265–6.
37 Williamson Murray, 'Retrospection' in John F. Kreis (ed.) *Piercing the Fog: Intelligence and Army Air Forces Operations in World War II* (Bolling AFB, Washington DC: Air Force History and Museums Program, 1996), pp. 411–13; Mierzejewski, 'Wheels Must Roll', pp. 410–12.
38 Annan, *Changing Enemies*, p. 117.
39 Mierzejewski, 'Wheels Must Roll', pp. 425–30; see also pp. 112–15, 137–42, 148, 158.
40 Terraine, *Right of Line*, pp. 547–8; Annan, *Changing Enemies*, p. 63.
41 Malcolm Smith, 'The Allied Air Offensive', *Journal of Strategic Studies*, 13(1): 77; Noble Frankland, *History at War* (London: Giles de la Mare, 1998), pp. 64–6.
42 Biddle, *Rhetoric and Reality*, pp. 270–86.
43 Denis Richards, *Portal of Hungerford* (London: Heinemann, 1977), p. 334.
44 Michael Howard, review of *The Strategic Air War Against Germany, 1939–1945: Report of the British Bombing Survey Unit* (London: Frank Cass, 1998) in *The Times Literary Supplement*, 21 August 1998, p. 10.
45 Sebastian Cox, 'An Unwanted Child – The Struggle to Establish a British Bombing Survey', *Strategic Air War*, pp. xvii–li.
46 Ibid., pp. xxxvii–xxxix.
47 David Eisenhower, *Eisenhower: At War, 1943–1945* (New York: Vintage Books, 1987), p. 257.
48 Eisenhower Papers, Post-PP, 1964, Box 47, Eisenhower Library, Abilene, Kansas.

12 Caen – the martyred city

Peter Gray

Many aspects of the air operations during World War II have attracted their share of myths and controversy. The efficacy of the strategic bombing campaign has been debated at length with considerable attention given to the primacy of targeting German morale and industrial capacity.[1] Individual raids such as the Dams, attacking the *Tirpitz*, and Dresden have also attracted much discussion.[2] It is, however, fair to say that this is not a new or even recent phenomenon; the various policies attracted debate and controversy both at the time and in the respective bombing surveys produced after the end of the war.[3] The ardent exponents of strategic bombing such as Air Chief Marshal Sir Arthur Harris and his US counterpart, General Carl Spaatz, decried any deviation of their assets from the attacks on the German heartland. Harris in particular resisted fiercely wasting time on what he called 'panacea targets'.[4] This debate reached a crescendo in the run up to, and immediate aftermath of, Operation OVERLORD – the Allied invasion of occupied Europe in June 1944. A relatively complicated command and control structure exacerbated the marked divergence of doctrinal (and dogmatic) priorities. The positions of senior airmen in the command chain may have been essential for pragmatic reasons – especially where specific assets, such as the heavy bombers, were kept separate from the force assigned to the Supreme Allied Commander. But these issues did little to harmonise relationships and will be discussed in greater depth below.

Out of all of the various myths, legends and controversies that have arisen since the liberation of France and the eventual overthrow of Nazi tyranny, few have left such a long-standing scar on the psyche of a city than the Allied bombing of Caen – the city that considers itself to have been martyred.[5] The strength of feeling is still evident today as any visitor to the memorial in the northern outskirts of the city is clearly able to see. In an area that is full of commemorations to the British, American and Free French forces, the poignancy of the Caen Memorial is most marked. Why should it be the exception? Any attempt to answer this question must include an examination of why Caen was subject to Allied aerial bombardment; that this question is regularly asked on staff rides and battlefield tours to the area adds to the need for some analysis.

This chapter will examine the various factors leading up to the bombing of Caen and the eventual capture of the city. It will therefore look at the planning for D-Day and the importance of Caen at the operational level of war. The planning will be set in the context of the air power strategy that pertained at the time with particular reference to the thinking on the support – direct and indirect – of ground forces. The chapter will also look at the command and control structures and examine some of the tensions therein. The decision-making process will then be set in the context of the progress of the air and ground war as it evolved. From this, it should be possible to show how events gathered momentum, resulting in the requests for aerial bombardment, its actual execution and eventual effectiveness.

The planning for OVERLORD

The prospect of a serious invasion of mainland Europe seemed remote in the dark days of 1940 and 1941. France had fallen and, although the Battle of Britain had been won, the contest in the Atlantic showed how tenuous Britain's survival was. The German invasion of Russia made a second front necessary as pressure in the East had to be relieved. For many long months, Bomber Command was the Allies' only option.[6] The entry of the USA into the war following Pearl Harbor and the German declaration of war made a second front not only vital, but also inevitable. The key question, however, was where this front was going to be. The Americans accepted a policy of Germany first; but the demand for settling scores with Japan meant that this would have to be done quickly. Churchill and his senior advisers considered a cross-Channel invasion (Operation SLEDGEHAMMER) to be too risky in 1942.[7] The decision was therefore taken to launch Operation TORCH in North Africa, thereby delaying the return to the Continent. Nevertheless, planning for an eventual invasion began in April 1942 with the tasking, by the British chiefs of staff, of General Sir Bernard Paget (C-in-C Home Forces) and Captain Lord Louis Mountbatten (Head of Combined Operations) to begin planning for Operation ROUNDUP. This early planning showed the potential of Normandy as a viable alternative to the Pas de Calais region which had seemed the most obvious choice of landing area (to the Germans as well as to the Allies). The Casablanca Conference of January 1943 saw the British chiefs of staff prevail over their US colleagues with action remaining in the Mediterranean with Operation HUSKY – the invasion of Sicily. Partly to keep the cross-Channel option 'in play', Lieutenant General Frederick Morgan was appointed as chief of staff to the supreme allied commander (designate). The acronym COSSAC was obviously less of a mouthful for those involved in the planning, which quickly gained momentum. By July 1943, the outline was in place for the invasion of Normandy with the target date of 1 May 1944.[8]

The Casablanca Conference was followed by a similar event in Quebec in August 1943. OVERLORD was high on the agenda, with the choice of supreme commander an important topic. The initial speculation was that the commander would be British and Churchill was keen for General Sir Alan Brooke (Chief of the Imperial General Staff and Chairman of the Chiefs of Staff Committee) to take on the role.[9] During the Quebec Conference, Churchill relented to American demands that their numerical superiority should guarantee them the key position. Underlying these discussions was a marked suspicion that neither Churchill nor Brooke was fully committed to OVERLORD. The almost automatic American nomination for the post was General George C. Marshall, the US Chief of Staff. President Roosevelt was reluctant to allow his key strategy adviser out of arm's reach, however, and General Dwight D. Eisenhower became the default option. Churchill had let it be known that Eisenhower was the only acceptable alternative to Marshall and his appointment was formally announced on 6 December 1943. Major General Omar N. Bradley was selected to command US ground forces. Competition for his British and Commonwealth counterpart was between Lieutenant General Bernard Montgomery and General Sir Harold Alexander. Churchill tended to favour 'Alex' while Brooke spoke strongly in favour of Montgomery. Brooke also doubted that Alexander had the strategic vision necessary to cope with OVERLORD. Eisenhower's marked preference was for Alexander – he considered Monty abrasive and difficult to control. The decision, in Montgomery's favour, was announced on 22 December 1943 with Alexander to remain in Italy where he provided much-needed continuity. This removed any lingering barriers to the appointment of Air Chief Marshal Sir Arthur Tedder as Eisenhower's deputy – air was going to be critical to the success of the European adventure.

Eisenhower's first impressions of the plan for OVERLORD were that the forces assigned were insufficient. Montgomery came to similar conclusions in parallel.[10] Popular myth has it that the latter was solely responsible for beefing up OVERLORD; while it is true that he became the architect for many of the changes, it is typical of the man that he claimed absolute credit. COSSAC was considerably expanded with many new faces, and detailed planning entered a new phase. Montgomery envisaged the rapid seizure of the main centres of road communication – Caen and Bayeux – and the high ground to the south and east of the former city. This area controlled the approaches and crossings of the Odon and Orne rivers and had to be captured early to prevent German reinforcement. This area would also provide vital land for the construction of airfields to reduce the flying times for close support aircraft. Montgomery also insisted on the use of airborne forces, on both flanks, to prevent German counter-attacks on the beachheads. The other element of Montgomery's thinking was the simultaneous attack on Caen, the high ground around it *and* the capture of Cherbourg by means of a Cotentin landing. Montgomery disregarded the risk of splitting his forces and not achieving sufficient concentration on Caen. He nevertheless believed that the battle would be lost or won in the British sector with considerable potential for the Allies to be repulsed by heavy Panzer counter-attacks.

As the planning matured, the importance of the capture of Caen became abundantly clear. The Allies would have to capture Caen and its associated river crossings: it could not just be bypassed. With characteristic boldness, Montgomery saw the city being taken by speed and aggression *on D-Day itself*. There was no question of using the city as 'a hinge' or maintaining a defensive posture on the flank.[11]

Air strategy

The planning requirements for air forces generally, and for those engaged in OVERLORD, were set in place at the Casablanca and Quebec Conferences. COSSAC effectively saw the air campaign in four phases.[12] The first of these was the continued strategic bombing of Germany. The second, or preparatory phase, saw the addition of communications targets, coastal defence batteries and airfields. The priority in the third phase would be the direct support of the invasion fleet. The fourth phase would be more of the same with the requirement to prevent enemy movement and reinforcement.

The Casablanca Conference set the tone for the use of air power for the remainder of the war in a number of ways. The first of these was the understandable, and laudable, aim to achieve complete mastery of the air. The Luftwaffe was to be dispersed, harried and destroyed by all possible means.[13] The second requirement was for the formation of large tactical air forces able to assert mastery over the battlefield and wield the firepower first seen in the desert. There was, however, less agreement on the utilisation of the bomber forces. The Casablanca directive read: 'The primary objective will be the progressive destruction and dislocation of the German military, industrial and economic system, and the undermining of the morale of the German people to a point where their capacity for armed resistance is fatally weakened'. As Biddle has pointed out, this contained something for everyone and gave the commanders a deal of latitude, both in target sets and methodology.[14] This allowed Air Chief Marshal Sir Arthur Harris (C-in-C Bomber Command) to pursue targets based on German industrial output and morale and the USAAF, under Lieutenant General Carl A. Spaatz, to attack key, or vital, centres such as oil manufacture and storage. Harris saw the diversion of his aircraft from Germany to gun emplacements and beach defences as a disservice to the army and, potentially, a disaster.[15]

Doctrinal issues were complicated by the appointment of Air Chief Marshal Sir Trafford Leigh-Mallory as Air Commander-in-Chief of the Allied Expeditionary Air Force. Neither bomber force took kindly to direction from a person that they considered to have only fighter experience.[16] That Leigh-Mallory had written extensively in the inter-war years on the use of air power in support of armies only served to deepen the antagonism.[17] The matter was only resolved in practice by 'direction' from Tedder, acting on behalf of the Supreme Commander.

To facilitate the second phase of pre-OVERLORD operations, Leigh-Mallory set up an AEAF Bombing Committee under the chairmanship of Air Commodore Kingston-McCloughry; its membership included Professor Solly Zuckerman. The latter argued that attacks on rail facilities would be the most efficacious means of disrupting German potential for reinforcement. Some 75 repair, servicing and similar targets were identified. Harris's objection that the necessary precision was beyond the capability of his crews was shattered on 6 March 1944 when 263 aircraft of Bomber Command dropped 1,258 tons of bombs on the railway centre at Trappes, south east of Paris. The centre was so hard hit that it was out of action for over a month.[18] The 'Transportation Plan' was formally adopted by the chiefs of staff and appropriate direction was issued to the strategic bomber commanders on 15 April 1944. Having had his objections swept aside, Harris put his command to the task with a vengeance and the plan was a considerable success.[19] Bomber Command, and their American colleagues, had by D-Day flown 21,949 sorties dropping 66,517 tons of bombs on 80 targets.[20] Targets were deliberately chosen to minimise collateral damage with a maximum acceptable potential French casualty toll of 150. As the RAF official historian points out, the French were stoical about the need for these operations – in marked contrast to the aftermath of Caen.

The third phase of the air campaign was conducted at the tactical level by aircraft under the command of Air Marshal Sir Arthur Coningham (Second Tactical Air Force) and General Louis Brereton of the US 9th Air Force. A range of targets were attacked from the Pas de Calais area down to the Cotentin peninsula. By this time the Luftwaffe had taken a pounding on all fronts. They were still able to operate on an occasional basis, but air superiority had been fought for, won, and then maintained primarily over the skies of their own heartland.

Command and control – the vexed issue of personalities

Supply of seriously good wartime commanders is always limited. It is therefore no surprise the same old list of 'usual suspects' keeps on reappearing – or stalwarts like Harris remain in post. With success inevitably comes an ego to match with Montgomery as the *primus inter pares*. There was no love lost between Tedder and Montgomery following their experiences in the desert campaign, but the greatest dissension was between Coningham and Monty. In the desert the two men had worked together exceptionally well, proving to be the model of co-located component commanders. By the time Normandy came round, the airman considered that his erstwhile colleague had slighted him. Coningham was, however, one of the most capable and experienced senior commanders available and Tedder may also have felt that he could be used as a foil to Montgomery. Both senior airmen considered that Montgomery had not made best use of air power in the desert and that he needed a strong team.[21] The batting order was enhanced further by

Air Vice-Marshal Harry Broadhurst who had fought with distinction in the Battle of Britain, North Africa, Sicily and Italy. He considered that the feud between Montgomery and Coningham was badly counter-productive and sought to minimise its impact. His sound relationship with Montgomery, whilst of considerable benefit to the conduct of the campaign, did little to improve his standing with Coningham and Tedder.

The battle of the egos found its culminating point in the need to capture ground suitable for the airfield sites necessary for the full exploitation of air power. This had been requested as a priority by Leigh-Mallory as early as 20 March. The tactical aircraft had relatively little combat task time over Normandy when operating from UK bases; this had been long recognised as a limitation to the choice of this region over the more logical Pas de Calais area. Leigh-Mallory saw tactical air as being key to the push to the Seine. During the planning phase, Montgomery refused to make promises that he could not guarantee keeping. But the airmen's demands for territory coincided neatly with Montgomery's own operational priorities. The eventual failure to take Caen and the surrounding area quickly provided the aviators with the ammunition with which to attack Montgomery.

The delay in capturing Caen also exasperated the Americans, who began to suspect that Montgomery was overly cautious. The importance of the British sector had not changed, but by 30 June Montgomery had begun to talk of containment rather than breakthrough. The lack of progress led to increasingly strident calls for Montgomery's removal – particularly from those that opposed his appointment in the first place. Bradley for example thought that it was typical 'Monty' – over-cautious, promising much and delivering little.

D-Day and beyond

Tidal conditions in the English Channel gave the Allies a narrow window for invasion in June 1944. A full-blown storm wrecked any chance of invasion on the morning of 5 June. Group Captain J.M. Stagg provided the meteorological brief for 6 June 1944. In what was probably the most critical met brief in the history of that rather inexact science (or black art), Stagg offered a glimmer of hope that Eisenhower and Montgomery seized upon, albeit to the scepticism of their air marshals.[22] The essential surprise was achieved, not least because of the marginal nature of the weather. Indeed, Rommel was in Germany on the strength of the weather-reporting! On D-Day itself, Bomber Command flew over 1,000 sorties dropping more than 5,000 tons of bombs as well as copious quantities of *window* (a codename for strips of aluminium foil used to confuse enemy radar). The aerial armada was reinforced by waves of transport and glider tugs carrying out the airborne landings on the flanks. British forces landed on their beaches at approximately 0700 with I Corps tasked to take Caen: in particular British Third Infantry Division was to 'capture Caen and secure a bridgehead over the River Orne at that place'.[23] The move inland from Sword Beach did not occur as rapidly as had been hoped, with elements of the division bogged down in front of the German fortification named 'Hillman'. By nightfall, a combination of the fortifications and elements of the 21st Panzer had effectively blocked progress towards Caen. Matters had not been helped by unusually high tides that restricted the amount of space on the beaches, which had in turn slowed the disembarkation of armour.

Hitler's prohibition to all commanders that they must not give up an inch of ground meant that they fought where they stood. Overwhelming Allied air power ensured that there could be neither re-supply nor reinforcement in depth. Counter-attacks were essential German doctrine. Set-piece battles were therefore the exception rather than the rule, with the war quickly degenerating into an attritional grind of vicious small-unit engagements. Much of this was inevitably the province of the infantry – and they were in short supply.[24] Likewise, close coordination between armour and infantry was frequently absent. In the face of highly effective anti-tank guns, determined Panzer divisions and brutal determination, the British forces made slow going. Arguably, had the Germans had even air parity, matters could have been considerably worse. Recriminations over lack of progress surfaced quickly with an overwhelming sense that these latter-day citizen armies were reluctant to commit to the type of warfare being fought. Commanders, from Montgomery downwards, were aware of the paucity of reinforcements, and most carried with them the legacy of the Somme and Passchendaele.[25]

In June, Montgomery made three major attempts to take Caen. The first of these was a direct assault as a continuation of D-Day operations on 7 and 8 June. He then tried to envelop the city in the Villers-Bocage operation of 13 June. Operation EPSOM followed on 25 June. This was to be a direct penetration by a powerful force involving all three corps. EPSOM, like its predecessors, was a dismal failure.[26] The best that can probably be said was that it prevented the Germans from mounting the expected counter-attack along the River Odon where much of the fighting took place.

By early July, Montgomery was running out of time and ideas. Caen was beginning to lose its strategic importance *per se* as the German reinforcements were tied down and the US army was making progress to the west. But the high ground to the south-east was still vital and as Caen could not be bypassed it would have to be taken – head-on if necessary. The planning for CHARNWOOD gathered momentum and with it the use of air power on the city.

The bombing of Caen

The first suggestion that heavy bombers be used to break the logjam in front of Caen came as early as 14 June when Leigh-Mallory flew to Normandy to see Montgomery. Relations between the two were strained because the airman had refused to sanction an airborne raid on the grounds of risk.

Montgomery, according to Leigh-Mallory's papers,[27] found the counter-proposal very attractive. The core idea had again originated with Kingston-McCloughrey and Zuckerman, and involved the use of the strategic bombers in direct support of the ground forces. This had only previously been done at Monte Cassino (15 February 1944) and Cassino (15 March 1944) in Italy. The concept was discussed further in a schoolhouse in Bayeux that was being used as the headquarters for the Second Army under General Dempsey. Their meeting was short-lived due to the arrival of Tedder, Coningham and Broadhurst. Neither Bomber Command nor the USSAF favoured the plan. More importantly, the nature of the terrain prevented the identification of a bomb line and suitable aiming points with the attendant risk of killing one's own troops. Furthermore, the target concentration was too low to justify the diversion of bomber assets.[28]

The politics and flexing of egos may have been sufficient for the plan to die stillborn. In reality, the practical problems spoke for themselves. Tactical air continued to be used with extra tasking against particular strongpoints – admittedly with only limited success. What was more relevant was that the kernel of the idea remained dormant for later use.

As Montgomery was putting together his plans for CHARNWOOD, he decided to try again for heavy bomber support. The German defences were known to be strong and intelligence suggested that they had recently been reinforced. The request envisaged the heavy bombers blasting a path through the defences in the northern suburbs of Caen. Leigh-Mallory and his staff considered the bid at their Stanmore Headquarters on 7 July. Tedder normally attended these meetings, but exceptionally, Eisenhower also attended this meeting – presumably to ensure that Montgomery received the full support that he had requested and coincidently would have no scapegoats should CHARNWOOD fail. With little apparent debate, the meeting agreed to task 450 heavy bombers for that night.[29]

Bomber Command launched its first attacks at approximately 2200 on 7 July using 1000lb bombs. Most were fused to explode six hours later to coincide with the ground advance. The operation lasted for about an hour and featured 467 aircraft dropping some 2,276 tons of bombs. The concept was almost identical to the plan rejected in June, albeit with the aiming points reduced to two. Notwithstanding German reinforcement, the target density was no better than when the concept had been rejected in June. The target area was a box 4,000 yards wide by 1,500 yards deep and included the northern part of the city. Care was taken to avoid fratricide, but this left some of the strongpoints untouched.

The aftermath

Two days of heavy fighting then ensued with little evidence to suggest that the defenders had been affected by the air attacks; the northern half of Caen was eventually secured by I Corps. Montgomery's victory was somewhat pyrrhic in that he had captured a ruined city at high cost. The Germans had also suffered heavily, but had dug into new positions on the south side of the river. They also retained the high ground to the south and east. Many of the desired airfield sites had not been reached and those in the bridgehead remained within artillery range. The breakout into Normandy was as elusive as ever and, despite favourable press, the pressure on Montgomery remained.

An immediate byproduct of the heavy bombing of Caen was that it was the first time that many of the soldiers had seen the full wrath of the heavy bomber force. General Dempsey was actually airborne with Broadhurst and watched the proceedings. Broadhurst recalled that his senior colleague had been shaken by the scale of the destruction – as well as by the damage done to their aircraft by anti-aircraft fire which necessitated a crash landing![30] Some reports suggest that this beneficial effect on morale extended down to those in the slit trenches facing Caen.[31] Montgomery claimed that the heavy bombing had been a vital part in the subsequent capture of Caen; he also praised Leigh-Mallory for his consistent support.[32] Later assessments of Montgomery's analysis range from fantasy to guilty conscience.[33]

Having been instrumental in the initial concept of using heavy bombers in support of the army, Kingston-McCloughry and Zuckerman conducted a survey immediately after the capture of Caen. They reported that there had been virtually no sign of enemy gun emplacements, tanks or casualties in the target area that the army had requested. This was in contrast with other areas close by that would definitely have been worthy of Bomber Command's efforts. The effect on friendly morale had been beneficial, but transitory. Kingston-McCloughry concluded that the air element of the operation was little more than a frill for a ground plan already made.[34]

The bombing created considerable quantities of rubble and impeded the advance into Caen. This restricted the access for armour, reduced the number of exits that the Germans had to defend and allowed extra scope for snipers against the exposed infantry. The obstructions also prevented the rapid seizure of the Orne bridges which were destroyed by the defenders.

The French population of Caen had been advised to evacuate the city by the Germans and their own prefect. About one quarter had taken this advice. Many of those who remained had expressed a rather fatalistic 'frying pan and fire' attitude, preferring to remain in their own homes.[35]

Conclusions

The military efficacy of Bomber Command's attack on Caen appears to have been somewhere between negligible and counter-productive. The effect on the residents was devastating. Any impact on the morale of either side was transitory with the Germans continuing to fight fiercely for two further days. The decision-making process was hasty and totally uncoordinated from the major land offensive. What had been decreed as being too barren in target density suddenly became worth the effort. There are therefore no easy answers, from a straightforward effects-based approach, as to why Caen was bombed.

It is, however, less cut and dried if one attempts to analyse how Caen came to be bombed. Montgomery was under increasing pressure to break the stalemate that had persisted for a full month after D-Day – the original target date. There can be no doubt that his later claims that he had always planned a 'holding' operation while the Americans developed their campaign in the West are anything other than fabrication. The balance of German forces in his sector may have made this reality into a slight virtue, but it was not pre-planned.

Tedder recalled in his diary on the day after the bombing that 'The problem is Monty who can be neither moved nor moved to action'. There is no doubt that he was under considerable pressure from Eisenhower – not least because the Supreme Commander was conscious that his fellow countrymen were becoming increasingly strident in their views that the war was being fought exclusively at the cost of American lives. There is some speculation that Montgomery was under pressure directly from Churchill; Kingston-McCloughry has suggested that the Prime Minister wrote to Monty along the lines that he must make progress or be replaced. It is feasible, and in character, that Churchill would so threaten. But as D'Este points out, it is inconceivable that Monty could have been removed at that stage. The wider message that such a move would have given – in Moscow, with Roosevelt, the British public and among the Germans – would have been unthinkable.[36] Nevertheless, Montgomery was not the sort of character who was going to risk future fame and fortune on such a gamble.

The personalities involved on the air side makes for somewhat unsavoury analysis. There was an unhealthy mix of egotism and ambition with many officers covertly looking forward to the appointments lists of the peacetime air forces. Kingston-McCloughry was an arch wheeler and dealer who had been involved in a number of backstairs controversies.[37] There was little chance that he and Zuckerman would be prepared to take a back-seat role. Likewise, Leigh-Mallory was frustrated with having so little genuinely to *command* – especially with the heavy bombers remaining under their respective commanders. He was determined that he would make his mark on the war and his casting of straws for Montgomery to clutch was a key factor in the eventual destruction of Caen.

The early appointment of Montgomery can be considered to be the starting point as he was neither a visionary leader nor someone capable of improvisation when matters turned sour. Failure to take Caen on D-Day accelerated the series of events with the direct attacks on D + 2 and D + 3, through Villers-Bocage and EPSOM to CHARNWOOD themselves as the key milestones. That they developed a momentum of their own helps to show *how* Caen came to be bombed, but cannot satisfactorily answer the question *why*.[38] This is why the normally stoic French response of 'it had to be done' is not always held to apply to Caen – hence the martyred city.

Notes

1 For authoritative accounts, see Richard Overy, *The Air War 1939–1945* (New York: Stein and Day), and more recently, *Why the Allies Won* (London: Pimlico, 1996). See also Noble Frankland, *The Bombing Offensive Against Germany – Outlines and Perspectives* (London: Faber & Faber, 1965).
2 For an account on Dresden see Peter W. Gray, 'Dresden 1945 – Just Another Raid?', *Royal Air Force Air Power Review*, 4(1): 1–14, and for the *Tirpitz* see John Sweetman, 'Barnes Wallis's other Bouncing Bomb: Plans to Sink the German Battleship *Tirpitz* in 1943', *Royal Air Force Air Power Review*, 5(2 & 3).
3 For the American version see the *Reports of the United States Strategic Bombing Survey* and subsequent debates on the subject: Gian P. Gentile, *How effective Is Strategic Bombing? Lessons Learned from World War II to Kosovo* (New York: New York University Press, 2001). The British equivalent is *The Strategic Air War against Germany 1939–1945: Report of the British Bombing Survey Unit*, republished by Frank Cass, London with introductory material by Sebastian Cox, 1998.
4 MRAF Sir Arthur Harris, *Bomber Offensive* (London: Collins, 1947), p. 220 et seq.
5 This remains the perception today – the martyrdom aspect is reflected in the City Memorial.
6 Discussions between Churchill and Stalin in August 1942 confirmed the grand strategic level direction for Bomber Command. The leaders agreed that not only should German industry be bombed, but also the population and its morale. Stalin stressed the importance of attacking Berlin and this cascaded down to Harris later that month. Stalin's appreciation of the efforts of Bomber Command was reinforced by Harris sending the Russian leader a book of aerial photographs of the damage wrought.
7 Carlo D'Este, *Decision in Normandy* (London: Robson, 2000), p. 25.
8 Ibid., p. 35.
9 Ibid., p. 43 and David Fraser, *Alanbrooke* (London: Harper Collins, 1982), pp. 332, 333.
10 D'Este, ibid., p. 61.
11 Ibid., p. 74.
12 Hilary St George Saunders, *Royal Air Force 1939–1945, Volume III, The Fight is Won* (London: HMSO, 1954), p. 84.
13 Overy, *The Air War 1939–1945*, p. 95.
14 Tami Davis Biddle, 'British and American Strategic Bombing', in John Gooch (ed.) *Air Power Theory and Practice* (London: Frank Cass, 1995), p. 120.
15 Saunders, *The Fight is Won*, p. 85.
16 Overy, *The Air War 1939–1945*, p. 97.
17 See for example the article by Wing Commander Trafford Leigh-Mallory in Volume 1 of *The RAF Quarterly*.
18 Saunders, *The Fight is Won*, p. 87.
19 As confirmed by Professor Zuckerman in his private diary; cited by D'Este, *Decision in Normandy*, p. 215.
20 Saunders, *The Fight is Won*, p. 88. Harris records that Bomber Command, by the end of June 1944, had flown 13,349 sorties dropping 52,347 tons of bombs with a casualty rate of 2.6 per cent. *Bomber Offensive*, p. 204.
21 D'Este, *Decision in Normandy*, pp. 218–19.
22 Ibid., p. 110.
23 Ibid., p. 120.
24 Ibid., pp. 252 et seq.
25 Ibid., p. 301.

26 Ibid., p. 245.
27 Reproduced in Bill Newton Dunn, *Big Wing – The Biography of Air Chief Marshal Sir Trafford Leigh-Mallory* (Shrewsbury: Airlife, 1992), p. 131.
28 D'Este, *Decision in Normandy*, p. 228.
29 Ibid., p. 310.
30 Ibid., pp. 314, 316.
31 Ibid., p. 316.
32 Bill Newton Dunn, *Big Wing*, p. 155.
33 Alexander McKee, *Caen, Anvil of Victory* (London: Souvenir Press, 1964), Chapter 14.
34 Cited in Ian Gooderson, *Air Power at the Battlefront; Allied Close Air Support in Europe 1943–1945* (London: Frank Cass, 1998), p. 136.
35 Max Hastings, *Overlord; D-Day and the Battle for Normandy 1944* (London: Pan, 1999), p. 263.
36 D'Este, *Decision in Normandy*, p. 311.
37 For a discussion on the political intrigue behind the downfall of Air Chief Marshal Sir Cyril Newall see Sebastian Ritchie's article in *War and Society*, 16(1): 83.
38 From a historiographical viewpoint, this should not be an issue. Some could argue that the functional approach is at least as valid as the causal; see for example E.H. Carr, *What is History?* (London: Penguin, 1987), p. 88. From a staff ride, or education, perspective, this debate adds to the value. It can be further enhanced by the importance contextual element added by R.W. Davies in the notes to the second edition. This aspect of military education is discussed elsewhere in this book.

13 Deception and the planning of D-Day

Mary Kathryn Barbier

When Allied troops stormed the Normandy beaches on the morning of 6 June 1944, their action was the culmination of years of preparation and anticipation. Victory was by no means assured. The Germans had had time to construct the Atlantic Wall and to erect their strongest defences at ports such as Calais. The Allies' operation at Dieppe in August 1942 had demonstrated several things, including the strength of the German position, the need for adequate training and preparation, and the importance of surprise. Consequently, as they began to plan the cross-Channel assault, the Allies chose to design and implement a series of deception operations to cover Operation OVERLORD.[1] The deception plan that had the most direct impact on the cross-Channel invasion was Operation FORTITUDE SOUTH, which was designed to pin down the German 15th Army in the Pas de Calais region of France. After the war, evaluators of the deception concluded that it was successful because the Germans failed to move the army for several weeks after the commencement of the Normandy invasion. Most historians have concurred with that conclusion. Few, however, have asked whether or not there were any reasons, besides the deception, that would explain why the 15th Army did not receive orders to move into Normandy. Before examining other factors that could explain this German decision, however, an understanding of the deception plan is necessary.

Two separate groups ultimately worked on a cover plan for OVERLORD – General Sir Frederick Morgan, the chief of staff to the Supreme Allied Commander designate (COSSAC), and his staff and Colonel John Bevan and his staff on the London Controlling Section (LCS). Bevan hoped to mask the build-up of US forces in Britain and was thus concerned by impending communications restrictions and the closing of frontiers in England, Scotland and Wales. He opposed the early closing of the frontiers because he believed that this might signal that the time of the invasion was at hand. Morgan, however, carried the day, choosing to emphasise tactical, not strategic, surprise. He stressed that the Allies would be unable to keep the build-up of troops a secret until D-Day. Therefore, it was his contention that the deception plan only had to hide the *target* of the Allied invasion.[2]

Because they had a high opinion of the German Intelligence Service, Morgan and his staff believed that they had to deceive the enemy in three separate ways – by intelligence, air reconnaissance and spies – which 'automatically implied an extensive programme of visual misdirection'.[3] The resulting vast nature of the deception scheme created problems for Allied commanders whose main concern was Operation OVERLORD. Because providing available troops, armaments, equipment, landing craft and other supplies for OVERLORD took precedence over making them available for other operations, including deception, the planners decided to coordinate the planning of OVERLORD and the cover plan to enable the sharing of physical supplies whenever possible. Planning for the deception operation, however, remained tentative until Allied leaders came to a final agreement concerning its nature and goals at the Teheran Conference in November 1943.[4]

While at the conference, Bevan received orders to develop a cover plan for the Normandy invasion. Upon his return to London, he and the LCS began work on an overall plan for the war against Germany in 1944. After three weeks of almost continuous effort, the LCS submitted a plan dubbed BODYGUARD to the British chiefs of staff, who approved it on 25 December 1943, shortly after Eisenhower's appointment as Supreme Allied Commander. Washington concurred with the British chiefs, and the combined chiefs of staff voted to proceed with the deception, which included several elements. The strategic goal of the plan was to convince the Germans to keep their troops in various locations around Europe even *after* OVERLORD had begun. To that end the plan even called for Soviet cooperation in a fictitious invasion of Norway. While much of BODYGUARD was designed to focus German attention in various parts of Europe, Operation FORTITUDE would have a direct impact on the upcoming D-Day landings.[5]

The goal of FORTITUDE was to convince the German High Command 'to make faulty dispositions in Northwest Europe before and after the Neptune assault'.[6] (Neptune was the codename for Operation OVERLORD.) Acknowledging that it would be difficult to conceal the build-up of Normandy invasion troops, Bevan increased the number of units involved in the deception to suggest forces sufficient for *two* invasions, by placing a fictitious army group in south-eastern England along with the true invasion force based more in the south-western part of the country. By doing so, the planners were able to use the Germans' own expectations that the Allies would cross the Channel at the Pas de Calais. Thus, the implementers hoped to convince the Germans that the Normandy invasion was merely a diversion for a second, more powerful landing near Calais. According to the fictitious plan, General Sir Bernard Montgomery would command one assault force, 21st Army Group, which would consist of British and American troops, while the Canadian and American forces of the First United States Army Group (FUSAG) would come ashore later near Calais.[7] Consequently, the deception scheme contained the right mix of actual fact and falsehood.

FORTITUDE had numerous objectives. The planners hoped to limit the 'rate and weight' of enemy reinforcement of Normandy prior to the assault, and to persuade the Germans to concentrate on fortifying areas outside the invasion site and focus their attention elsewhere. In addition, they wanted to convince the Germans to keep their troops away from Normandy for as long as possible. Although the deception had two parts, only FORTITUDE SOUTH, which suggested a threat to the Pas de Calais, had a direct impact on the D-Day invasion.

Allied leaders divided FORTITUDE SOUTH into two phases – pre-invasion and post-invasion. During the pre-invasion phase, the implementers hoped to convince the Germans that the main invasion would occur in the Pas de Calais *45 days after* the real invasion. During the post-invasion phase, the Allied leaders wanted the Germans to conclude that the Normandy assault was a diversion designed to draw their reserves from Belgium and the Pas de Calais. The goal was to convince the Germans to leave their 15th Army in Calais for as long as possible after D-Day.[8]

As noted, three methods would be used to implement the FORTITUDE deception – wireless transmissions, physical displays and double agents. The planners assigned the code word QUICKSILVER to the numerous ways in which the deception would be implemented. QUICKSILVER I referred to the two phases of ground force activities by 21st Army Group, commanded by Montgomery, and FUSAG, initially under the command of General Omar Bradley. FUSAG would set up camp in east and south-east England, supported by the Ninth US Air Force. Following the Normandy invasion, 21st Army Group would persuade German reserves to move toward the Allied beachhead, which would allow FUSAG and the Ninth US Air Force to assault the Pas de Calais area. The armies involved would participate in invasion exercises prior to launching their attack.

The wireless part of the plan, simulating the radio traffic of the non-existent FUSAG, was QUICKSILVER II. The wireless stations would initiate operations on 24 April. The plan scheduled 'two notional combined exercises, the first DRYSHOD the second WETSHOD . . . by the 4 Canadian Infantry Brigade assisted by Force G' for 16 and 25 April.[9] QUICKSILVER III referred to 'craft indication'. The planners ordered that 270 dummy landing craft be displayed in Yarmouth, Lowestoft, Waldringfield, Wolverstone, Dover and Folkestone to support the deception in the event that the enemy flew reconnaissance flights to verify the existence of an invasion force in the south-east. Naval wireless traffic would simulate the presence of craft in designated areas.

The air threat to the Pas de Calais received the QUICKSILVER IV designation. Prior to D-Day, air forces would suggest long-term preparations for the D plus 45 target date in several ways. Fighter squadrons based in southern England would engage in flight training exercises. High speed air sea rescue launches and air sea rescue squadrons stationed in south-east England would also practise. Fighters and bombers would participate in a 'large-scale air operation' in east and south-east England approximately three days before the Normandy invasion. By using 'careful manipulation of call signs, arrangement of deliberate indiscretions by R/T [radio telephony] and very strict orders as to the height at which aircraft are to fly', the air force would attempt to 'conceal' the movement of aircraft to Kent and the Thames Estuary from southern England. The construction of 'dummy hard standings' would supplement the normal activity on airfields in the south-east. Small-scale fighter and bomber practices would also occur in the same area and include 'deliberate indiscretions on R/T and manipulation of call signs'. Immediately before the invasion, the air force would bomb beaches and rail targets in the Pas de Calais area as part of the tactical railway bombing initiative.[10]

Orchestrating increased activity by Combined Headquarters, Dover, QUICKSILVER V would perpetuate the menace to the Pas de Calais. Combined Headquarters, Dover (in reality, II Canadian Corps Headquarters) undertook special work to create the illusion of 'extra tunnelling and the erection of further wireless stations'. New wireless circuits would go on line to supplement the deception. The plan also contained a provision for night-time activity: QUICKSILVER VI. Beginning in the middle of May, QUICK-SILVER VI included the erection of night lighting installations and imitated activity in areas such as Great Yarmouth, Lowestoft, the River Deben and the River Orwell.[11]

The deception was much more complex than one might suppose. In agreement with the LCS, the Supreme Headquarters Allied Expeditionary Force (SHAEF) devised a wide-ranging cover plan that incorporated implementation by all branches of the military, including naval diversionary operations, as well as several subsidiary plans.[12] By March 1944, thousands of real and imaginary American soldiers began arriving in Great Britain. While the real units joined Bradley's Twelfth US Army Group, the imaginary troops reported to the Third US Army in south-east England, which had recently received a new commander when Bradley was transferred. Command of the fictitious FUSAG now fell to General George Patton, which allowed the deception planners to take advantage of the enemy's fears; because they considered Patton to be 'the most able [Allied] battlefield commander', the Germans were quite certain that he would command the most important force involved in the impending invasion. In reality, because he had recently fallen from favour, Patton only received the responsibility of preparing the Third Army for future action in France.

The arrival of American troops in the UK began to lend an air of realism to the deception. In order to facilitate it further, several American units received orders to conduct their training in south-east England. Some of the men erected dummy army camps, fake airfields and dummy landing craft. After additional training, others provided the wireless traffic to simulate the existence of real forces engaged in invasion exercises. Wireless traffic for FORTITUDE SOUTH officially opened on 26 April 1944.[13]

Planning for the wireless component of the deception, however, had begun much earlier. Designed by COSSAC, the initial wireless plan dictated periods of wireless silence and intense activity for FUSAG and 21st Army Group. The length of silence periods varied from two to ten days, with the first scheduled to begin on 25 December 1943 and the last to end on 5 September 1944. Within each period the participating formations began and ended at different times. In late February 1944, SHAEF allocated deception units and equipment for the FORTITUDE scheme. The Supreme Commander received three deception units from No. 5 Wireless Group, which would establish one static monitoring section, one divisional section and one monitoring section. The Allied naval commander, the Expeditionary Force, the 21st Army Group commander in chief and the air commander in chief, AEAF all received three deception units, which were the 3103rd US Signal Service Battalion and two units from No. 5 Wireless Group, one of which would establish two divisional sections, while the other would set up a mobile monitoring section.[14]

The purpose of the wireless part of the deception was to reinforce the physical aspects of the plan. Although American troops helped erect physical displays, the main responsibility fell to the British. Montgomery formed a deception staff called G(R) or 'R' Force, appointed Colonel David Strangeways as its commander, and instructed him to implement the physical aspects of the FORTITUDE SOUTH deception. 'R' Force had to produce the illusion of another invasion force, FUSAG, by 'providing troop concentrations, vehicle parks, guns, tanks, and landing craft throughout southeast England'.[15]

Deception crews constructed fake troop camps, including 'tent cities', field kitchens, ammunition dumps, vehicle displays and whatever was needed to add realism. Canvas tent sides fluttered in the wind; field kitchen chimneys emitted large amounts of smoke daily to suggest the preparation of meals for the fictitious soldiers. By driving army trucks back and forth to leave visible tyre tracks, American engineers laid tracks to connect existing roads. Movie-set designers from Shepperton Studios provided rubber tanks, artillery, trucks and landing craft for some of the FUSAG displays. Using fiberboard, wood, canvas and sewer pipe, the studio's craftsmen constructed a dock and 'a large oil-storage complex near Dover'. To perpetuate the illusion of functional facilities, both King George VI and Montgomery 'inspected' the new dock and during a dinner at a hotel in Dover, Eisenhower addressed the workers who had built the dock and the storage complex. In addition, RAF fighters patrolled the skies overhead to enhance the illusion.[16]

However, implementation of the deception plan involved more than physical displays, wireless traffic and a flamboyant American commander. SHAEF and the LCS also decided to use double agents to reinforce the physical aspects of the deception. Special Means and the Double-Cross Committee had been cultivating several double agents, including 'Garbo', 'Brutus', 'Tricycle', 'Treasure' and 'Tate'. While some double agents had been captured and 'turned' by the British, others volunteered to work against their German masters.

Dusko Popov, or Tricycle, was a Yugoslav businessman who unwillingly began working for the Germans shortly after the war broke out. Within a year, the Germans had sent him to England. By 1944 not only had Tricycle established himself as a reliable double agent, he had also become 'the *Abwehr* paymaster in England'.[17] The Double-Cross Committee decided to use Tricycle and other agents to provide the enemy with information about FUSAG and the threat to the Pas de Calais in the hope that the Germans would reach the following faulty conclusions. First, the Pas de Calais region would be the primary location of the impending Allied assault. Second, following the initial landing, the Allies would launch a second more powerful attack in the same area. Third, the possibility that the Allies might launch a diversionary attack in the Bordeaux area to draw enemy troops from the invasion area was real. Finally, the Normandy invasion in early June would be a diversion, while the main attack would be the Pas de Calais assault near the end of June. According to Popov, 'Never did we say anything directly about the Pas de Calais. Naturally we couldn't say things right out. We had to give the Germans indications that would make them draw these conclusions themselves'.[18]

Of the double agents who participated in the deception, the most notorious was Juan Pujol Garcia, or Garbo. A trusted member of the German intelligence network, Garbo amassed a fictitious ring of 24 agents, all of whom provided various pieces of the puzzle that would help the Germans reach the intended conclusions about Allied plans. Consequently, he succeeded in presenting the Germans with a wide range of information for the FORTITUDE scheme. Some of it was gathered so that Garbo could respond to questionnaires sent by his German contact. The information was all plausible and authoritative, including details of the movement and training of Allied troops, which suggested that the Pas de Calais was indeed the true target of the upcoming Allied offensive.[19]

As D-Day approached, Garbo prepared to perform his most important work. In late May, his German contact in Madrid enquired about a division located near Glasgow. He also wanted an estimate about 'how much time will be lost from the moment the division starts its embarkation operation until news reaches you for transmission to us by message'.[20] One of Garbo's agents had observed the division in question. Garbo instructed him to keep close watch on a fleet in the area, because its departure would indicate the commencement of an invasion. In addition, he wired Madrid that he could transmit the information within 12 hours, which meant that the receiving station would have to stay open past its normal shutdown time of 11.00 p.m.

It was a truly dangerous game. Now, in order to maintain his credibility, Garbo would have to notify the Germans about the start of the Normandy invasion. Although he initially opposed such a move, Eisenhower eventually agreed, but stipulated that the message could go out no sooner than three and a half hours prior to the initial landing of Allied troops. Ironically, the Madrid receiving station was closed when Garbo tried to wire the message in the early hours of 6 June. Consequently, in addition to being unable to announce the start of the invasion, Garbo could not communicate his most important message until two nights later. Even so, Garbo's superiors in Germany raised his level of credibility based on the information that he provided about the Normandy invasion. As a result, his continuous assertion that Normandy was but a diversion and that the main invasion was yet to come and would take place at Calais carried more weight.

Thanks to the FORTITUDE deception, by the time the vulnerable Allied forces landed on the beaches at Normandy on 6 June, the Germans were apparently convinced that the enemy had enough troops stationed in the UK to launch more than one invasion. Intelligence indicated that the Germans believed that the Allies would take the shortest route across the English Channel, from Dover to the Pas de Calais. Hence, the Germans put most of their efforts into defending Calais and were quite reluctant even after the invasion to transfer their 15th Army from the Pas de Calais to Normandy. They did, however, reinforce the battlefield with divisions from other parts of France and from as far away as the Eastern Front.

No one can doubt that the FORTITUDE deception plan had an effect on the Allies' success in Normandy, but the extent of that effect can be questioned. When reaching a conclusion about the importance of FORTI-TUDE one must first consider whether or not the deception operation was a success. Most historians who mention the deception do so in terms of the *success*, not the *importance*, of the scheme. Several of them intimate that success and importance are synonymous and praise FORTITUDE, because it appeared to be successful. They fail, however, to address the issue of which part or parts of the operation – wireless transmissions, physical displays or double agents' messages – successfully transmitted the cover story to the Germans.

In general, historians rely upon analyses of the deception's outcome by Sir Ronald Wingate and Roger Hesketh. Both men served on the LCS and wrote accounts of the planning, implementation and outcome of FORTI-TUDE. Although he suggested that the deception succeeded in disguising the time and place of the Allied invasion from the Germans, Wingate conceded that not all aspects of the plan contributed to the Germans' acceptance of the fictitious threat. According to Wingate, the OKW *Lagebericht* (intelligence summary) indicated that the Germans accepted all of the imaginary formations that participated in FORTITUDE as real. He admitted, however, that the OKW might not have obtained its information about these formations from the wealth of wireless traffic sent out over the airwaves as part of the deception: 'It is rather surprising to note that the OKW *Lagebericht* provides no single example of [the] wireless programme having brought any item in the FORTITUDE story to the knowledge of the

Germans in the first instance. There are a few rare cases where the "Y" report purports to confirm Intelligence which has already been supplied by one of the controlled agents'.[21]

In addition, the Germans apparently failed to observe the numerous displays of fake landing craft, supply depots, airfields and army camps. The OKW *Lagebericht* did not, according to Wingate, indicate the presence of landing craft in south-east England, primarily because few German aircraft succeeded in flying reconnaissance missions over the area either before or after Allied troops arrived in Normandy. Wingate concluded, 'every phase in the story can be directly attributed to the three double-cross agents, GARBO, BRUTUS, and TRICYCLE. Individual messages can be checked with passages in the German Intelligence Summary'.[22] Wingate did not, however, suggest that Allied deception teams should not have transmitted wireless messages or displayed dummy landing craft, which he called 'valuable insurance, the omission of which might on another occasion cause disastrous results'. Although the lack of enemy reconnaissance flights explained the Germans' lack of awareness of the physical displays, Wingate admitted that he did not understand why the wireless programme failed to garner German attention.[23]

Hesketh concurred with some of Wingate's conclusions. He acknowledged that the dummy landing craft did not contribute to the deception. Like Wingate, he compared the physical displays to having an insurance policy. Because British intelligence had captured all the German agents who entered Great Britain, no uncontrolled spies could provide the Germans with information about the displays. Noting the limitations of wireless deception, Hesketh stated, 'even if one has the resources and the skill to disclose false intentions by controlled leakage, one can scarcely hope that the enemy will always be listening at the right moment, nor can one be sure that faulty reception may not prevent him from hearing if he is listening'.[24]

Consequently, he admitted that the most reliable aspect of FORTITUDE SOUTH was the role played by the double agents. Throughout his report, however, Hesketh reiterated his opinion that FORTITUDE succeeded beyond their initial expectations in convincing the Germans that the assault on Normandy was a feint and that the Allies would invade later in the area around the Pas de Calais.

If one accepts the assertions made by Wingate and Hesketh, then one can legitimately attempt to ascertain the dependability of *Abwehr*, which was the principal German intelligence service from 1935 until 1944. The Germans made incorrect assumptions about the how, when, where and the strength of the Allied invasion because of a failure in the 'estimative process', which resulted from poor intelligence. After crediting the Allies with a system of intelligence that provided their leaders with an accurate portrait of German defences, coastal obstacles and troop strength and placement, Major Anton Staubwasser asserted, 'As to the sources of German military intelligence . . . in Great Britain and the USA, H Gp B knew that we did not have one single agent in these countries that were on the defence, who had any insight to the Allied invasion plans, and that the whole intelligence service against the western Allies was exceedingly faulty'. Staubwasser went on to say that the Allies had 'been very clever at playing no end of false reports into the hands of the German command . . . The *Oberkommando* of H Gp B was well aware of the complete lack of agents having insight to Allied invasion plans'.[25]

An analysis of the German Intelligence Service after the war reinforced Staubwasser's perception of inadequacies. Part of the problem was attributed to Admiral Wilhelm Canaris, the head of *Abwehr*, who was apparently a bad judge of men. In addition, he was a poor organiser. There is some evidence to suggest that *Abwehr* officers 'sat in Paris and Athens, in Biarritz and Estoril, enjoying the opportunities for self-indulgence provided by these resports [*sic*], undisturbed (thanks to a complete lack of centralization at Hq), so long as a quota of reports was sent in'. The validity of these reports was unimportant: ' "It was better to have a controlled agent than none at all", observed one cynical officer when it was suggested to him (correctly) that his principal source of information was under Allied management'. Another officer reacted in horror at the thought that his agent was controlled by the enemy: 'If he were to admit that to his chief, he said, he would be shot for defeatism'.[26]

The fact that John Masterman, who ran the Double-Cross Committee, asserted that the British captured and turned every agent that the Germans sent could imply a certain degree of ineptitude on the part of the Germans either in the people whom they chose to be agents or in the level of training they received. There is no denying that the British excelled at identifying possible enemy spies. The exploits of Garbo and Tricycle, as portrayed in their autobiographies and their case files, seem at times a bit far-fetched; therefore, one has to wonder why the Germans failed to question their reliability and appeared to accept all of the information that these two and other spies provided.[27] According to 'Johnny' Jebsen, a double agent known as 'Artist', Canaris 'did not care if all the agents in Britain were fakes as long as he could go to Field Marshal Keitel, the head of the German high command, and report that he had twelve agents in Britain, each of them writing a letter once a week'.[28] In addition, it is possible that by the end of the war several *Abwehr* officers were no longer employing agents despite the fact that they were still providing information from them. Several officers pocketed the money meant for their agents and either fabricated the information or obtained it from the newspapers.[29]

Despite the possible failings of the *Abwehr* and other German intelligence agencies, Wingate, Hesketh and many historians judge the FORTITUDE deception as wildly successful because the Germans failed to move the 15th Army from the Pas de Calais to Normandy. They credit the deception for the enemy's decision not to transfer the army, but they fail to ask an important question. Are there any other reasons why the Germans decided to leave the 15th Army where it was? There are several factors to consider here.

Because they had concluded months earlier that the Allies might launch several assaults, some of which would be diversionary, the Germans could not immediately react to the Normandy invasion as if it were the main attack.[30] As a result, they did not transfer their Panzer reserves immediately to Normandy. Some historians emphasise the role of Garbo's 8/9 June message for the cancellation of Gerd von Rundstedt's order transferring the 1st SS Panzer Division to Normandy. The 1st SS Panzer did, however, move to Normandy a week later. Even if the Germans had tried to transfer the division earlier, its movement would have been harassed by Allied air forces and the forces of the Resistance, which would have delayed its arrival.[31]

Prior to D-Day, the Allies instituted the Transportation Plan, which was an air offensive aimed at isolating Normandy to prevent German reinforcement of the battlefield. By attacking road and rail bridges across the River Seine, Allied aircraft performed a twofold function. They intimated the Pas de Calais as the site of the impending invasion and they limited traffic from the Pas de Calais into Normandy. Allied bombing forced the Germans to send supplies and troops to the battlefield via indirect routes, often through or around Paris, which frequently delayed their arrival for several days. By D-Day no routes across the River Seine north of Paris remained open. Allied bombers were particularly successful in attacking the railway bridges across the River Seine and the Paris-Cointure railway junctions prior to D-Day, which forced the Germans to disembark from trains north of the Seine and travel to Normandy by road. Before the invasion, the Germans could only use three road bridges across the river between Paris and the sea. As a result, the Germans had to *ferry* troops, supplies and vehicles across the river, which greatly impeded their ability to reinforce their troops in Normandy.

Continuous attacks on railways by Allied bombers after D-Day caused the Germans to experience further delays in reinforcing the battlefield. For example, damage caused by Allied aircraft and the French Resistance hindered the movement of the 9th and 10th SS Panzer Divisions, which the Germans transferred from the Eastern Front. It took less time for the two Panzer divisions to travel from the Eastern Front to France than it did for them to proceed from eastern France to Normandy.[32] In addition, shortly after the invasion, Allied aircraft succeeded in obstructing the major railways across the River Loire, which hindered the movement of German forces and supplies into Normandy from the south. By closing the Loire rail lines, the Allied air forces completely isolated the Normandy battlefield. During the first week of the invasion, the Germans failed 'to run a single supply train into Normandy across the Seine and Loire'.[33]

Evidence of German difficulties with regard to the movement of troops and supplies beginning in early May can be found in the *Ultra* intercepts. On 1 May, Keitel complained about inadequate repairs to railways damaged by air attacks. Two days later there were complaints about 2nd SS Panzer Division's deficiencies in motor transport and 12th SS Panzer

Division's lack of fuel for training. On 8 May, according to C-in-C West, 'the enemy is already effectively hampering our supply and troop movements, and in the event of active operations would hamper the latter in particular . . . Latterly the enemy has also been attacking important railway bridges on the lower Seine. The supplying by air of agents and of the Resistance Movements has been stepped up very greatly and acts of sabotage, especially on the railways, have increased'. Reports in this vein continued well after the invasion began. By early June, approximately 15th per cent of German fuel supplies for the Western Front were 'backlogged' throughout France. By 12 June, the extremely strained fuel situation resulted in unnecessary travel being forbidden and the use of fuel from state of emergency stocks. By the middle of June, German forces in Normandy received daily deliveries of munitions that replaced less than 15 per cent of what they expended in a day. By the end of June, the 7th German Army had received only 37 per cent of the munitions that had been sent.[34]

However, transportation difficulties did not prevent the Germans from reinforcing the Normandy battlefield. Although the 1st SS Panzer Division was rerouted to the Pas de Calais area for a week before being sent to Normandy, Rommel immediately transferred the 21st Panzer Division to the battle area, and within 24 hours he ordered the movement of the 2nd Panzer Division. Von Rundstedt obtained the release of three divisions of the OKW reserve – the 12th SS Panzer, the 17th Panzer Grenadier and Panzer *Lehr* – within 12 hours of his request. Although the 12th SS Panzer Division arrived in Normandy on 7 June, Allied aircraft delayed Panzer *Lehr*'s arrival for two days. By 13 June two more German Divisions – 2nd Panzers and 17th SS Panzer Grenadiers – entered the battle. A few days later the 1st SS Panzer Division, which the Germans held as a reserve behind the 15th Army, travelled to Normandy.[35]

In addition to Panzer divisions, the Germans immediately began to transfer two types of infantry division to Normandy – static and attack. Between 6 and 7 June, the Germans committed six static divisions to the fighting. Two of the 15th Army's static divisions received orders for immediate transfer to Normandy and were subsequently integrated into the 7th Army. Numerous infantry divisions stationed around France received orders to proceed to Normandy. Although the remainder of the 15th Army did not receive transfer orders, several factors would have made it difficult for it to move from the Pas de Calais to Normandy. Much of the 15th lacked transport, suitable equipment and armaments. Many of the men were not well trained and were either very old or very young. Of the 11 infantry divisions attached to the 15th Army, 7 were static divisions, which meant that they were trained for defence, and 2 were Luftwaffe in origin. Furthermore, many of the 15th Army formations were not battle-ready.[36]

Although the 15th Army formations might not have been combat-ready, the fact remains that the German High Command did not order the transfer of the 15th to Normandy for several weeks. Apart from the FORTITUDE deception, there is another reason that is equally important in terms of the German decision. According to several *Ultra* intercepts, the Germans were beginning to focus their attention on Normandy during the month before the invasion. Based on Allied air attacks on railroads and waterways, they concluded 'that landing is planned in the area Le Havre – Cherbourg, is confirmed once more'.[37] In early May, the Germans were aware of the 'Anglo-American landing exercise "Fabius" in the area of the Isle of Wight, [which] provides evidence for the conjecture that the enemy, in view of the outer beach obstacles known to him, is attempting to achieve a modified landing and battle technique for his foremost landing wave'. According to the same communication:

> C in C West appreciates the situation as follows: Invasion preparations by the Anglo-Americans in the English Motherland are completed. Despite the fact that visual and photo recce has not yet been able to include the whole of the English south coast, the observed concentrations of landing shipping space, especially in the area north of the Isle of Wight (Portsmouth – Southampton), nevertheless give a clear picture of a main concentration defining itself in that area. Tonnage of shipping space for landings which has so far been observed can be assumed to be sufficient for 12 to 13 divisions . . . for fairly short sea-routes . . . The point of main effort within the whole threatened Channel front stretching from Schedlt to the northern tip of Brittany, appears to be roughly from Boulogne as far as Normandy inclusive. In this connection, the enemy's chief concern must be to gain possession of large harbours with good performance. Of primary importance as such would be Le Havre and Cherbourg, and of secondary importance (in respect of performance as well) Boulogne and Brest . . . The enemy landing exercise which took place most recently indicates that the enemy attaches special importance to recognising and clearing the outer-beach obstacles at low water . . .[38]

This communication, which was sent during the time when the Allies were implementing the FORTITUDE deception, seems to suggest that von Rundstedt, at least, was aware of the threat to Normandy. Although the wireless component of FORTITUDE SOUTH did not open until late April, the Allies had begun passing the cover story through physical deceptions and double agents much earlier. Despite the deception, some Germans did realise that the threat to Normandy was real.

Operation FORTITUDE was a well-organised, complex plan that its creators and implementers wanted to believe was instrumental in making Operation OVERLORD a success. Just as the Germans had preconceived ideas about the importance of the Pas de Calais, so Allied officials had a preconceived notion of what FORTITUDE would accomplish. Because the 15th Army remained in the Pas de Calais until mid-July, they concluded that the deception had achieved its objective. A new look at the evidence, however, suggests that other factors, in addition to FORTITUDE, influenced the German decision not to transfer the 15th Army immediately to Normandy. While FORTITUDE helped the Allies successfully invade Normandy, it is time to consider that the importance of the deception has been overrated.

Notes

1 Peter Snow, 'Operation FORTITUDE: The Deception Tactics Used for the D-Day Landings, Normandy 1944', *Dirty Tricks*, BBC radio programme, 134493/ 2, recorded 7 October 1993 by the Imperial War Museum Sound Archive.

2 Major General Whiteley, letter dated 9 September 1943; R.F. Hesketh, Appendix 'C', dated 30 August 1943 in WO 219/250, PRO; Sir Ronald Wingate, *Historical Record of Deception in the War Against Germany & Japan*, Volume II, DEFE 28/49, PRO, p. 391.

3 Wingate, ibid. Wingate was Bevan's second in command in the LCS.

4 Ibid., p. 391.

5 Ibid., p. 361; Roger Hesketh, *Fortitude: The D-Day Deception Campaign* (London: St Ermin's Press, 1999), pp. 17–19; Michael Howard, *Strategic Deception in the Second World War* (London: Pimlico, 1990), pp. 107–9.

6 Exhibit 62, in Document 9 – 'Operations in Support of NEPTUNE: (A) Plan FORTITUDE, 26 February 1944, Exhibit "6" of C & D Report ETO', in John Mendelsohn (ed.) *Covert Warfare, Volume 15 – Basic Deception and the Normandy Invasion* (New York: Garland Publishing, 1989), p. 1.

7 James Bowman, 'Fortitude South: The Making of the Calais Hoax', a 1,000 page manuscript and clippings file, Eisenhower Center, New Orleans, Part II, 2–1, Part III, 2–9, 2–10.

8 Hesketh, 19–20; Wingate, Volume II, 392–5; 'Cover Plan – Fortitude (South)', N.J.C./00/261/33, in WO 205/173, PRO.

9 Ibid.; 'Order of Battle for S.E. Force', Appendix 'A' to Part I, NJC/00/261/33, in WO 205/173; 'Wireless Layout S.E. Force', Appendix 'B' to Part I, NJC/00/261/ 33, BLM 102, Imperial War Museum.

10 'Cover Plan – Fortitude (South)', WO 205/173; 'Cover and Diversionary Plans', BLM 102; Part I of 'Cover Plan – Fortitude (South)', *Covert Warfare, Volume 15 – Basic Deception and the Normandy Invaison*; 'Appendix D to Part I – Fortitude (South) – Air Plan', WO 205/173; Hesketh, p. 93.

11 Hesketh, p. 93; 'Order of Battle for S.E. Force', Appendix 'A' to Part I, NJC/00/ 261/33, in WO 205/173, PRO; 'Cover and Diversionary Plans'; N.J.C./00/261/33, BLM 102, IWM.

12 Tactical and Staff Duties Division (Historical Section), Naval Staff, Admiralty, Battle Summary No. 39, Volume 1, 'Operation "Neptune", Landings in Normandy, June 1944', ADM 234/366, 38, PRO.

13 Howard, p. 121; Wingate, Volume II, p. 407.

14 'Operation "OVERLORD" Wireless Deception', Appendix 'A' to COSSAC/2355/ Ops, dated 9 December 1943, WO 219/2208, PRO; 'Plan "Fortitude" ("Neptune") – Allotment of Wireless Deception Units and Major Equipments', Appendix 'B' to SHAEF (44) 21, dated 26 February 1944, WO 219/1847, PRO.

15 Len Whittaker, *Some Talk of Private Armies* (England: Albanium Publishing, 1984), p. 72.

16 William Breuer, *Hoodwinking Hitler* (Westport, CT: Praeger, 1993), pp. 113–15 and *The Secret War with Germany: Deception, Espionage, and Dirty Tricks* (Novato, CA: Presidio Press, 1988), pp. 233–5.

17 Howard, pp. 16–18, 121, 223; Hesketh, pp. 53–4; Dusko Popov, *Spy/Counterspy* (London: Weidenfeld & Nicolson, 1974), pp. 14–58, 69, 97, 99–101, 188–92. See also Russell Miller, *Codename Tricycle: The True Story of the Second World War's Most Extraordinary Double Agent* (London: Secker & Warburg, 2004).
18 Popov, p. 224.
19 Hesketh, pp. 47–9; Howard, p. 231.
20 Juan Pujol and Nigel West, *Operation GARBO: The Personal Story of the Most Successful Double Agent of World War II* (New York: Random House, 1985), p. 129. See also *GARBO: The Spy Who Saved D-Day* (Richmond: Public Record Office, 2000).
21 Wingate, Volume II, pp. 407–8.
22 Ibid., p. 408.
23 Ibid., pp. 408–9.
24 Hesketh, pp. 351–4.
25 T.L. Cubbage, II, 'The German Misapprehensions Regarding OVERLORD: Understanding Failure in the Estimative Process', in Michael I. Handel (ed.) *Strategic and Operational Deception in the Second World War* (London: Frank Cass, 1987), p. 124; Anton Staubwasser, 'The Enemy as Seen by the Oberkommando of the Heeresgruppe B before Invasion (Time: End of May – Beginning of June 1944)', MS # B-675, dated 1 October 1947, pp. 9–10, 13–14. Document furnished by Professor Russell Hart, Hawaii Pacific University.
26 'The German Intelligence Service and the War', p. 4. Norman Holmes Pearson Papers, Beinecke Library, Yale University.
27 J.C. Masterman, *The Double-Cross System in the War of 1939 to 1945* (New Haven, CT: Yale University Press, 1972), pp. 3, 6–7. For more information about the exploits of Garbo and Tricycle, see the following books: Dusko Popov, *Spy/Counterspy* (London: Weidenfeld & Nicholson, 1974); Juan Pujol and Nigel West, *Operation GARBO: The Personal Story of the Most Successful Double Agent of World War II* (New York: Random House, 1985); *GARBO: The Spy Who Saved D-Day* (Richmond: Public Record Office, 2000); and Russell Miller, *Codename Tricycle: The True Story of the Second World War's Most Extraordinary Double Agent* (London: Secker & Warburg, 2004).
28 Miller, p. 184.
29 'The German Intelligence Service and the War', p. 4.
30 Nr. 007774.43 g, K. WFSt/Op., Keitel directive dated 12 December 1943, *Führer Directives and Other Top-Level Directives of the German Armed Forces 1942–1945*, translation (Washington, DC: n.p., 1948), pp. 110–15. AL768, Imperial War Museum.
31 Howard, pp. 188–9.
32 Sir Arthur Travers Harris, *Bomber Offensive* (Don Mills, ONT: Stoddard, 1990), p. 207; Forrest C. Pogue, *United States Army in World War II: The European Theater of Operations, Volume 3 Part 4, The Supreme Command* (Washington, DC: Office of the Chief of Military History, Department of the Army, 1954), pp. 132–4; Russell A. Hart, 'Feeding Mars: The Role of Logistics in the German Defeat in Normandy, 1944', *War in History*, 3 (1996), p. 420; Richard Overy, *Why the Allies Won* (New York: W.W. Norton, 1995), p. 167; Lieutenant Colonel A.E. Warhurst, the Historical Section of the Cabinet, Section D, Chapter II (Book One), 'OVERLORD: D-Day 6 June 1944', pp. 23–5, CAB 44/243, PRO.
33 Hart, pp. 423, 425–6.
34 C/6431 from Boniface to Loxley, dated 6th May 1944, HW 1/2765, PRO; CIBS/PM/497 dated 3rd May 1944, signed Brooke, CIGS to the Prime Minister, HW 1/2761, PRO; CX/MSS/T183/84, KV 37663, dated 8 May from Commander-in-Chief West, HW 1/2784; Hart, pp. 419–21, 425, 434. According to Russell A. Hart, 'The interdiction campaign had thus already seriously compromised the

German ability both to redeploy forces to Normandy and to resupply such forces once committed'. See 'Learning Lessons: Military Adaptation and Innovation in the American, British, Canadian, and German Armies during the 1944 Normandy Campaign', dissertation, Ohio State University, 1997.

35 Howard, pp. 187–8.

36 Niklas Zetterling, *Normandy 1944: German Military Organization, Combat Power and Organizational Effectiveness* (Winnipeg, Manitoba: J.J. Fedorowicz, 2000), pp. 396–400; Craig Bickell, 'Operation FORTITUDE SOUTH: An Analysis of its Influence upon German Dispositions and Conduct of Operations in 1944', *War & Society*, 18: 105–21; David Westwood, 'The German Army in France 6 June 1944', paper presented at 'Normandy 60 Years On' conference, University of Wolverhampton, July 2004.

37 CX/MSS/T178/86, KV 3242, dated 8 May 1944, from Luftflotte 3, IC, NO7228/44, HW 1/2781.

38 CX./MSS/T.183/84, KV 3763, 'Appreciation by Charlie in Charlie West Eight May', HW 1/2784, PRO.

14 Intelligence and OVERLORD

A snapshot from 6 June 1944

John Ferris

Allied intelligence for OVERLORD is usually seen as a success story. That is the truth – just not all of it. Intelligence revealed German expectations, understanding and intentions. It showed the enemy was behaving as OVER-LORD assumed, how the Allied deception plan, FORTITUDE, was working, and the weakness of enemy wireless intelligence and aerial reconnaissance. MI5's control over German agents revealed enemy expectations, and shaped them. *Ultra* and *Magic* showed that German generals and Adolf Hitler exaggerated Allied forces in Britain by 200 per cent, the initial strength of a seaborne assault by 400 per cent and remained fixed on the Pas de Calais. However, during May 1944 they were paying increasing attention to Normandy and strengthening its garrison.[1] Intelligence was excellent on great ·issues yet mediocre about major ones, like enemy strength in Normandy on 6 June 1944. Scholars have noted these facts but not explained them. In 1994, Alexander Cochrane described intelligence and deception as the 'missing dimension' of studies in OVERLORD.[2] In 2006, planning and intelligence in OVERLORD remain mutually exclusive topics. That problem cannot be solved in 8,000 words or so, but this chapter will examine Allied assessments before the invasion of the enemy's combat strength in France, and consider why intelligence success and failure marched hand in hand for OVERLORD, and how far either mattered.

OVERLORD involved a struggle between two sides in military rationality, intelligence and deception. The Allies won in every sphere. Reason led both sides to conclude that the ideal place for an Allied attack would be the Pas de Calais, with Normandy second and anywhere else a distant third; and an attacker would have great logistical problems. Thus, the Germans assumed any Allied attack must aim immediately to seize a major port. They spread their bets everywhere, but above all at the Pas de Calais. The Allies put all theirs on Normandy, where they faced just a fragment of enemy strength and evaded most of it – and carried a port in their hands. Again, OVERLORD was the first priority for Allied intelligence services, aided by specialist organs focusing on issues like beach topography. They had good human sources, excellent imagery and *Ultra*, and fused them. German sources failed in coordination and quality. Their spies were controlled by MI5, their imagery was spotty and their signals intelligence mediocre, missing truth and eating lies. German commanders paid almost as much attention to deception as Allied ones, leaking false news about their strength in defences and divisions – to no avail.[3] Conversely, FORTITUDE reinforced German preconceptions which the Allies predicted by reason and detected by intelligence.[4]

In planning for OVERLORD, military rationality always came first, intelligence second. Operational decisions were made by middle-level planners at Chief of Staff Supreme Allied Commander Designate (COSSAC), Supreme Headquarters Allied Expeditionary Force (SHAEF) and 21st Army Group, by the Supreme Allied Commander and the Chief of 21st Army Group, Dwight Eisenhower and Bernard Montgomery, and sometimes by the British Chiefs of Staff (COS). The key decisions were made purely on the basis of military rationality, with intelligence irrelevant, by COSSAC in July 1943, to avoid the Pas de Calais and strike Normandy, *tant pis*; and by Eisenhower and Montgomery in January 1944, to double the frontage and strength of the initial attack. Intelligence was secondary even in the formulation of the initial plan for OVERLORD, though it became central when that plan was refined and applied between April and June 1944. Most decisions emerged through the routine interaction of mid-level military bureaucrats, their arguments, agreements and differences.

This was especially true of intelligence. The British Joint Intelligence Committee (JIC), MI14, the German branch at the Military Intelligence Division, and mid-level figures in COSSAC, SHAEF and 21st Army Group, dominated estimates. Specialists handled collection and deception. These officers were able, experienced and British. Montgomery and his chief of intelligence, Edgar 'Bill' Williams, had served harmoniously for two years. Montgomery's chief of staff, Freddie de Guingand, thought Williams 'the most able and clear-headed' general staff intelligence 'I have ever met'. From January to May, General John Whiteley, an operations officer trusted by Eisenhower but not Montgomery, and without experience as an intelligence chief, ran SHAEF G-2. He was replaced just before D-Day by Ken Strong, Eisenhower's intelligence chief in 1943 and first choice for SHAEF G-2.[5] MI14 and JIC reports went only to top commanders and staff officers; so too, some assessments by SHAEF G-2 and Williams, though all staff officers and commands to division level received their weekly estimates. During the planning for OVERLORD, MI14 and JIC dominated analyses of strategic issues and enemy organisation, while Whiteley and Strong harmonised all sources for their commander and his forces. After D-Day, SHAEF G-2 dominated intelligence in the west, seizing power from MI14 and Williams, but until then it was a fifth wheel. The 21st Army Group dominated operational planning, and Williams the intelligence for it.

Tensions there were within intelligence, because of opinion, personality and tangled lines of command. Thus, in February 1944, the senior operations officer at SHAEF thought Williams was addressing 'a problem of a much larger nature than any with which he had been previously faced'.[6] Yet they also pulled together. Williams told Whitely, his senior in hierarchy but junior in experience:

> I do not want to be preaching a contrary doctrine to yours, for I feel there is real value in an agreed text. If we are to be wrong, let's all be wrong together. At least then our Commanders will not have had muddled counsel. You will remember the loss of confidence in the Middle East caused by the internecine but public disputes between the 'I' people which helped nobody, least of all the disputants.[7]

These officers avoided disputes, but agreed texts were hard to find, because they confronted a situation up to 12 months away. They made and argued over predictions as much as assessments; all strove for accuracy, each understood its limits. COSSAC's July 1943 plan for OVERLORD noted:

> As it is impossible to forecast with any accuracy the number and location of German formations in reserve in 1944, while, on the other hand, the forces available to us have been laid down, an attempt has been made in this paper to determine the wisest employment of our own forces and then to determine the maximum number of German formations which they can reasonably overcome. Apart from the air situation, which is an over-riding factor, the practicability of this plan will depend principally on the number, effectiveness and availability of German divisions present in France and the Low Countries in relation to our own capabilities.[8]

Commanders and planners thought less about Germany's current strength in France than how it would meet amphibious attack, its power relative to Allied forces in recent battles, its uncommitted forces across Europe and their speed of deployment. When making these decisions, Allied planners used whatever intelligence they had. It served them well. Yet between the time plans were made and executed, much might change; and many key points did not lie simply in the sphere of intelligence – like how good the enemy would be, and how it would prepare its defences and counter-attack. The value of intelligence was defined by its ability to support planning based on predictions of power and military rationality.

This produced characteristics in preparations for Normandy. Intelligence and planning were never effectively combined on paper, only in the minds of commanders. The planning applied on 6 June 1944 rested on old estimates, not current ones. Most planning was done by April, reflecting estimates of that era. Even more, these estimates and plans recognised a wide range of possibilities. Assessment had to be fluid, because enemy strength and intentions were changing, and rapidly. The Allies originally planned to attack on 1 May. Had they done so, Normandy would have had barely

50 per cent of its garrison of 6 June, which in turn might have received the extra few divisions needed to force the postponement of OVERLORD had the attack waited until 1 July. If the enemy guessed right, it could defeat OVERLORD, or deter it. Meanwhile, a dynamic tension emerged between worst-case and better-case assessments. Worst-case logic has a bad reputation, because in open-ended circumstances it causes timidity and costs opportunity. Yet in OVERLORD, uncertainty on basic issues and the need to control risks were unusually high. Caution was the better part of error, doubly so because planners and commanders recognised they were applying worst-case logic, tried to minimise its impact, and sought to understand how the Germans (not the Allies) would act.

COSSAC assumed the quality of enemy units would remain constant and the enemy would use them as well as it could. COSSAC's July 1943 assessment of the air aspect of OVERLORD was a classic statement of worst-case planning:

> The following estimates and appreciations are based on factual intelligence and consider the scale of enemy air effort possible under ideal conditions, not taking into account any effect that the present Allied air offensive may have on the G.A.F.'s fighting value in the future . . . Furthermore, the rates of reinforcement are those of which the enemy is physically capable, considering the scale of efficiency of his organization as a whole, and do not take into account the effects of any counteraction by Allied forces. The scale of effort envisaged assumes also that the enemy would concentrate the maximum strength possible even at the expense of adequate defence elsewhere.[9]

In this instance, worst-case logic was accurate: during June 1944 the Luftwaffe did throw most of its remaining aircraft across Europe into the battle of Normandy. Had that logic been applied to land forces, planners would have had to abandon OVERLORD; here, the worst case centred on the nature and the number of 'full-strength first quality divisions' Germany could use against OVERLORD. In July 1943, COSSAC concluded that OVERLORD had a 'reasonable chance of success' only if German forces and defences in Normandy, its reserves in the West and all aircraft deployable there, did not rise above the level of 30 July 1943, including 12 'full-strength first quality divisions' in France; if no more than three such formations joined the local forces of three infantry divisions on D-Day, five by D + 2 and nine by D + 8; and if no more than 15 good formations moved in from other theatres by D + 60.[10]

Soon, the quality of German forces sagged, and was seen to be sagging. In July 1943, COSSAC calculated Germany had 1,740 first-line aircraft in the West, but its key concern was the 'steady rise' in fighter strength, which must be 'checked and reduced' before invasion. Air intelligence estimated that between 1 January and 1 August 1943, German first-line strength in fighters had grown by 245 aircraft to 1,340 (or 2,260, counting second-line reserves), and in the West from 305 to 600 machines.[11] In February 1944, planners expected to confront 1,650 first-line German aircraft on D + 1, perhaps soon joined by 950 more but, like COSSAC, they noted the Luftwaffe's lack of 'appreciable depth' and inability to sustain losses. Soon, SHAEF thought German fighter pilots 'vastly inferior in quality' to American ones. By May, the British COS agreed that the Luftwaffe's strength exceeded July 1943 levels by 5,250 to 4,870 aircraft, including 2,700 fighters versus 2,175 (first-line and all reserves), but this was irrelevant: its decline in quality, production and reserves changed the meaning of the numbers.[12] These figures still distorted German air strength – the Luftwaffe did throw most of its fighters into OVERLORD, but they numbered barely 1,300 – yet that problem was minor. All planners abandoned the worst case about the Luftwaffe save Trafford Leigh-Mallory, commander of the Allied Expeditionary Air Force; this provoked needless debate over any part of OVERLORD related to air support, crippled the use of airborne forces and made decisions imperfect, but not seriously so. Worst-case logic ruled the air equation and also the naval one, but caused little worse than waste.

The story was different regarding assessments of the German army. As COSSAC wrote, the issue was not so much 'the precise number' of enemy divisions as their 'effectiveness': if they 'are below strength or of low morale, or if German ability to move them is reduced, we can face and defeat a proportionately larger number'.[13] When assessing the balance between the Allied and German build-ups in Normandy, a major figure in the operations section at SHAEF, General H.R. Bull noted:

> we are tempted to look on the enemy forces as fully-equipped, fully-trained, battle experienced 1940 divisions, instead of regarding them as 1944 divisions, diluted by foreign elements, and in several cases far from being up to strength or effectively trained . . . I feel that the whole difficulty in estimating the enemy's course of action lies in appreciating what real strength we are up against as opposed to theoretical strength. This, I think, must be evaluated in the monthly estimate of the rate of reinforcement, to avoid giving us the one-sided impression a purely logistical calculation is apt to do.[14]

Great problems emerged in understanding the enemy's real strength. Several good sources, *Ultra* above all but also agents in France and imagery, kept an extraordinary grip on the enemy's order of battle. From August 1943 to June 1944, the number of German formations in France constantly shifted, as did Allied estimates of them, reflecting both knowledge and ignorance. Until April, when SHAEF thought its information 'unsatisfactory', they included several German formations which were not in that theatre.[15] Estimates were filled with speculation about the value and name of formations. Given the nature of planning and the situation, these problems were hard to avoid and errors often cancelled each other out. At any time, Allied intelligence was good on the identifications, numbers and locations of formations in, entering or leaving the theatre, and almost perfect on these matters in the weeks before D-Day. It gave commanders accurate information they trusted, reinforcing their faith that enemy strength was still within the COSSAC conditions.[16]

Yet, simply to identify the quantity of divisions was not enough; their *quality* was of equal importance. Virtually every formation in France was rebuilding, some starting in early 1944 from just 10–25 per cent their establishment of equipment and trained soldiers; to determine how good they would be on the day, one needed to know not just their current strength, but how far and fast each would improve. Two types of formation proved especially hard to assess. 'Training' divisions, infantry and armoured, had an uncertain value: though usually that title described their function, rarely they did serve in combat, and over time their rating could rise. Meanwhile, the Allies ranked German infantry divisions either as field infantry, capable of independent assault in mobile operations, or lower establishment (LE), defensive formations ranging from poor to decent in quality, about half having just two instead of three regiments, including some '*Ost*' battalions (with German officers and ex-Soviet soldiers). The Allies had mixed success in determining the 'real strength' of most enemy infantry, and also of its best forces.

Ultra illuminated the manpower and training of Panzer, Panzer grenadier and paratroop formations, but not their equipment. *Ultra* and the Combined Service Document and Interrogation Centre (CSDIC), which collected and assessed material from prisoners and captured documents, offered good material about LE divisions.[17] The Allies' grasp of these formations was sound, no easy task, yet not perfect. Conversely, intelligence on field infantry was lacking, and estimates of their value were arbitrary and erroneous. These problems were fundamental to planning, though not on the battlefield, fortunately. JIC's last full estimate of German strength in France identified 14 field infantry divisions there. It overrated by 33 per cent the manpower of four of them, and that of eight others and most LE formations by 10 per cent. JIC slightly underrated the quality of the best infantry in France, 3 Paratroop Division, which also had 33 per cent more soldiers than expected – 18,000 men, twice the strength of the average infantry division in France. With that exception, every other so-called field infantry formation had just 50–66 per cent the manpower of average ones of 1939.[18] Only one of them, 5 Paratroop Division, had the strength even of German formations that in 1943 the British termed '2nd quality infantry divisions' (12,000 soldiers), while four were much weaker than 'defensive infantry divisions' (10,000 men).[19] Manpower was only one indicator of combat value, but a central one, and the Allies knew German infantry placed increasing reliance on organic firepower. All told, Allied intelligence distorted the combat quality of German infantry – in reality, only one field infantry division stood in France, 3 Paratroop. The rest were just slightly better

LE formations, and many of the latter were far worse than even that title would indicate.

A little intelligence and knowledge of standard enemy practices provided a fair, if overstated, account of the number of flak guns which could be deployed at Normandy, calculated at around 1,300.[20] This approach failed in another sphere. In its greatest technical failure before D-Day, Allied intelligence did not know the number of tanks in Panzer divisions, or the number of divisions in France, and knew it did not. This failure stemmed from limits in *Ultra*, which did worse in tank counting than ever since 1941, because changes in the way German formations reported their tank strengths stymied Bletchley Park. *Ultra* solved messages, but could not understand their meaning. Bletchley began to overcome these problems on D-Day itself, but all prior calculations rested on guesses.[21] These took many forms. Allied planners knew the number, location and manpower of armoured formations in France, but errors over tank strength crippled views of their combat value. The Germans had fewer tanks than Allied intelligence feared, but more than Allied planners assumed. On 6 April 1944, *Ultra* showed that the German commander in the West, Gerd von Rundstedt, aimed to make his three Panzer training divisions combat worthy as quickly as possible. Williams, thinking this 'a desperate improvisation', never took it seriously, at most seeming to think each might provide a combat worthy battlegroup. Before von Rundstedt's message, the JIC rated these formations and all non-divisional armour as together matching two divisions in strength. In early April, conversely, MI14 expected each Panzer training division to be fully operational by D-Day. By 30 April, JIC rated them as equal to two operational divisions; by 25 May it thought only 'elements' of each 'are at present capable of employment in an offensive role'. In fact, they did not fight until the last days of Normandy, with mediocre quality.[22] Yet throughout this period, these formations were always counted at face value on the books, crediting the enemy with three more Panzer/Panzer grenadier divisions in France than the seven which were there on 6 June. Hard intelligence on these formations was scanty – one training division had no Panther battalion and was short of motor transport; 2 SS Panzer and 17 SS Panzer grenadier lacked motor transport while 12 SS Panzer did not; 'slight evidence' suggested 21 Panzer had two tank regiments (in fact, it had one weak regiment).[23] The absence of intelligence drove the Allies to predict German tank strength by their understanding of enemy establishments. This approach usually caused overestimates, as the Allies understood these establishments no more than the Germans followed them.

MI14, thinking it knew from *Ultra* the formal establishment of Panthers in Panzer divisions but ignorant of their real strength, assumed all but training divisions had a full strength battalion with 81 Panthers, unless it had proof to the contrary, reversing the analytical process used to determine the number of Panzer divisions in France.[24] MI14 and SHAEF's grasp of the strength of Tigers and Panthers in non-divisional units was accurate enough

(135 Tigers and 283/320 Panthers, against in reality 102 and 250 on 6 June, or the armoured elements of three Panzer divisions). They were, however, wrong on important elements of German organisation. They did not know 21st Panzer Division lacked its Panther battalion, while those of two armoured formations and a training one were at 50–66 per cent their establishment strength; and thought four assault gun battalions were additional non-divisional units, rather than being part of formations. Predictions of strength derived from establishments could take many forms. If one added the figures for non-divisional armour and assault guns to seven Panzer divisions on what was taken to be full establishment, plus one Panther regiment above establishment, and three training divisions weak in Panthers, one had some 1,750 armoured fighting vehicles (AFVs) – or 1,560, if the training divisions were entirely removed from that figure.

In reality, even the low-ball projections exaggerated the problem. On 6 June 1944, in France the Germans had 1,891 AFVs, including 179 captured ones, 39 Mark IIIs (for command purposes), 758 Mark IVs, 102 Tigers, 655 Panthers and 158 assault guns. Of these, 12 per cent had little combat value (captured tanks and Mark IIIs), while another 15 per cent, the 253 Mark IVs and 40 Panthers in training divisions, were irrelevant until 25 July 1944, leaving 1,420 battleworthy AFVs on 6 June 1944. German strength was hard to determine. Allied estimates of it varied wildly, and many were grossly wrong.

Just before D-Day, Third US Army thought the Germans had 1,750 to 2,600 tanks. The First United States Army Group, relying on estimates of enemy strength from February, assumed each of the seven Panzer and Panzer grenadier divisions it thought were in the theatre would have what it took to be a full complement of 160 tanks, but ignored non-divisional forces and training divisions, for a total of 1,120. MI14, the JIC and SHAEF thought the Germans had 800 to 850 to Panthers alone, though they could not offer 'a reliable estimate', and 'may possibly' have a total of 3,000 tanks – 159 per cent above the true strength.[25] The figure of 1,120 came from knowledge of average German complements; so too that of 3,000, added to every piece of certain and uncertain information, including aircraft sightings of empty flat cars, commonly used to carry Panthers on trains, moving eastward toward the Rhine, indicating they had done so in an unobserved inward trip. At the strategic level, imagery on train movements created more mysteries then it solved. However, Allied estimates of German tank strength were wrong, in many ways, not just one. They were all over the map. The problem was uncertainty rather than error. This caused debate at the strategic level, but little harm, since the issue was academic and the mistakes cancelled each other out. Greater problems emerged at the tactical level.

The issue was not just the enemy's total and real strength, but also how much of it could intervene in the battle, and when. This matter, central to planning for OVERLORD, is too large for proper analysis here. Briefly, Allied planners were split on this point. Most grossly overestimated the problem, but Williams came close to the truth, and 21st Army Group acted on his assessments. On 6 June, the Normandy garrison was stronger than any analyst predicted before 25 May – past the level COSSAC thought manageable. This rise in strength did not produce failure, but it did prevent success. After 6 June, conversely, German reinforcements were smaller and slower than any Allied analyst dared predict, though close to the level Williams hoped. By D + 12 (18 June), five Panzer/Panzer grenadier divisions, three infantry divisions (including 3 Paratroop) and elements from two more reached Normandy. Compared to SHAEF's predictions of 3 June,[26] this was 66 per cent the expected level of reinforcements in armoured formations and 40 per cent in infantry, producing a total of 60 per cent the mechanised divisions (six) and 65 per cent the infantry (nine divisions and three battlegroups) at the front. Even more, two of these Panzer divisions were not yet in action. By D + 25 (1 July), another infantry division, elements of four others and two Panzer divisions reached the front. Compared to SHAEF's predictions of 3 June, this was 100 per cent the expected gains in armoured formations but only 20 per cent of the infantry, producing at the front 80 per cent the Panzer/Panzer grenadier divisions (eight) and 47 per cent the infantry – much less, given their losses (ten divisions, and elements from another seven;) in both cases, battlegroups were treated as 33 per cent of a division, an overstatement which perhaps balances 3 Paratroop's superiority over any other German division. On these issues, Williams was much more accurate than any other analyst, and good by any standard. All Allied analysts, however, were wrong on two major matters. On 6 June, 19 per cent of German tanks in France (including 40 per cent of their Panthers and Tigers) were in non-divisional units. Planners never forecast their arrival, which shaped the fighting. Roughly half these tanks reached the front by D + 12, the rest by D + 25. Meanwhile, no analyst predicted the main German transfer to France, the return from Poland of 9 and 10 SS Panzer Divisions, with 15 per cent the total tank strength in France on 6 June. Thus, the Germans transferred as many elite forces to France from outside it as the Allies ever feared, but only one other infantry division. These transfers were smaller than Allied analysts had predicted before 25 May, but larger than they had hoped just before D-Day.

Compared to what *did* happen, Williams's assessments of what *would* happen were good, but not perfect. He slightly underrated enemy capabilities, which all other analysts significantly exaggerated. Allied planning followed his estimates, gaining from their strengths and losing from their flaws, which stemmed less from intelligence *per se* than its relationship to planning. The Allies could use strategic intelligence until the moment landing craft were launched, but just in one sense, to postpone OVERLORD. Tactical intelligence could be incorporated up to 48 hours before, but only in matters like fire plans on the beaches. From mid-May, however, operations and operational intelligence were prisoners of prior planning. The naval commander forbade any change to plans for D-Day involving seaborne landings or supply. Except on the Cotentin peninsula, where in late May airborne attacks were changed to reflect enemy redeployments, the planning applied on D-Day was made between February and April. It rested on Williams's estimates from that period, the most optimistic reading of evidence from the most optimistic time, which no one entirely accepted on 5 June. These plans assumed the enemy would have fewer formations at Normandy between D + 8 and D + 20 than SHAEF expected and more than 21st Army Group did; and that the Normandy garrison would be weaker than every analyst thought it was.

Williams rightly predicted the value of German infantry and armoured divisions, and their strength in formations around the beachhead by D + 8 and D + 20. When these plans were formulated between February and April, he was more right on those issues than anyone else; and so too when they began to be executed. Yet his estimates on the day of execution were different from those during the days of planning. Again, because he accurately assessed the numbers of combat-worthy formations in France, his estimates were upset more by unexpected matters, like the rise in the Normandy garrison just before OVERLORD, or the arrival of 9 and 10 SS Panzer Divisions, than were those of other analysts, with fat free from their worst cases to cover underestimates elsewhere. The Allies paid for Williams's accuracy in assessment by underestimating the enemy in important particulars, though the gains were worth the costs. Again, by 5 June Williams had a remarkably good picture of the enemy which, alas, could not help units on 6 June, though it guided actions in coming days. Like other planners at 21st Army Group, he was more accurate about numbers of enemy formations than the situation they would produce once battle was joined. His estimates and their planning attempted precisely to gauge the nature of many variables and their interactions and combine them into one whole. He and they were remarkably accurate, but imperfect, and the battle took a different form than they had expected. This should not be surprising. Normandy was a hard operation; it only seems easy because it was done so well, something critics often forget. OVERLORD, the most complex operation of the Second World War, faced interlocking problems that required precise and accurate solutions. Either inaccuracy or imprecision could hamper operations or wreck them; yet the more precise planning was, the less accurate it could be, because chance must strike like a tsunami. Planners for OVERLORD controlled just one part of a reciprocal system. They determined what to do on the basis of guesses about what the enemy would do, and the interaction between their wills and actions and chance. The 21st Army Group understood these facts. It played to the odds and understood them. What went right outweighs what went wrong, and avoided the worst of outcomes; but still some mixed ones occurred, because of the way the Allies made decisions.

Some aspects of OVERLORD were planned in a tight and centralised way – in particular, anything to do with seaborne issues, like beach assault and logistics – others not. OVERLORD, after all, was defined by a staff without power or responsibility. Its land component was refined by another staff parachuted in five months before the attack; and it was fought by armies of several nationalities, each with its own command, doctrine, training and preparations on stream. This produced a strikingly loose approach to intelligence, planning and training. Estimates of German armoured strength were imprecise, contradictory, and left that way – every authority was free to believe what it wished; so too, views of enemy strength between D-Day and D + 25. The 21st Army Group followed Williams, while American forces were more pessimistic. In May 1944, FUSAG's version of Neptune used for intelligence an estimate of 10 February 1944, so old that many of the formations it listed were no longer in the West, while others known to be there were not mentioned. The Third US Army gave its forces an assessment based on SHAEF's views of 17 April.[27] That every command had its own estimates created some confusion on 6 June. Above all, it blinded generals and units to tactical realities. In preparing for OVERLORD, the Allies faced three circumstances, each requiring complex and distinct training: beach assault, attrition and mobile war. Everyone expected and trained for the best case – quick breakthrough leading to mobile war – and ignored the prospect of having to fight through the *bocage*, which seemed pessimistic and old-fashioned. This issue fell through that gap in intelligence, planning and training. No Allied commander matched Montgomery in the ability to fight this kind of battle, but even his plans did not play to this strength. He knew how to handle these circumstances, but hoped they would not happen. Where British and Canadian units had a tribal understanding of how to fight such a battle, American units did not, and their commanders ignored these weaknesses. This shaped a key phenomenon of the first six weeks of the Battle of Normandy: the failure of the American army.

This problem grew because the Allied ability to gain what usually is the easiest material to find, tactical intelligence, was constrained. In the 50 days before 6 June, eight dedicated squadrons aimed to conduct 735 photographic reconnaissance (PR) missions in north-west France, including seven overflights of the main beachhead up to 4,000 yards inland, and detailed coverage of beach gradients and enemy forces. Yet the Allies could not focus these resources on the real target for fear of tipping their hand. They sought to fly two imagery missions elsewhere for every one flown over Normandy, a high price for security and deception, beyond the reach of poorer powers and expensive even for them. Tactical ignorance was the cost of strategic security. When free to concentrate on the real target, PR was far more effective – from 6 June 1944, 380 sorties were flown over Normandy each day.[28] Had this effort been possible before OVERLORD it might have solved the problems in tactical intelligence. So too, in February 1944, the Allies ceased trying to take prisoners or conduct seaborne reconnaissance in Normandy, though they knew this would cripple the collection of tactical information. The only such mission run thereafter, aimed to examine outer beach defences, was done at the Pas de Calais, for security reasons and with effect – though the Germans detected the mission, it reinforced OKW's predisposition to fear for that region.[29] The Allies hoped to make up for the damage to tactical intelligence by interrogating prisoners taken in Italy who previously had been in Normandy, with mixed success.[30] Allied forces in Italy did not capture prisoners from any division presently in Normandy, though some based there in 1943 did illuminate old procedures, while other captives gave excellent and recent accounts of defences and their defenders in Brittany, Belgium and the Netherlands.[31] CSDIC provided useful background to assessments of defences in Normandy, but nothing concrete; imagery provided many facts, which guided planners and commanders, and the maps issued to assault units, but much was missed. Whenever the Germans changed anything in Normandy, the Allies could not know of it for days or weeks.

These circumstances and constraints prevented good intelligence services from discovering basic points. Errors that normally would be inexcusable were unavoidable. Few things should be easier in intelligence than to determine the strength and defences in a tactical sector one plans to attack; but this proved beyond the grasp of services which otherwise achieved marvels. Though prior planning and the initial assault rested on a good picture of the topography and defences on the beaches, the Allies missed important details: and at H hour, a prior failure to locate individual guns could have deadly costs. In particular, they were unsure of the deployment of two of the enemy's seven divisions in Normandy, its best formations there, standing precisely at places the Allies must attack on D-Day: 352 Infantry Division raised by 150 per cent the strength of the garrison on Gold and Omaha Beaches and made them formidable, while 21 Panzer placed its anti-tank units and half its infantry between the River Orne and Caen, key British targets on D-Day, with its armour in easy reach behind. This position was well suited to its task and its enemy – the Germans deployed their forces as well in Normandy as they did badly in other parts of France.

Allied intelligence looked hard and objectively for information on these forces. Williams suspected, but could not prove, they might be near their true locations. His last report before D-Day, of 4 June, warned 352 Division might be where it really was but 21 Panzer was unlocated, though thought to be entirely outside the assault area, from which it would advance toward Caen as a whole around H + 12. Williams was wrong about where enemy armour would be met, but right on its strength. He warned his forces that they might engage 280 AFVs on D-Day; the two armoured formations in the sector actually had 276, though poor German decisions kept 12 SS Panzer with its 164 tanks from the battle until D + 1. Second Army intelligence, conversely, warned its units to expect immediate local counter-attacks by some armour, while between H + 12 and H + 24, they might encounter 540 tanks (twice the real strength at hand), and perhaps 160 more from 17 SS Panzer Grenadier Division (which had only 42 assault guns).[32] Second Army correctly warned some armour might be met before Caen, and more there, but distorted that strength, in one of the greatest examples of worst-case logic before OVERLORD. As with the JIC or SHAEF in similar instances, Second Army probably was not stating its real beliefs, but defining the absolute worst case to make people think about the problem in advance, to show the limits to bad news, and for the record. This warning, however, was too big and vague to help; only a more precise and timely statement could have done so. In fact, if it was right, all that could be done was cancel OVERLORD – the Allies could not possibly defeat a force so much larger than that defined in the COSSAC conditions.

Williams's last estimate reached divisional commanders only as they were at sea, but that of Second Army was known to all units. They treated it as academic – above their pay grade. Units prepared only for what they could handle. They focused on known problems like hitting the beaches and forming up to advance, which already were necessary, difficult and time-consuming. They tended to ignore problems which would emerge later, doubly so because these circumstances were unpredictable and estimates of them constantly changing. Units simply assumed they would drive straight off the beaches and first meet enemy forces around Caen, in an encounter battle, possibly with Germans attacking British positions, rather than charging themselves into enemy units deployed in defensive systems. They expected to meet much enemy armour after Caen, but little before it. Nothing but a clear warning weeks in advance that the enemy already controlled the approaches to Caen in force could have affected their attitudes. Williams would have issued such a warning had he been able to, as might have been the case had the attack waited a few days – by which time, of course, more Germans might have reached Normandy. Even such a warning could only have saved some tanks and, above all, confidence in high command; the real problem was that the Germans held Caen, not that this surprised the Allies. These failures in intelligence cost lives, but not the battle. Even had they known the truth, the Allies would have had to advance on 6–7 June, and largely as they did – otherwise they would have been damned for passivity. So too, sure knowledge of the location of 352 Division could have done nothing to stem the slaughter at Omaha Beach. These intelligence failures were indicative, but not influential.

More significant was a muted version of an old problem. When CRUSADER was launched during 1941, British intelligence was precise in classic ways – 99 per cent accurate on the enemy's order of battle and numbers of tanks – and let the British time their attack with optimum effect. Yet they were grossly wrong on basic matters, like the quality of enemy forces and weapons relative to their own.[33] Meanwhile, an extremely precise plan relying on intelligence collapsed, as did the Eighth Army. Poor training negated good intelligence. British intelligence was more accurate before CRUSADER than OVERLORD, and integrated as much into planning; but by 1944, Allied armies, plans and commanders were better. Even so, before OVERLORD the Allies misinterpreted the relationship between terrain and tactics. Planners and units assumed that once ashore they would quickly enter the rolling country inland from Normandy, and fight mobile battles. Even an able 'tactical study of the terrain correlated with the latest Intelligence estimates of enemy capabilities' of 7 May, which discussed fighting in circumstances like and roughly on the line of 28 June 1944, was over-optimistic. It defined that territory as 'not an easy one for forces to advance through rapidly in the face of determined resistance, but it will likewise be most difficult for the enemy to prevent a slow and steady advance by infiltration'. It was 'difficult to judge' whether the *bocage* would better suit attacker or defender; tactics for the matter 'should be given considerable study by formations to be employed therein'. This advice was not followed.[34] Allied planners knew they might be forced into a battle of attrition in terrain well suited to the defender, but units did not train for it. They knew Panthers, Tigers and 88s were formidable, not that they would be attacking the largest force-to-space densities in these weapons the Germans ever managed on the defence, in terrain well suited to their strengths and Allied weaknesses. Through these gaps in operational expectation and tactical intelligence flowed tragedies.

The conventional assumption is that intelligence for OVERLORD was precise and powerful, and almost everything right and certain, with some errors. In fact, as many things either were erroneous or uncertain as they were accurate and trusted, though the latter category included most key matters. Allied intelligence was filled with errors, but they were not systematic, so most cancelled each other out, or else shaped things which did not matter – as did many successes, including the most famous or complex. Too much attention has been paid to *Ultra*, too little to the main sources of tactical intelligence and their limits. Success was most pronounced at the strategic level, where Allied intelligence bracketed the truth closely enough to show where it was, or was not. Since planners and commanders cared about gaps in their information at the strategic level, intelligence was fundamental as a source of knowledge and psychological certainty. Even so, even here key issues were filled with uncertainty and error, like enemy armoured strength and the speed and scale of reinforcements. These problems were fundamental to planning but had little negative impact on operations, either because their practical significance was small, or 21st Army Group made the least mistakes and acted on its own views.

The biggest intelligence failures occurred at the tactical and operational levels. In principle, they might have had major consequences, as on 6 June tactical problems could trigger operational ones. However, one may doubt that these failures (as against the realities they masked) mattered much in practice, or that successes would have done so. The point of intelligence is to aid action. Its value depends on the circumstances. Good tactical intelligence allowed useful changes in the plans for assault on the Cotentin peninsula, where enemy forces were weak and scattered, the Allies had room to manoeuvre, and forces to redeploy or add. It could have done little to change the outcome on Omaha Beach, or the Anglo-Canadian front from D + 3 to D + 60, where the Allies had to fight strong forces which could not be sidestepped. Good tactical intelligence might have led Anglo-Canadian forces to think better in advance about how to handle their circumstances of H + 12 to H + 36, but to what effect? As it was, they knew this battle would be hard and the enemy strong. They fought well enough to make the enemy focus on them, abandoning the initiative and their hopes to annihilate the Americans. Better advance preparations might have let every Allied force, especially the Americans, do better than it did between D + 3 and D + 45, but they had been warned of the problems they might face. They would not have done better unless weeks or months ahead of D-Day, at a time when units still could have improved their preparations for a prolonged and intensive battle in close country, 21st Army Group and FUSAG had made them do something they did not want to do, at the expense of preparing for other matters. As this would have had to happen before 352 Infantry and 21 Panzer Divisions reached Normandy, it was less a failure of intelligence than command. Perfect knowledge of these movements might have made the Allies in the week before D-Day realise attrition was unavoidable; but what good would that have done? Intelligence failures did little harm to the Allies. The successes did some good, and FORTITUDE still more, but they could not win the battle. On 6 June 1944, the problem was the enemy, not intelligence about it. Allied intelligence had done as much as could be expected. The rest was up to the men.

Notes

The RG 331 and RG 165 series are held in the National Archives, Washington, and the PREM and WO series at The National Archives, London. All citations appear with permission from the copyright holders.

1 MI14 Weekly Summaries, 15.5.44., 5.6.44., 'The OKW and Allied Intentions–Apr 1944', *passim*, WO 208/4312; JIC (44) 221 (0) Final, 29.5.44, RG 331/3/131; F.H. Hinsley, E.E. Thomas, C.A.G. Simkins and C.F.G. Ransom, *British Intelligence in the Second World War, Its Influence on Strategy and Operations, Volume Three, Part II* (London: Cambridge University Press, 1988), pp. 49–65, 790.

2 Alexander S. Cochran, 'ULTRA, FORTITUDE and D-Day Planning: The Missing Dimension', in Theodore Wilson (ed.), *D-Day, 1944* (Lawrence, KS: Kansas University Press, 1994), pp. 63–79, assesses the literature well. The best study of intelligence and OVERLORD, an excellent one, is Hinsley *et al.*, *British Intelligence*, Three, II. The best account of planning before Normandy, Carlo d'Este's, *Decision in Normandy, 50th Anniversary Edition* (London: Harper, 1994) offers good but brief accounts of intelligence.

3 Interrogation of General Gerd von Rundstedt, 4–14, 1.2.46, WO 205/1020.

4 For FORTITUDE, cf. Michael Howard, *Strategic Deception, British Intelligence in the Second World War, Its Influence on Strategy and Operations* (Cambridge: Cambridge University Press, 1991); Michael Handel (ed.) *Strategic and Operational Deception in The Second World War* (London, 1989). The chapter by Katherine Barbier in this volume, and John Ferris, 'The Roots of Fortitude: The Evolution of British Deception in the Second World War', in Thomas Mahnken (ed.), *The Paradox of Intelligence: Essays in Memory of Michael Handel* (London: Frank Cass, 2003).

5 'Notes taken at a meeting of Army Commanders and their Chiefs of Staff, at HQ 21 Army Group, 7 Jan. 1944', WO 205/16; Francis de Guingand, *Operation Victory* (London: Hodder & Stoughton, 1947), p. 106; Nigel Hamilton, *Montgomery, Master of the Battlefield* (New York: Hamish Hamilton, 1983), p. 144.

6 West to Whiteley, 17.2.44., RG 331/12/9.

7 Williams to Whiteley, 2.2.44., RG 331/12/9.

8 C.O.S. (43) 416 (O), 'Operation "Overlord", Report and Appreciation', 30.7.43., p. 4, PREM 3/342/2/8.

9 Ibid., pp. 1, 69.

10 Ibid., p. 25, *passim*.
11 CCS 309, 15.8.43., PREM 3/333/15.
12 Fourth Draft, 30.1.44., 'Neptune, Initial Joint Plan', WO 205/15, 1.2.44., Neptune, Initial Joint Plan, WO 171/126; SHAEF *Weekly Intelligence Review*, 6(11), RG 165/79/2566; PREM 3/342/10, COS to Churchill, 23.5.44., 'Opposition to Overlord'; Hinsley *et al.*, *British Intelligence, Volume Three, Part II*, pp. 35, 103–25. The discrepancies between these figures occur because Allied estimates of what German air strength would be on 31 July 1943 changed, while two different issues were being assessed, the 'initial establishment' of first-line units, and total *Luftwaffe* strength, including second-line reserves.
13 'Overlord', p. 10, PREM 3/342/8.
14 Bull, Assistant Chief of Staff, G-3, to Assistant Chief of Staff, G-2, SHAEF/17100/12/Ops, 24.2.44., RG 331/29A/119.
15 SHAEF to AGWAR, S-50558, 21.4.44., RG 331/1/114.
16 Material on these matters is contained in RG 165/79/2566, RG 331/29A/119, RG 331/12/9, RG 331/1/114, RG 331/1/59, WO 208/4312 and WO 171/102.
17 CSDIC (UK) SIR Nos. 110, 115, 117, 119, 236, 256, 277, 340, RG 165/179/659; CSDIC (UK) No. 293, RG 165/179/660.
18 Compare JIC (44) 215 (0) 25.4.44., RG 331/3/131, to the figures in David Westwood, 'The German Army in France 6 June 1944', paper presented to the conference on Normandy, Wolverhampton University, July 2004.
19 Appendix 'E', COSSAC (43) 4, RG 331/3/124.
20 JIC (44), 215 (0), 25.5.44., RG 331/3/128.
21 Ralph Bennett, *Ultra in the West*, (London: Hutchinson, 1981), pp. 29–57.
22 Hinsley, *British Intelligence*, 3(11): 72–7, 814.
23 JIC (44) 215 (0) 25.5.44., RG 331/3/131.
24 'Allotment of Panthers to Armoured Divisions in the West', MI14 /Apprec/8/44, 18.5.44., WO 208/4312; JIC (44) 215 (0) 25.5.44., RG 331/3/131.
25 *After Action Report Third U.S. Army, 1 August 1944–1 May 1945* (Scholarly Resources), Reel One, Chapter 2, p. 10; 'Operation Neptune'; FUSAG, 20.5.44., *First United States Army Group, Report of Operations, 23 October 1943–1 August 1944*, Reel Two, Book Two (Scholarly Resources), 'Allotment of Panthers', WO 208/4312; JIC (44), 215 (0), 25.5.44., RG 331/3/128.
26 SHAEF, 'G-2 Estimate of the Enemy Build-Up Against Operation 'OVERLORD', 3.6.44., RG 331/1/59.
27 *First United States Army*, SR, Reel One, Book One, 20.5.44., HQ First US Army, 'Operation Neptune'; *After Action Report Third U.S. Army*, Reel One, Third United States Army Outline Plan, Operation Overlord, n.d.
28 'Operation Neptune, Joint Commanders-in-Chief Memorandum No. 7, Air Reconnaissance – Requirements and Resources', NJC/00/74/6, 15.4.44., WO 205/15.
29 Hinsley *et al.*, *British Intelligence*, 3(11): 89; Helmut Heiber and David Glantz (eds) *Hitler and his Generals, Military Conferences 1942–1945, The First Complete Stenographic Record of the Military Situation Conferences, from Stalingrad to Berlin* (New York: Enigma, 2003), p. 434.
30 3rd Joint Commanders in Chief meeting, 22.12.43., WO 205/12; SHAEF/45BX/1/INT, 9.2.44., SHAEF/17/225/Ops, 12.2.44. RG 331/12/9.
31 CSDIC (UK) SIR Nos. 130, 132, 136, RG 165/179/659; CSDIC (UK), Nos. 160, 213, 260, RG 165/179/660.
32 Hinsley *et al.*, *British Intelligence*, 3(11): 847–51.
33 John Ferris, 'The "Usual Source": Signals Intelligence and Planning for the Crusader Offensive, 1941', in David Alverez (ed.), *Allied and Axis, Signals Intelligence during the Second World War* (London: Frank Cass, 1999), pp. 84–118.
34 21 A Gp/20651/55/G (Plans), 7.5.44., 'Appreciation of Possible Development of Operations to Secure a Lodgement Area, Operation Overlord', WO 205/118.

15 Reconstructing D-Day

6 June 1944 and British documentary films

Michael Paris

Veterans of the Second World War have usually been scathing about attempts to recreate the experience of that conflict on film. Indeed, many seem to believe that there were actually two wars – the real one in which they fought and endured, and the guts and glory version that has emerged from the imagination of populist film makers. Steven Spielberg's *Saving Private Ryan* (1998) has proved to be a notable exception, and was highly praised by survivors of D-Day for its realism, particularly the reconstruction of the initial landings on Omaha Beach. But generally, war films have had a cool reception from those who had first-hand experience of the war. Historians, especially military historians, have also expressed reservations about the use of film as a legitimate historical source or as a medium through which to reconstruct the past. Let a commercial film maker use the wrong model of tank, the wrong type of aeroplane or uniform, and immediately the whole production becomes suspect. Grudgingly, sceptics might concede that original newsreels or documentaries shot by combat cameramen at the time are of some value, but there is still an ingrained resistance to accepting film as a valid window on the past. Certainly, film can never replace the traditional sources of the historian in search of the complete story – film cannot deal adequately with causation or with complex political issues, for example; but what it can do is enable us to share in a historical experience in a way that no other source can.

Through the painstaking work of many historians who, over the years since 1944, have unravelled the complex story of the Normandy invasion, we now have an incredibly detailed understanding of the sequence of events of D-Day. Sixty years after the events themselves we probably know almost all there is to know about the planning and execution of Operation OVERLORD, the sequence of events, the parts played by individual units, the facts and figures and so on. Through diaries, autobiographies and oral history projects, we have equally gained some insights into the personal experiences of participants, enabling us to understand something of what it was like to storm the beaches of Normandy, to wade ashore under the guns of the enemy, to be a part of one of the most significant moments of the Second World War. But here our knowledge is somewhat less than complete, for although sensitively written accounts can help us to understand something of the realities of combat, and particularly the danger of taking part in a high-risk seaborne invasion, we really need to have taken part in those events or at least to have witnessed them first-hand, before we can claim any sort of real understanding of what being in battle is really like. This point was made explicit in the testimony of Cliff Morris, a young commando, recorded for a recent television documentary. Morris took part in the landings on Sword Beach, and described how on 6 June he left his invasion barge, struggled through the water, then crossed the beach where 'bodies and body parts lay around him, where the moans of the wounded mingled with the shriek of bullets and the screaming of shells', and then concluded, 'all this has to be *seen* before the full effect of what war really means can be understood'.[1] What Morris experienced on D-Day is almost impossible to capture in words. Even the most eloquent and powerfully descriptive writing cannot convey the full meaning of what men endured in combat. But if we could see it for ourselves, we might gain a more complete understanding, and that is the value of film; it is simply the only medium through which we can reconstruct the past in all its dimensions, as it actually happened.

At its most basic, film is a simple visual record, but the real popularity of cinema is located in the manner in which audiences can be drawn into the unfolding narrative on the screen, identifying with the characters and, in a sense, sharing their experiences. Clearly it is this aspect of film, what we might call the 'magic of cinema', that accounts for the enormous impact of the landing sequence in *Saving Private Ryan*. Here for a short time it is almost as if we are actually on Omaha Beach, sharing the mind-numbing chaos of combat, and experiencing just what it was like to be a part of the invasion of Europe – and that's due to the magic of cinema. I'm not sure that any other source can give us that same shared sense of 'being there'. That so many films have unfortunately sacrificed historical accuracy in pursuit of box office success is not an inherent fault of the medium but a conscious decision by the film maker to make their work more appealing, more saleable, to a mass audience. The most effective and persuasive form of cinema is the feature film, the drama, which so easily draws us into its narrative, but documentaries, making use of actuality footage shot at the time, can still provide us with that same sense of being there and experiencing war in a more realistic way than any other source. The purpose of this chapter, then, is to provide an overview of the way in which D-Day has been recorded in British documentary films, from the first newsreel reports to the most recent television documentaries made to commemorate the sixtieth anniversary of the Normandy landings, and to explore some of the ways in which producers have attempted to recreate the experience of participants as realistically as possible.

For the public, the first news of D-Day came from a BBC bulletin at 9.32 on the morning of the 6 June, read by John Snagge:

This is London. London calling in the Home, Overseas and European services of the BBC and through United Nations Radio Mediterranean, and this is John Snagge speaking. Supreme Headquarters Expeditionary Force have just issued Communiqué Number One. Under the command of General Eisenhower, Allied naval forces, supported by strong air forces, began landing Allied armies this morning on the northern coasts of France.

This came as little surprise – almost everyone had known the invasion was imminent; troop movements and the build-up of military might along the south coast were obvious and resulted in endless speculation, much of it surprisingly accurate. The only question had been: exactly when and where would the Allies land?

But as soon as Eisenhower's statement had been broadcast the public were anxious for details, for this was what the British had been waiting for, the beginning of the end of a long and bitter war. But for a public hungry for news, details of the invasion were scarce over the next few days. The BBC and newspapers gradually added detail but the information they released was still cautious and it was difficult to piece together exactly what the invasion had been like from these reports. One can fully understand why the authorities were so reticent. While preparations for OVERLORD had been meticulous, invasion was still a risky business. The disastrous landings at Dieppe in 1942, which had seen over 50 per cent casualties among the attackers, cast a long shadow over the planning for D-Day and was a constant reminder of just how dangerous such seaborne invasions could be. Even Alan Brooke, Chief of the Imperial General Staff, noted in his diary on 5 June that the offensive upon which they were embarking could be a 'ghastly disaster'.[2] Thus, until the Allies were firmly established, it was simply common sense not to say too much. However, what the public wanted was to see the landings for themselves. Through cinema newsreel reports and government information films that had become increasingly common through the early years of the war and through the graphic moving images recorded by combat cameramen almost sharing, albeit artificially, the experiences of those at the sharp end of war, they had become accustomed to 'seeing' the news. But even the most enthusiastic advocate for the use of film as a historical source would have to admit, the film shot on 6 June by combat cameramen was disappointing, for while it does provide a simple visual record of some aspects of the landings, it offers remarkably little detail.

The Army Film and Photographic Unit (AFPU) had been established in 1940 under the control of the Directorate of Public Relations at the War Office. In the aftermath of Dunkirk, confidence in Britain's military was at an all time low, and it was felt that something was needed to redress the balance. Film, the most popular method of mass communication, was thought to be the most effective channel through which to redress the army's image, so the Unit's initial function was to sell the army and its leaders to the public;

to produce a visual record of military operations and to make footage available to the commercial newsreels. The AFPU was based at Pinewood Studios and eventually included over 80 cameramen working in a number of self-contained units.[3] For the invasion of Europe, seven cameramen of Number Five section were detailed to go in with the assault troops – all had volunteered for the assignment. They were not told what to shoot, simply to accompany the military units to which they were attached, stay as close to the fighting as possible, and film as comprehensive a record of the action as they could. In addition, automatic movie cameras were mounted on invasion barges and tanks to record the actual landings. Operated by clockwork, these were to be switched on by naval personnel prior to landing. Unfortunately, most were broken in the assault or were not switched on. The Americans, in comparison, had some 23 cinematographers to cover the landings on Omaha and Utah Beaches.[4] While British cameramen were not excluded from filming anything, there were accepted conventions of self-censorship. There was, for example, a reluctance to show dead Allied soldiers or distressing injuries – the wounded shown usually had 'cosmetic' wounds, such as bandaged heads, arms, legs and so on. This was usually due to the fact that cameramen knew such shots would be 'wasted film' in so far as such scenes would be censored; or because they had become part of a military unit and were as distressed as anyone at the sight of a dead or badly injured comrade.[5]

The first newsreel reports about the invasion reached British cinema audiences on 8 June, but these showed nothing of the actual landings, rather shots of the preparations and of the invasion fleet setting sail. *Gaumont British News*, *British Movietone* and *Pathe Gazette* were all released on the same day and used much the same footage. Under the heading 'The Hour of Liberation', *Gaumont British* reported the communiqué from Supreme Headquarters and showed Winston Churchill's visit to the invasion ports, paratroopers preparing their equipment and a night bombardment of a distant coastline. Significantly, the commentary pointed out that it was 'four years to the very month, since we were hurled off the Continent of Europe', a reference to the evacuation of the British Expeditionary Force from Dunkirk that was picked up by most of the other newsreels. *Pathe Gazette's* report even included a short visual sequence of the 1940 evacuation to remind its audience of that humiliating episode. *Pathe* used similar footage of Churchill's visit to the invasion fleet and a close-up of Eisenhower's communiqué, but told its audience that while these were the 'first pictures of the opening of the Second Front', security demanded they should be 'meagre at this stage'. However, the commentary went on to point up the significance of the moment: 'Four years ago Europe was Hitler's. The lights of freedom went out. Now the world of free men strikes in all its assembled might at the weakening chains of bondage'.

But while these first reports captured something of the intense excitement of the moment, they offered no evidence of the actual experience of landing on the beaches under the guns of the German defenders. Audiences had to wait a further week until the first pictures of the landings were screened; and even then they were impersonal and disappointing for who wanted to understand something of the experience of the men who had taken part in that historic moment.

Arguably the most dramatic film report was that of the 15 June issue of *Pathe Gazette*, under the title:

INVASION
Pictorial Reports from France

In this report audiences could almost gain some sense of the drama and excitement of the landings. The opening shot – taken from the rear of a British landing craft packed with Canadian troops by a clockwork camera mounted at the back of the vessel and operated automatically – shows the craft approaching Juno Beach; the doors open and the soldiers disembark, one places his hand on another's shoulder – a small gesture of support and comradeship. The staccato commentary reinforces the drama of the moment:

> French rooftops over the bows of Allied landing craft beaching on the Normandy shore. There comes the grinding of heels on shingle and our troops spill ashore across that open stretch menaced by enemy gunfire. Newsreel and Allied service cameramen go in with the landing forces. The pictures they take make up this lengthened edition of *Pathe Gazette*.

While the commentary creates a sense of immediacy, the report seems to combine the initial landing with footage taken later. Thus much of the drama of the landings is lost. In this report, the second scene is taken from further up the beach looking back to the disembarking troops and one soldier appears to stumble and fall, suggesting enemy resistance. However, the scene is immediately followed by others which undermine the intensity of the opening sequence and can only have been filmed later: tanks and heavy equipment coming ashore, the camera lingering on wrecked enemy gun emplacements, and finally Montgomery coming ashore and posing for the cameras before overseeing the advance inland. But even this report did not offer those dramatic pictures of combat that audiences had come to expect from the war films they had seen and which had been artfully reconstructed in the studio – shells exploding, men fighting, the wounded, the burnt-out tanks and the shattered debris of the battlefield. In contrast, newsreels could offer only an impression of events, a factual record that could not deal with personal experience. Thus, dramatic imagery was largely missing from the D-Day footage, which presented the landing as a highly successful but almost mechanistic event, a sanitised view from which almost all the real drama of war is missing, and particularly the personal experience.[6]

While the British celebrated the success of the landings, albeit with images that played down the human cost, so German newsreels tried to ignore the events of 6 June altogether. News of the invasion was long delayed and when newsreel reports were finally released they were highly selective in their view of events. German cameramen had little opportunity to film the actual landings, thus the report from *Die Deutsches Wochenshau*, the official German newsreel, issued on 20 July, was largely comprised of old footage from the archives accompanied by a confident narrative that suggested that the invaders were being contained and that their losses had been heavy. Reinforcing such claims were scenes of abandoned Allied landing craft, wrecked gliders, and shots of dazed and wounded prisoners – probably stock footage of Canadians captured during the disastrous raid on Dieppe in 1942. Interestingly, much of the footage here had already been used in a late June report from *France Actualities*, the official newsreel of Occupied France. Here, the commentary was anxious to stress that not only were the British and Americans being contained but that the invasion was causing great suffering for the French people through air raids and the bombardment of Norman towns. For example, over a sequence of a devastated town, the commentator claims: 'Every minute Frenchmen are dying and French homes crumble to dust. How many other Norman cities are now ghost towns or cemeteries?' The message was clear – the Allies, in their relentless war against Germany, have little concern for innocent French civilians or their property – and invited the audience to consider whether these pitiless men really were the noble 'liberators' of France.

So while British audiences may well have wanted to share the drama and the danger of the invasion through the moving image, they were offered only short newsreel reports that dealt with some of the facts but ignored the wider experience of those involved. As we know there was a little more footage, but by the time that was available, the invasion story had moved on to the advance into the heartland of Normandy. The experience of 6 June, as far as the newsreel companies were concerned, was 'old' news. The D-Day film reports, however limited, did of course fulfil one of the basic functions of documentary cinema – the creation of a visual record of events. But as the Allies secured their position in France and the Normandy campaign got underway, film shot on D-Day was worked into more a more detailed record of events in the official documentaries produced by the Ministry of Information, through which audiences could learn more and share something of the experience of the men who took part. These later films made use of other footage, establishing material that showed something of the background to invasion, and added a narrative which again increased the level of detail.

From autumn 1944 a number of British documentary films about D-Day began to appear. *Towards the Offensive* (1944) and *The Air Plan* (1945) were both from the Royal Air Force Film Production Unit and detailed the RAF's preparations for D-Day and the battle for air supremacy over the Continent. The RAF Film Unit had been established in September 1941 to create a film record of air operations, produce documentaries and training films, and provide footage for the commercial newsreels. Implicit in the creation of such a unit was to ensure that the RAF gained its share of publicity. The Unit however, was not simply concerned with air combat. Its cameramen were active in filming on the ground – not only on airfields but equally in forward combat zones where they often worked alongside their army colleagues.[7] *Towards the Offensive* dealt with the build up of air and other units for the Allied invasion, a story that was continued in *The Air Plan* which focused on the part played by the RAF and other air forces in the Normandy landings. Here the emphasis of the narrative, spoken by the actor Eric Portman, is that the Normandy invasion had been a 'combined operation' where the RAF had significantly contributed to the success of the landings. The film begins with combat footage of the battle for air supremacy, and details the offensives against enemy coastal defences, communications and supply centres. There is some excellent footage of the air cover provided for the invading troops, and the building of forward airstrips once the Allies were established in Normandy.

What the RAF films ignore, of course, is the antipathy of Arthur Harris and Carl Spaatz – the British and American bomber barons – who believed that invasion was an unnecessary diversion from the main business of bombing Germany which would inevitably lead to the complete collapse of the Third Reich. A short report on the Allied air forces pre-invasion bombing of northern France was also included in issue six of the RAF's own newsreel *The Gen*, but the main report was included in issue eight under the title 'The Day'. Included here are some brief but telling shots of air attacks on German coastal defences and the dropping of airborne forces. However, as the report was issued some time after the invasion, the assumption was that the audience would already be familiar with the story.[8] In 1944 the RAF Film Unit also began production on a docudrama that would tell the story of the RAF's support of the Resistance movements in France which had played a significant role in intelligence-gathering and in disrupting enemy communications before and after D-Day. The film, however, was not released until June 1946 under the title *School for Danger*. The film was interesting, however, in that real agents were asked to play themselves in a reconstruction of their experiences in occupied France, thus establishing a precedent for 're-enactment' in the documentary form.[9]

These documentaries were accompanied by other productions which explored events after the landings such as *A Harbour Goes to France* (1945) which told the extraordinary story of the mobile floating harbour (*Mulberry*) used by the Allies to bring in supplies and reinforcements immediately after the landings. But the most important of these later documentaries was *The True Glory* – the official Anglo-American documentary record of D-Day and the subsequent campaign in Europe – and one of the most powerful of all feature-length wartime documentaries.[10] Directed by Carol Reed and the American Garson Kanin, the film's commentary had clearly been inspired by Laurence Olivier's highly successful film version of *Henry V*, released in

November 1944, which dealt with an earlier and equally successful invasion of France. *The True Glory* was originally intended to cover only the Normandy campaign, but inter-service rivalries and disagreements between the British and American production teams delayed the project. In October 1944 it was decided to extend the film into one which would cover subsequent events down to Germany's surrender. Consequently it was not completed until the summer of 1945.

The film was introduced by Supreme Commander General Dwight D. Eisenhower, who emphasised that the focus of the film was on the 'really important men in this campaign, the enlisted soldiers, sailors and airmen' – and the film does precisely that by relating what happened to these ordinary men at key points in the campaign. A commentary in blank verse, clearly inspired by Shakespeare, links these episodes of personal experience and creates a sense of the past impacting on the events witnessed on the screen. Over a hand-drawn map of the Channel coast, the verse narrative explains:

> We planned to breach the wall and smash the German spine,
> but where?
> We searched the coast of Europe like fierce eagles,
> Between low Flushing and deep-harboured Cherbourg,
> Our eyes sought out the place of the assault . . .

Until finally 'All resolved on Normandy, on Caen': 'So on five miles of still unblooded sand; the fretful course of fate would be assailed by armoured nations'.

The film sequences dealing with 6 June combine footage from Allied service cameramen and captured German film and provide the backdrop for the personal testimony of participants, delivered in everyday language by a variety of voices and in perfect counterpoint to the high rhetoric of the verse narrative. Indeed, it is surprising that men who had so recently been a part of this enormous and highly dangerous enterprise could be so matter-of-fact about their experiences. For example, a Scottish soldier relates how on GOLD Beach, 'It wasn't too bad getting ashore. After that it started, we had to fight for every bloody field. And it was the same each time; crawling on your belly, keeping your backside down like you'd been told, chucking a few grenades then rush them. Sometimes they killed us, but we were killing more of them . . .'.

The True Glory made a brave attempt to document the personal experiences of those taking part in D-Day; and audiences found it a far more absorbing film than the usual documentaries issued by the Ministry of Information, but it was still in stylised, semi-official form and far removed from the intensely dramatic and emotional reconstruction of events than can be created in narrative films, and which cinemagoers looked to in order to experience how such momentous events impacted upon the individual soldier, sailor or airman. Nevertheless, *The True Glory* established the format for most of the post-war documentary films about the invasion – the narrative of events against a background of original footage and interludes of personal experience of combatants. The film, however, was almost the last of the war documentaries made for a cinema-going public. The waning popularity of cinema audiences through the post-war years and the increasing popularity of television meant that by the 1950s, documentary films had become the exclusive preserve of television producers; and the major problem faced by these television historians was simply that the lack of detailed archival footage prevented them from exploring the story of 6 June in terms of personal experience. Thus producers were forced to develop new techniques, new approaches, in documentary film making that would enable them to recreate the experience of the individual.[11] And in the years since D-Day, successive generations of documentary film makers have extended to the story of the D-Day landings1944, adding more detail to the original core footage, and attempting to find more 'realistic' ways of recreating the experiences of those who were there.

The tenth anniversary of D-Day more or less coincided with the screening of the first significant television history series, *War in the Air*. Made by BBC Television and the Air Ministry, the series has frequently been overlooked by historians, yet it was a ground-breaking precursor to television histories such as *The Great War* and *The World at War*. Written and produced by John Elliott, in 15 parts, its major focus was on the part played by the RAF in the Second World War; nevertheless, the coverage the of the war as a whole is generally good. The episode 'Overlord' (Programme 10) offers us useful insights into the landings. Starting with the tenth anniversary commemorations at Arromanches-Les-Bains – seemingly a remarkably low-key affair compared to the recent sixtieth anniversary celebrations, the programme concentrates on the air aspects of the invasion. There is considerable detailed coverage of the bombing raids and fighter sweeps that prepared the way for the landings, and clearing the Channel of enemy shipping – mostly footage from *The Air Plan* and other RAF productions. D-Day is covered by shots of the armada of troop transports crossing the Channel, the bombardment of the enemy defences and the landings, again using the original AFPU footage. However, the film offers some new insights: the deception techniques over the Pas de Calais, the landings of the airborne divisions and the reinforcements going in after the initial landings. Like *The True Glory* the film adopts a linking narration, interspersed with episodes of personal testimony. Although these are clearly read by actors, such as Sam Kidd, Ferdy Mayne and Marius Goring, such interludes offer a personal view of D-Day and should be praised for their diversity – including as they do a French airman, an American war correspondent, a British sailor and a French woman who thanks the Allies for liberating her country from the Germans.

Significantly, *War in the Air* makes use of scenes from earlier documentary films and even wartime docudramas such as *Target for Tonight* and *Journey Together* in an attempt to capture a more personalised approach. While its focus is on the RAF, *War in the Air* was not just made for the domestic market. The high cost of television productions, even ones which relied largely on pre-existing film, meant that producers had to appeal to a wider market. Consequently, it became mandatory for documentaries to include more than just national experience, and to explore the American and Commonwealth contribution to victory as well – an increasingly important factor in British television production which aimed at a world audience.

Twenty-two years after the *War in the Air* Thames Television screened its acclaimed series *The World at War*, which although not without its critics, is now generally considered to be one of best visual histories of the Second World War yet produced. Programme 17, 'Morning', dealt with events during June and August 1944. Taking its lead from the newsreels of that year, 'Morning' prefaced its D-Day programme with a reminder of the humiliation of Dunkirk, and then focused on the inherent danger of seaborne invasion with a brief report on Dieppe. Coverage of the landings began by examining the detailed preparations coupled with the comments of significant figures like Mountbatten and Dr John Stagg, the meteorologist, as well as less distinguished participants – the ordinary soldiers and sailors, British, French and American. The series adopted the 'talking head' approach but the original film footage is shown uncut, thus we see casualties and other distressing scenes so obviously censored out when originally screened for wartime audiences. Viewed today, *The World at War* stands up remarkably well as a thoughtful and concise visual history of the Second World War.

From 1939 until the immediate post-war period, documentaries had been made for an audience intimately connected to the war – it was 'their war', after all; and even in the longer post-war period such films appealed to viewers who had experienced at least some aspects of the war themselves and who wanted to know more, or perhaps how their small part in the conflict contributed to the bigger picture. However, by the late 1970s, while such films still played to a section of the audience who remembered the war, they also had to appeal to an increasing number of viewers who had no direct connection with the war and who could look back at the conflict with detachment. Primarily this new audience wanted to know the story of the war but they wanted above all to be entertained. They did not want detailed and complex explanations of how and why, rather they wanted to see it for themselves. Thus, producers were required to make films for a mass audience that were entertaining, visually exciting, but informative enough to satisfy a minority of viewers who wanted more than a Noddy in Toyland version of events. Thus not only has the documentary film maker to find the right level of detail for an audience which is extremely diverse, but their task is overshadowed by the driving force of being entertaining, while still striving to present 'good' history.[12] It would probably be impossible to produce a documentary in the style of *The World at War* today with any real hope of it being transmitted on a major network. Thus, in the drive to be entertaining it is obvious that not only have producers turned to the latest developments of visual technology, but have also drawn closer to the style of populist film makers. Where these factors come together most clearly are in the films that were made for the anniversaries of D-Day in 1994 and 2004.

The fiftieth anniversary of D-Day in 1994 saw a considerable number of documentaries produced,[13] though most offered very little that was new, with perhaps the exception of BBC Television's *Destination D-Day*, which used original combat footage and veterans' testimony with studio reconstructions. But two of the major productions made for the recent sixtieth anniversary, *Ten Days to D-Day* (Channel 4) and the BBC's *D-Day, 6.6.44.* are worth discussing because they have incorporated interesting new approaches to documentary film making culled from the world of popular cinema in an effort to recapture something of the personal experience of participants. A third film, *D-Day in Colour* from Carlton Television, made at this time is, despite the interesting contributions of historian Steven Badsey, little more than an attempt to cash in on the anniversary by cobbling together all the original colour footage. Most of this had been taken by American cameramen and had already been used in earlier films such as *From D-Day to Berlin* (1985). However, little colour footage of the actual landings was taken and the programme is padded out with material that is too often irrelevant.

Ten Days to D-Day was based on David Stafford's popular book of the same title. It tell the story of the invasion through the experiences of ten participants: the story of commando Cliff Morris; Juan Pujol (codenamed 'Garbo'), the agent responsible for one of the major deceptions; Andre Heintz, a French resister in Caen; an American infantryman, and so on. Their stories are told through personal testimony, original wartime footage and dramatised scenes of their experiences. As docudrama it works reasonably well. For example, as Cliff Morris relates his memories of the landings, on the screen we see genuine combat footage supplemented with reconstructed scenes of his own experiences. The original footage is not always well used, but it offers a lively, accessible and reasonably accurate visual account of personal experiences on D-Day with a degree of realism that would be difficult for the historian to create using words alone.

The BBC's *D-Day 6.6.44.* is remarkably similar in structure, even duplicatng some of the case studies – 'Garbo' and Andre Heintz, for example – and a cross-section of others – an American, a Canadian and a German soldier, and, perhaps most interestingly, a reconstruction of the experience of photographer Robert Capa during the first landings. The inter-cutting between original footage and reconstruction is sometimes brutal, and there are some truly bizarre computer-generated graphics which appear to have been heavily influenced by the Disney Studio, and sound effects taken directly from *Saving Private Ryan*. Only the veterans' voice-overs remind us we are not watching a *wunderkinder* director desperately attempting to make a sequel to Spielberg's film. Nevertheless, some episodes do work well – the re-enactment of 6th Airborne Division attacking the Merville battery, for instance. And it is through these reconstructions that, when they are well done, we can come close to sharing the experience of those who participated in the Normandy invasion.

But what is obvious in both of these documentaries is the influence of popular films such as *The Longest Day* and *Saving Private Ryan*. Both adopt the episodic approach of the former and the shaky, hand-held cameras and washed-out colour film of the latter. This, in itself, is no bad thing, because most audiences who watch history on the screen today want something more than an ageing historian talking to the camera. The docudrama, properly made by a knowledgeable and honest film maker, is probably as close as we will ever get to reconstructing the past, and the most effective way in which the viewer can be drawn into becoming a participant in the events portrayed. Both the historian and the documentary film maker are, in essence, tellers of stories; the only real difference between them is the integrity with which they tell them.[14]

Notes

1 Morris's testimony is cited in the docudrama *Ten Days to D-Day* (Channel 4, 24–5 May 2004).
2 Alex Danchev and Daniel Todman (eds) *Field Marshal Lord Alanbrooke, War Diaries, 1939–1945* (London: Phoenix Press, 2002), pp. 553–4.
3 See James Chapman, *The British at War: Cinema, State and Propaganda, 1939–1945* (London: Tauris, 1998), pp. 138–54.
4 See Toby Haggith, 'D Day Filming – For Real: A Comparison of "Truth" and "Reality" in *Saving Private Ryan* and Combat Film by the British Army's Film and Photographic Unit', *Film History*, 14: 332–53.
5 Ibid., p. 346.
6 *Pathe's* coverage of D-Day, including the report cited, is included on the DVD, *1939–1945* (Telstar, 2003).
7 See Chapman, *The British at War*, pp. 155–8.
8 *The Air Plan* is available on video from After the Battle video, and *Gen* from the Imperial War Museum and DD Video.
9 Clive Coultass, *Images for Battle: British Film and the Second World War, 1939–1945* (Newark, DE University of Delaware Press, 1989), pp. 166–7.
10 *The True Glory* (MoI, 1945) is available on video from the Imperial War Museum and DD Video.
11 The issue of television history is discussed in Taylor Downing, 'History on Television: The Making of "Cold War", 1998', in Marcia Landy (ed.) *The Historical Film: History and Memory in Media* (London: Athlone Press, 2001), pp. 294–302.
12 On this point see the interesting discussion by Jerome Kuehl, 'History on the Public Screen, II', in Paul Smith (ed.) *The Historian and Film* (Cambridge: Cambridge University Press, 1976), pp. 177–85.
13 See for example *D-Day Eyewitness* (DD Video, 1994); *British Campaigns: D-Day Heroes* (InterVision, 1994); *D-Day – The Secret Battle* (DD Video, 1994); *D-Day 6th June – the Official Story* (Castlevision, 1997); *D-Day – The Best Kept Secret* (IMC Vision, 1999).
14 *D-Day in Colour, Ten Days to D-Day* and *D-Day 6.6.44.* are all currently available on video and DVD.

16 D-Day in Hollywood motion pictures

A brief history of changing perceptions of war

Carsten Hennig

Introduction: film and history

There has been a considerable public debate in Germany concerning the scheduling of Steven Spielberg's *Saving Private Ryan* on German television. In its wake, the FSK (*Freiwillige Selbstkontrolle*)[1] and the television station in question organised a symposium on war and its depiction by the media in Berlin in September 2003. Attending this conference, I found myself in a conversation with a history teacher. He was airing his disappointment with today's students, who, in his view, did not seem to have any interest in history any more. The insufficient knowledge they had, he claimed, mainly stemmed from motion pictures. I argued that, if he already knew about his students' interest in films dealing with certain events in history, he had a great opportunity to go on from there. So we started playing movies back and forth in our heads, thinking about what issues would have to be considered when incorporating film into a history seminar.

Narrative, history and the movies

A central issue concerning the representation of historic events in film is the discrepancy between the necessity for narrative dramatisation of cinematic content and the demands concerning the accuracy of pictured history as claimed by scientific approaches.[2] However, the issue of bridging the gap between fact and fiction, between chronicled events and dramatised attractions, is not entirely new.[3] When discussing whether the work of a professional historian should or even can be reduced to just chronicling and interpreting events, we will have to keep in mind the problematic relationship between history and its developing means of mediation, and the challenges every new medium presents. First, some clarifying comments on narrative form, and its role in the processes of constructing history, seem necessary. The main features in constructing an ideal narrative have been characterised by Kenneth Gergen.[4] According to him, introducing a final goal that contains some moral or ethical value has to be considered a narrative's central issue. This value introduces strong cultural influences into the story, because that value is determined in relation to a cultural background. Events within the story will all be structured in view of the narrative's ultimate goal, and all characters carry a fixed identity. Also, a narrative ideally offers explanations, often through selected events which are causally linked and woven into the plot, and there are markers for the beginning and the end of a story, or formal conventions as symbols for entering the world of the narrative (like opening credits and end titles of a film). These features of narrative help to create a feeling of coherence and direction with respect to events; incidences receive meaning, and life starts to make sense. Furthermore, there are culturally specific forms of narrative, used frequently, easily recognisable and highly functional. The function of narratives, according to Gergen, lies in the expression and production of cultural values: by defining an ultimate goal and its value, by populating a story with certain actors and events, the narrator enters the realm of moral and political judgement.[5] Certain patterns of behaviour (such as trying to win as opposed to obvious signs of competing), of social structures (such as individual heroes and villains instead of anonymous communities), and of allocated meanings (such as perceiving the world as being material rather than spiritual) are propagated. A credible narrative has to take into account specific cultural and sub-cultural achievements, and it is crucial to understand these as social forms of objective judgement. That means a true story does not necessarily represent an account of things that really happened, but rather registers a certain state of affairs in relation to a specific community. Narrative accounts are important parts of continuing patterns of social behaviour, which are often institutionalised, argues Gergen, and in this sense they serve to create cultural traditions and help to keep them alive (and sometimes to end or change them).

According to Gergen, history's ability to create truth has to be considered as culturally defined. The measurements of its correctness need to specifically correspond to certain communities, and the scope in which they may be kept up depends on the steady ability of this community to (re-)negotiate reality constantly.[6] That means history, and the narrative thereof, is unavoidably tied to cultural values and moral standards, and to lend credibility to certain traditions is, in effect, silent support for the sense of goodness they represent. Consequently, representations of history only partly deal with the past. More importantly, the meaning of the past is constructed with respect to the cultural life and its range of values offered by the present. It is the way in which we presently attain our sense of right and wrong which achieves a shared worldview to build a common future upon.

While certain movie genres and, due to the nature of their content, war movies in particular, link fiction with reality by constructing a dramatic story in front of a historical background, accurate depiction of history has never been one of the strong aspects of Hollywood. Instead, the cinema strives to entertain; it offers the possibility to take part emotionally in the stories it has to tell. Turning around the argument, it does not seem unfair to declare that 'pure' chronicles have difficulties trying to provoke an emotional response, even if the recipient does have an above average general interest in history as such. The cinema presents us with the opportunity to really immerse ourselves in the experiences it evokes. The structure of our experiences, according to David Carr, is a function of narrative as embodied in our way of life.[7] He identifies this narrative structure as the organising principle of identity as such, on the level of both the individual self as well as the story of a community, and thus narrative as a feature of historical existence. Jürgen Straub in turn argues that 'historical realities are constructs',[8] which occasionally attain a certain degree of objectivity through technical recording or material form, such as texts, monuments, museums and other important objects or places created and shaped through creative acts.[9] From these two perspectives, added to Gergen's insights about narrative, we may conclude that products of popular culture dealing with aspects of history do have an impact on a society's self-perception. This is especially true for those products conforming to narrative forms, because they correspond with our perception of reality. Even though Straub does not specifically mention the cinema, his rather broad definition is perfectly suited to include war movies which, we have to conclude, must have considerable impact on the way history is perceived today, because they link strong emotional responses (intense experiences) with dramatised history (narrative form).

D-Day made in Hollywood

According to Jeanine Basinger, the combat film is perfect for Hollywood:[10] 'It provides ready-made conflicts that are easily simplified and clarified – and reversed'.[11] She argues that the genre of war movies embraces the virtues of both cinematic action and drama, while it 'brings its own credibility, since it is based in reality'.[12] She observes an evolutionary process in the course of development of the combat film genre, in which it defines itself, then repeats itself, and finally varies itself to adjust to the changing contexts of its times. Looking at a longer period of change, these variations can reveal what audiences expected to learn from the genre during a certain era, making it clear how important such shifts in ideologies are for the construction of movie genres, and how these shifts are used to demonstrate different political attitudes to the past, the present and the future:

> When war nears, we make films about it. When it goes away, we make films about military battle maneuvers, or films about how awful the war was (awful, even if glamorous). We also make other genre films that serve similar purposes, of course. As war nears, we change our minds, and get involved in the new mechanized war and a new understanding of it. To do all this, we tell stories in the old way, updating them with new equipment and new ideology, slowly moving toward a new period of time when the new war breaks out and the issues it will provide can be amalgamated into the story.[13]

Following from these processes of development described by Basinger, we may argue that film can actually preserve the contemporary views and opinions concerning its general subject, and by looking at the genre of war movies we can get an impression of a society's changing attitudes and values towards war in general (since war as a general subject basically transcends the genre's development). In her book, Basinger presents a very detailed analysis of the evolutionary process of the World War II combat film genre. The first films of this genre were made as attempts to create stories about the real thing, incorporating narrative aspects in order to let events come to life for the audience. Viewers had the chance to participate in the war, learning about the new ways it had to be fought: 'Presumably, this process also created patriotic pride and fervor, a desire to win the war'.[14] Soon, the films started to develop an awareness of genre rules, establishing a visual shorthand for viewers. While their realism was still based on the war itself, the presentation started to be increasingly distanced, turning the story of World War II into myth and legend. Going to see war movies had turned into a ritual with the social function to let the American public relive the war, veterans and civilians sitting side by side. The genre had turned into a uniting force, creating consent on how to remember the war, bridging the gap between memory and imagination to create a national heritage of victory and success. More and more, the films started to draw their material from other films instead of representing reality, even though they did keep events of history as points of reference. This way, 'war was now war movies', states Basinger, arguing that the 'displacement of fact of history by legend is well known to historians in all fields. In film, we can *see* it happen'.[15] The key to film's central meaning for the representation of history is connected to memory as mental image. While visualised recollections of past events fade over time, film images remain as they were. They may be refreshed by watching them again, that way replacing mental images of reality even in those who actually saw combat.

With respect to D-Day, Ulrike Klein identifies the mechanisms of remembering the past through mass-mediation as processes of secondary communication that have the ability to reinforce selected events in our memory. The mass media's influence on our perception of the past has at least an equally great effect as our history books do, and eventually collectively remembering the past is nothing other than 'forming public opinion on a shared past'.[16] Considering this mediated process of remembering, the D-Day films are particularly interesting, because not only do they cover a fairly large time-span of war film history (thus offering an exemplary sketch of the genre), but they also all cover, more or less, the same point of reference in history, and thus invite comparison. Some details of the films' content can serve as an example of how the cinematic construction of collective memory integrates cinematic events of past and present. Furthermore, the creators of the two most central D-Day films, Darryl Zanuck and Steven Spielberg, have commented on, and thus displayed an awareness about, the relation of film and collective memory. Zanuck, according to Lawrence H. Suid, was convinced that his film would not just portray history:

> He maintained that any picture 'made on such a scale and with so much effort must say something'. He felt it was important to convey through the film a message about the current world situation and the threat to 'our way of life'. He wanted his movie to serve as 'a reminder to millions and millions of people that the Allies, who once stood together and defeated an evil because they stood together, can do so again in a different situation today which in some way is similar to what they faced in 1940.'[17]

While Henry Koster's *D-Day, 6th of June* (1956) is mainly concerned with a triangle relationship in front of a World War II backdrop, and thus addresses common domestic issues of its time, its combat sequence is centred on assaulting Pointe d'Hoc. Darryl Zanuck's *The Longest Day* (1962) already features the first major reoccurrence, for here, too, this assault is covered. The film itself impresses through its sheer scope. Parallels have been pointed out between its incredible production efforts and logistics and those of Operation OVERLORD, and imitating the undertaking it tries to portray really adds to the films credibility. Lawrence Suid compares Zanuck's efforts to the preparations made for D-Day when he describes the producer as 'a supreme commander in assembling his staff, in supervising all aspects of the production, and in all decision making'.[18] *The Longest Day* breathes the spirit of its time, when the epic greatness of Hollywood-CinemaScope seemed to state that if it was not on film it never happened. Consequently, the movie displays the attitude of a documentary. Central characters and places of action are introduced via subtitles, original language is preserved in dialogue, the story basically sticks to factual chronological development, and it seems to cover all major events of the operation in fair enough detail. The complexity of events leaves little time to develop characters in depth. To cover up this drawback, screen-image is employed deliberately. Zanuck cast a large number of international stars to appeal to his audience, and one of them was John Wayne, whom we know as a great warrior from many combat films, and who thus gives credibility to his role as commanding officer of a paratrooper unit – or rather makes us believe the real officer surely was a man somewhat like John Wayne. More importantly, we encounter the legendary Bangalore torpedoes for the first time, and of course we are allowed to look at the first blueprint of Spielberg's famous half-hour landing sequence. *The Longest Day* relishes the magnitude of the operation with a very upbeat ending:

> Until the early 1960s, most Americans perceived the nation's armed services as an all-conquering and infallible force that could protect the United States from any threat and project the national interest to any

corner of the world. Conveyed in history books, popular literature, and the mass media, this image received its highest expression in the military's overwhelming success in World War II.[19]

Before the mid-1960s, war movies tended to show the glamorous side of combat, and the victories of the almighty American military. While not necessarily depicting battle as a positive experience, film makers established pain and suffering as important ingredients of victory. Later films included more implicit criticism of war. Robert Aldrich's *Dirty Dozen* (1967) and Brian Hutton's *Where Eagles Dare* (1968), even though not D-Day films as such (they present commando operations in preparation for the invasion), both feature actors who had just recently established a new screen image of the anti-hero, replacing the clean-shaven hero of the fifties: Charles Bronson and Clint Eastwood characterise ruthless killers and brutal criminals who make fun of war and disrespect the military establishment. Both of them had starred as the main character in a new kind of western created by the Italian director Sergio Leone (*A Fistful of Dollars* [1964] and *Once Upon a Time in the West* [1968]), which established a major shift in representing heroism in the cinema, be it Western or war film, mirroring the general change in public opinion constituted by the problems of the conflict in Vietnam.

In *Patton* (1970), Made during the decline of Hollywood's epic Cinema-Scope era, Franklin Schaffner characterises the American military commander General George S. Patton. While D-Day is only referred to in a short newsreel scene, the hero is shown as somehow larger than life and full of himself, giving the film an ironic twist and thus questioning the motives of both the soldier and the war. Schaffner also presents the three major stages of invading the European Continent by visiting northern Africa, Italy and France. Samuel Fuller does the same thing in his *The Big Red One* (1980); however, he is pushing this even further, 'culminating with the liberation of a concentration camp in Czechoslovakia and final victory in Europe'.[20] In this graphic (and coloured) recollection of D-Day events, we also encounter the nameless soldier being shot underwater and the blood-red sea washing up on the shore, as well as the Bangalore torpedoes. Fuller made this film to memorialise his own World War II experiences, establishing characters that did their job fighting a necessary war, caring about survival and performing bravely. He managed to capture the nature of combat, periods of anxious boredom suddenly interrupted by bloody moments of sheer terror, making it clear that 'even when it may become necessary, war still had few socially redeeming qualities'.[21] Nevertheless, Fuller's film somewhat rehabilitated the military, helping to give new life to the war film genre.

Starting with Samuel Fuller's *The Big Red One*, the war movie genre explored various directions during the eighties and nineties. There were further efforts to rehabilitate the military image, and many of the movies about Vietnam were still full of self-criticism, while the appearance of Rambo in Ted Kotcheff's *First Blood* (1982) marked a counter-current in this area as well. After the Cold War ended, the old enemies were gone. In addition, there have been moral insecurities fuelled by the USA taking part in international conflicts (such as Somalia and the Balkans). By the end of the nineties, criticism of war seemed to have become relative through efforts of reassurance. That goes for *Saving Private Ryan* (1998) as well, and to make his point, Steven Spielberg obviously did have a whole sub-genre of combat film to draw from. Covering the invasion of Normandy he is using all the familiar devices from the history of D-Day films to appeal to the audience to live as good (American) citizens. By showing us the landing craft and the soldier being shot underwater, the blood-red sea washing ashore, the Bangalore torpedoes, the soldier adding a can of French sand to his collection of African and Italian sand (film cans, by the way), he does not merely display his ability to recreate the images of a popular genre in a modernised version. Spielberg reminds us of what we have come to know about D-Day from his colleagues, and in the same way he wants to bring across his message: he wants to remind us that we are supposed to make the sacrifices others made for us count, in this case the eight lives sacrificed to save the one life symbolic of an American value (however, why all four of Mrs Ryan's sons had to go to war in the first place is never questioned).

The evolutionary process of genre development shows how a set of useful characters and situations has been created to present us with new insights. While ideologies may shift over time, the strategies to communicate them basically stay the same, modifying themselves with the medium they choose to employ, and adapting its narrative characteristics accordingly. Considering this perspective on D-Day films, it becomes clear why, for example, the work of Spielberg is quite important.[22] His *Survivors of the Shoah Visual History Foundation* testifies to the director's conviction that film is the ideal medium to create and store collective memory. The traces of his conviction are found in his other works as well, especially in films like *Schindler's List* (1993) and *Saving Private Ryan*, and of course in the television mini-series *Band of Brothers* (2001), which is closely connected to *Saving Private Ryan*. The series may be interpreted as a popularised background story for the movie, and as an experiment in applying the principles of creating consent on collective memory through collecting personal impressions of participants, mixing them with dramatisation in the form of popular mass media. One could argue that the loose connection between *Schindler's List* and the visual history project has been structurally developed into *Band of Brothers*, the difference being only that its contents have been inspired by the events of D-Day and those of the following invasion until the end of World War II in general. We may even argue that this aspect of the work of Steven Spielberg has vaguely been anticipated by Zanuck's attempts to make a film that is 'both a pseudo-documentary history and a commercial drama',[23] and by Fuller's cinematic recollections of his own wartime experiences, representing roughly the same structure of events. These parallels only underline the work of Spielberg being an excellent example for Klein's argument about how a collective past is growing out of shared cultural identities and mainly shaped by a public discourse to form consent on a common history. Basinger's work summarises the role and function of a specific form of media and conforms with Klein, who is in line with Carr, Straub and Gergen.[24] Ulrike Klein, however, is the only one who explicitly expresses the conclusion following from the work of these scholars when she notes that different cultural spheres (or, in our sense, other collective communities) may have differing attitudes to how a common past should be formed, and, more importantly, what it should contain. That means public discourse about history is of considerable political importance, since it is 'a question of communicative negotiation which version of history will gain the upper hand'.[25] While the proverbial history books written by winners may conform to a colloquial form of Klein's argument in some part, it certainly is too far fetched to see propagandistic motivations as the major force in written history. Nevertheless, negotiating consent about shared history most certainly has some aspects of strategic structural acquisition, and as an aspect of defining cultural identity deserves attention in terms of its importance for the social function and the political meaning of history.

Collective memory and the cinema

As has been shown, the cinema, as an American form of social consciousness, has always offered the American culture part of the material to shape its attitudes about war through war movies. Since its declaration of war against global terror, the USA has gone to a state of war once more. Indications for the scope of this development can be found in the contemporary products which have come from Hollywood since 11 September 2001. Films like Ridley Scott's *Black Hawk Down* (2001), John Woo's *Windtalkers* (2002), Randall Wallace's *We were Soldiers* (2002), Gregory Hoblit's *Hart's War* (2002) and Antoine Fuqua's *Tears of the Sun* (2003) come to mind; others, like Peter Weir's *Master and Commander* (2003), Edward Zwick's *The Last Samurai* (2003) and Wolfgang Petersen's *Troy* (2004) follow. As Virchow and Thomas have already made clear, on 9/11 some of these had already been more or less in production, but even those almost finished by then had to undergo a process of revision and adjustment before being released.[26] Consequently, the films that were produced and came out post-9/11 should give us even more insight into the currents of culture, politics and war. While some of these films do not relate directly to wars the USA participated in, they nevertheless present a possibility to take a closer look at contemporary representations of today's culture of war. Even though, unfortunately, no film has been produced dealing with the events of D-Day since then, looking at the steps the genre has taken, it immediately becomes clear that a considerable shift must have occurred.

Most of these films' heroes have become traumatised heroes. Interpreting their standards and values makes it clear that criticism of war has moved into the background. As in the later Vietnam films, coping with traumatic experiences of war is an important role for the hero's psyche. However, his strategies to deal with the problems have changed considerably. The hero seeks catharsis through reliving the traumatising situation; he wants to redeem his failure through success, through martyrdom, if necessary. The film hero, who had evolved into an opponent of war in search of his inner self during the last two or three decades, suddenly finds himself thrown into a massive regression. The armed conflicts of the American past are defining the framework of his war trauma, and become stylised depictions of national myths in themselves. The hero's inner journey to overcome war as a form of pre-civilised conflict management has been replaced by dying in the line of duty. He has become the uncritical and patriotic arm of political and military violence, for whom death has turned into a necessity of war, symbolising a part of constant social renewal. The war heroes' struggles serve as examples for dealing with the 'dark hours' of American history, offering strategies to reintegrate them into the national psyche and thus symbolically to cope with the shock of 9/11. Fighting has again become a cause, death has once more a meaning for the greater good. With this in mind, it is particularly interesting to notice a rising number of films dealing with the myths and circumstances of early American wars, especially the Civil War – for example, Ronald F. Maxwell's *Gods and Generals* (2003), Anthony Minghella's *Cold Mountain* (2003) and John Lee Hancock's *The Alamo* (2004). However, other films borrow from the myths of the early American wars as well, especially *We were Soldiers* and *The Last Samurai*. The Civil War in the movies has a long tradition of being used to symbolise the trauma of the American nation. The struggle for unification, one of the dark chapters in US history, in combination with the traumatised war hero and his strategies to overcome defeat clearly show how films attempt to reintegrate American traumatisation into the dynamics of national identification. Because of the central role of films dealing with the Civil War, in combination with trying to overcome a nationwide trauma, I have come to label this phenomenon in today's Hollywood cinema 'rebirth of a nation'.[27]

The themes of war depicted in contemporary American cinema resemble efforts to process and integrate the trauma of 9/11 into the national myth. Since the emotional experiences and the psychological mechanisms of narrative offered by the war movies of today constantly contribute to the negotiations about our collective past, the interpretations of history they offer, particularly through redefining social values, and through reframing political phenomena, mark a considerable shift towards a determinist perception of war as a result of evolution, modernisation and technological development. Thus perceived, war becomes a phenomenon of nature, and as such cannot be questioned any more, it can only be handled as advantageously as possible, which obviously means winning. In that way, however, war has left its role as an object of representation and become a subject of presentation. It has become a prerequisite, a presumption of its own discourse. The new cinema of war, through its strategies of representing heroes of war combined with the traditions of depicting national myths, has extinguished decisive steps in the evolution of one of the most traditional film genres. Analysis of the new war films illustrates efforts to reintegrate American traumata into the dynamics of national identification, and to reframe public opinion to raise acceptance of the war effort and the culture of war. Normalisation of armed intervention is presented as an implicitness of national and individual American self-conception, while public opinion is shifting from seeing war as a man-made means of politics towards considering it an unavoidable socio-historic phenomenon.

Conclusion: notes on a motion picture lesson in history

After discussing various aspects of cinematic representations of history, the history teacher and I agreed that it could be quite useful to make use of the medium in the classroom to catch the students' attention and to arouse their curiosity, motivating them to approach history from a new point of view. Going even further, by looking at the development of films dealing with history, it might be possible to discover certain dynamics, narrative or other, that can tell us something about the effects the general and mass mediation of history has on the way we perceive the past, arrange ourselves in the present, and prepare ourselves for the future. There could be discussions about the purpose of history, something students most likely would be happy to discuss, especially in relation to popular fiction and entertainment. Maybe these discussions would shed some light on how professional historians should approach new trends in the development of the media, and what the connection is between the social functions of communication technologies and related assumptions on the content they carry, be it religious paintings, historical books or popular films. Most likely, each of them has its own form of narrative, waiting for audiences, be it contemporary or future ones, to tell this story.

Notes

1 Freiwillige Selbstkontrolle ('voluntary self-control'): a volunteer initiative of Germany's media industry consisting of independent experts to ensure the compliance of media products with German laws for youth protection via self-censorship as a precautionary principle (comparable to the movie ratings of the Motion Picture Association of America).
2 Narrative is one major device in Hollywood movies, amongst others, which are much more typical for film, to create the drama which makes a film exciting and successful at the box office. In the context of cinema and for our purposes, narrative does not literally mean a story with a narrator. The term refers to the characteristics of story construction. Films not based on narrative structure do exist, however, for our purposes, they are not of interest.

3 Hayden White theorists of history have kept pointing out how our tradition of historiography is closely related to the western culture of storytelling. See Hayden White (trans. P. Kohlhaas), *Metahistory: Die historische Einbildungskraft im 19. Jahrhundert in Europa* (Frankfurt am Main: Fischer Verlag, 1991).

4 See Kenneth J. Gergen (trans. J. Straub and A. Kochinka), 'Erzählung, moralische Identität und historisches Bewußtsein. Eine sozialkonstruktionistische Darstellung', in J. Straub (ed.) *Erzählung, Identität und historisches Bewußtsein. Die psychologische Konstruktion von Zeit und Geschichte* (Frankfurt am Main: Suhrkamp Verlag, 1998), pp. 172–6.

5 Ibid., pp. 184–8.

6 Ibid., pp. 198–202.

7 See David Carr, *Time, Narrative, and History* (Bloomington, IN: Indiana University Press, 1991).

8 See Jürgen Straub, 'Geschichten erzählen, Geschichte bilden. Grundzüge einer narrativen Psychologie historischer Sinnbildung', in J. Straub (ed.) *Erzählung, Identität und historisches Bewußtsein*, p. 84. The original quote is 'historische Wirklichkeiten *sind* Konstrukte' (trans. Carsten Hennig).

9 See Straub, 'Geschichten erzählen, Geschichte bilden', p. 85.

10 Even though Basinger and Suid use terms like 'combat film' and 'war movies' or 'genre' with different intent, for our purposes a slightly wider approach is necessary, mainly due to the lack of large numbers of war films related to the subjects discussed in this chapter.

11 See Jeanine Basinger (updated filmography by J. Arnold), *The World War II Combat Film: Anatomy of a Genre* (Middletown, CT: Wesleyan University Press, 2003), p. xii.

12 Ibid.

13 Ibid., p. 108.

14 Ibid., p. 111.

15 Ibid., p. 141.

16 See Ulrike Klein, *Das internationale Medienereignis D-Day: Presse und kollektives Erinnern nach 50 Jahren* (Bochum: Verlag Brockmeyer, 1996), pp. 28–9. The original quote is 'öffentliche Meinungsbildung über eine gemeinsame Vergangenheit' (trans. Carsten Hennig).

17 See Lawrence H. Suid, *Guts & Glory: The Making of the American Military Image in Film* (Lexington, KY: The University Press of Kentucky, 2002), p. 172.

18 Ibid., p. 178.

19 Ibid., p. xi.

20 Ibid., p. 425.

21 Ibid., p. 427.

22 See Robert F. Daniel, *Erinnerung als ethisches Projekt: Aufarbeitung der Vergangenheit im Filmwerk von Steven Spielberg* (München: KoPäd-Verlag, 2001).

23 See Suid, *Guts & Glory*, p. 184.

24 See Klein, *Das internationale Medienereignis D-Day*, p. 15.

25 Ibid., p. 25. The original quote is 'eine Frage der kommunikativen Verhandlung, welche Version der Geschichte die Überhand gewinnt' (trans. Carsten Hennig).

26 See Tanja Thomas and Fabian Virchow, 'Militainment als "banaler" Militarismus. Auf dem Weg zu einer Militarisierung der politischen Kultur?', in M. Löffelholz (ed.) *Krieg als Medienereignis, Bd. 2. Krisenkommunikation im 21. Jahrhundert* (Wiesbaden: Verlag für Sozialwissenschaften, 2004), pp. 299–300.

27 See Carsten Hennig, 'Rebirth of a Nation: Das Kino im amerikanischen Kriegsdiskurs', *Newsletter Arbeitskreis Militärgeschichte*, 23: 37–40.

Index